The Literature of Cinema

THE LITERATURE OF CINEMA presents a comprehensive selection from the multitude of writings about cinema, rediscovering materials on its origins, history, theoretical principles and techniques, aesthetics, economics, and effects on societies and individuals. Included are works of inherent, lasting merit and others of primarily historical significance. These provide essential resources for serious study and critical enjoyment of the "magic shadows" that became one of the decisive cultural forces of modern times.

Motion Pictures
and Standards of Morality

Charles C. Peters

ARNO PRESS & THE NEW YORK TIMES

New York • 1970

Reprint Edition 1970 by Arno Press Inc.
Library of Congress Catalog Card Number: 72-124030
ISBN 0-405-01648-4
ISBN for complete set: 0-405-01600-X
Manufactured in the United States of America

MOTION PICTURES AND
STANDARDS OF MORALITY

❖

CHARLES C. PETERS

PROFESSOR OF EDUCATION,
PENNSYLVANIA STATE COLLEGE

NEW YORK
THE MACMILLAN COMPANY
1933

THIS SERIES OF TWELVE STUDIES OF THE
INFLUENCE OF MOTION PICTURES UPON
CHILDREN AND YOUTH HAS BEEN MADE BY
THE COMMITTEE ON EDUCATIONAL RE-
SEARCH OF THE PAYNE FUND AT THE RE-
QUEST OF THE NATIONAL COMMITTEE FOR
THE STUDY OF SOCIAL VALUES IN MOTION
PICTURES, NOW THE MOTION PICTURE RE-
SEARCH COUNCIL, 366 MADISON AVENUE,
NEW YORK CITY. THE STUDIES WERE DE-
SIGNED TO SECURE AUTHORITATIVE AND
IMPERSONAL DATA WHICH WOULD MAKE
POSSIBLE A MORE COMPLETE EVALUATION
OF MOTION PICTURES AND THEIR SOCIAL
POTENTIALITIES

AUTHOR'S PREFACE

THIS monograph undertakes to give factual evidence on the question of the amount of divergence of commercial motion pictures from current standards of morality in respect to the conduct exhibited in them. This question has been hotly debated, but too often the argument has turned upon exceptional cases of good or bad pictures rather than upon a careful comparison of prevailing tendencies among motion pictures and the actual mores of our society. In the study we were obliged to invent new techniques for measuring the mores on the one hand and the movies on the other. During the progress of our effort to find objective methods for studying this subtle problem we alternated between despair and high hopes. We ourselves feel that hope triumphed, and trust that the technique herein developed may prove useful in further researches on problems similar to this one and that our findings may constitute a substantial factual basis from which a constructive consideration of social policy toward the movies may proceed.

The author is under incalculable obligation to his graduate assistant, Robert P. Wray, for assistance in the study. Without his indefatigable labor on the statistical work, his insight into the nature and the demands of our problem, and his excellent organizing ability, the study could not have been completed. Miss Catherine E. Geary and Mr. John Dubbs also rendered valuable assistance in setting up the scales and developing effective methods for using them. For the clerical and other necessary expenses of the investigation we are indebted to the Payne Fund.

C. C. P.

State College, Pa.,
July, 1933.

TABLE OF CONTENTS

MOTION PICTURES AND STANDARDS OF MORALITY

CHAPTER I

MORALITY AND THE MORES

IT is most convenient to approach the problem of this chapter through reference first to *folkways*. This topic has been most extensively studied by William Graham Sumner, late Professor of Political and Social Science at Yale University. The folkways are patterns of conduct that groups of people develop, sometimes by accident but more often as the result of an unconscious selection of the more efficient and safe methods of responding to types of situations.

The operation by which the folkways are produced consists in the frequent repetition of petty acts, often by great numbers acting in concert or, at least, acting in the same way when face to face with the same need. The immediate motive is interest. It produces habit in the individual and custom in the group. It is, therefore, in the highest degree original and primitive. . . . We have to recognize it as one of the chief forces by which a society is made to be what it is. . . . The folkways are not creations of human purpose and wit. They are like products of natural forces which men unconsciously set in operation, or they are like the instinctive ways of animals, which are developed out of experience, which reach a final form of maximum adaptation to an interest, which are handed down by tradition and admit of no exception or variation, yet change to meet new

1

conditions, still within the same limited methods and without rational reflection or purpose.[1]

The *mores* grow out of the folkways. Man finds it annoying to break a habit, to change his ways. He naturally comes to think of his ways of doing things as the "nicest," the "most convenient," and the "best" ways and to oppose any influences that urge him to change. Groups act in the same manner in regard to their habits. Thus the folkways, after being practiced for some time, come to take on values; the members of the group are emotionally disturbed when anything tends to upset these established practices.

After practicing certain folkways for an extended time people acquire the conviction that they are indispensable to the welfare of society. . . . It is with the addition of this welfare element that folkways become mores. . . . The mores are social ritual in which we all participate unconsciously. . . . Each does as everybody else does. For the great mass of mankind as to all things, and for all of us for a great many things, the rule to do as all do suffices. We are led by suggestion and association to believe that there must be wisdom and utility in what all do.[2]

The term *mores* is the plural form of the Latin *mos*, meaning custom. The mores rest primarily on custom and are supported by feeling; they are not the product fundamentally of a process of ratiocination. Nevertheless even primitive groups are likely to rationalize about them, so that the system of mores comes to be shaped up into something of a philosophy of life, especially in the minds of the members of a reflective temperament.

When the elements of truth and right are developed into doctrines of welfare, the folkways are raised to another plane. They then become capable of producing inferences, developing

[1] Sumner, W. G., *Folkways*, Ginn & Co., 1906, pp. 3–4.
[2] Sumner and Keller, *The Science of Society*, Yale University Press, 1927, II, 33–34.

into new forms, and extending their constructive influence over men and society. Then we call them the mores. The mores are the folkways, including the philosophical and ethical generalizations as to societal welfare which are suggested by them, and inherent in them, as they grow.[3]

By reason of the accidental factors involved in their origin, the mores may differ markedly from group to group. They are always basically a single-group affair, even though they have analogues in other groups. Of course there is likely to be considerable similarity in the folkways of different groups, out of which the mores spring, because many of the situations with which these groups deal are essentially the same and require much the same practices for effectively dealing with them. Nevertheless there is also a surprising amount of difference. The literature of anthropology is extremely rich in examples of "queer" approvals.[4] There is perhaps not a single vice in the code of our own society that some other group has not considered a virtue—murder, theft, dishonesty, torture, suicide, adultery, and the rest. In these other tribes a man's conscience hurt him, and public opinion was against him, if he did not do one or more of these things, just as our own conscience hurts us, and public opinion is against us, if we do them.

The members of a group are customarily quite unconscious of their own mores. Like habits, these function automatically. It never occurs to the members that these acts could be done in any other way. If you ask a primitive man why his people do so and so, he merely laughs at you for asking a foolish question. Civilized people become aware of their mores only when they come into contact with other groups which have different customs. It requires some sort of

[3] Sumner, *Folkways*, p. 30.
[4] See, for examples, Westermarck, E., *The Origin and Development of Moral Ideas*, The Macmillan Company, 1906, Vol. II.

conflict to raise the mores above the limen of consciousness. Usually moral sanctions are attached chiefly to *vital* folkways. But in primitive societies even very commonplace acts are often treated as moral acts. "Tylor relates that the Dyaks of Borneo, when shown a more efficient manner of chopping wood with a V-shaped cut, not only refused to adopt it, but fixed a fine upon anyone who should employ the new method." [5] In our own society we think we take seriously only matters of vital importance, but an impartial evaluation might reveal us as attaching moral importance to some things that really make little difference.

Now society's moral code is simply its system of mores. Morality is conformity to the mores; immorality consists in failure to conform. There is, therefore, a difference between morality and fundamental rightness, if this latter means such conduct as an omniscient judge would prescribe as the "best" way. Morality is always limited by the knowledge and the experience of the group. There is no certainty that what is "moral" in this generation will continue to be so in the next generation. Perhaps it should not be. For morality should change as conditions change—a thing it stubbornly resists doing. Folkways are at their best when they continue changing so as to keep best adjusted to the changing situations with which they must cope, and morality is at its best when it lends sanctions to the most "fit" folkways.

It is our purpose in this study to learn whether motion pictures conflict with morality, as morality stands in our society. We are concerned to know whether the acts depicted in commercial motion pictures conform with the mores of our society. Or, if they deviate, we wish to learn at what points, in what direction, how frequently, and how far.

[5] Ames, E. S., *The Psychology of Religious Experience*, Charles Scribner's Sons, 1912, p. 61.

This is evidently a very different thing from asking whether the movies are "right" or "wrong," "good" or "bad." This latter question the author, at least, is incompetent to answer, because he is too much imbued with the outlook of his age. Very few persons are competent to answer it, though many think they are. But we can set the whole problem of evaluating motion pictures in relation to morality in better perspective when we have before us detailed factual evidence as to where and how the movies deviate from present moral standards. Seeing just where these deviations lie and how great they are, we can then think on a factual basis about the question as to whether these deviations are toward better or toward worse. Perhaps we may even wish to lay these factual findings before a jury of far-visioned "philosophers" and ask their verdict as to whether these tendencies seem to point upward or downward.

CHAPTER II

DEVELOPING SCALES FOR MEASURING
THE MORES

OUR problem is to study the relation of commercial motion pictures to the mores. Is the conduct depicted in the movies parallel to the mores? Or does it deviate from these approved modes of conduct? If there is deviation, how frequently, in what direction, and to what degrees? Answers to these questions we want not on the basis of impressions, which are likely to be affected by biases, but on the basis of quantitative measurements among which there is no room for wishes.

If we are to study the parallelism, or lack of parallelism, between the mores and behavior in motion pictures, and are to indicate in quantitative terms the amount of divergence between them, it is evident that we must have measures of both of these in terms of the same units. Unfortunately there are at present no such measures of either. No one has up to the present made a quantitative study of the status of the mores. Studies of the moral value of motion pictures have been made, but mostly in terms of general impressions rather than in terms of such specific units as we must employ in our investigation. How we undertook to measure motion pictures we shall explain in a later chapter; how we developed scales for measuring the mores is the theme of this chapter.

It is very difficult to study morality scientifically.

Custom is by its nature a floating and undefined conception, and is accepted as a sort of pervasive and irreducible feature of

6

life. In its varieties it is highly interesting and can be profusely and edifyingly illustrated, but to deal with it scientifically is difficult. It lends itself to irresponsible speculation just because it is diffuse, evasive, and resistant to scientific devices for analyzing phenomena, reducing them to orderliness, and handling them in the search for truth. [1]

Certainly no group is in position to look objectively at its own mores, because it is too much enmeshed in them. The mores go simply unnoticed because they are so familiar. Even the learned members are scarcely in position to reflect critically upon the approved customs of their group because their point of view, too, is biased by the social pressure. As Sumner says:

> It is vain to imagine that a "scientific man" can divest himself of prejudice or previous opinion and put himself in an attitude of neutral independence towards the mores. He might as well get out of gravity or the pressure of the atmosphere. The most learned scholar reveals all the philistinism and prejudice of the man-on-the-curbstone when mores are in discussion. The most elaborate discussion only consists in revolving on one's own axis. [2]

Since the mores go normally unnoticed, the only way in which to make them articulate (unless to an outside observer to whom the group is wholly strange and "different") so that they may be studied objectively, is to produce conflicts with them. We can at any time bring them to the level of focal activity by outraging them. This may be accomplished by performing in life acts that lie beyond the limits of routine approvals. Or it may be achieved in some degree by having these acts performed, under the observation of the members of the group, in some symbolic fashion that gives a realistic semblance of life activities—as in pictures or in verbal

---

[1] Sumner and Keller, *The Science of Society*, I, 30.
[2] Sumner, *Folkways*, p. 98.

narratives that generate vivid images in the minds of the beholders. In our study it was not feasible to utilize the conflicts that normal social life affords, since these come too sporadically. We tried the device of producing these conflicts by means of motion-picture scenes, but to get a sufficiently wide sampling by this method was too costly. We resorted, therefore, to described bits of conduct, hoping that we could make these serve the purpose of producing in the reader a response similar to that which would be called forth by the corresponding real scene, or at least enable him to know how he does respond in life to scenes of that sort. For this purpose we constructed a series of scales, each describing bits of conduct of varying degrees of "badness"—the extent of badness being measured (as will be explained in detail later) by the degree of shock indicated by the proportion of members of the group aroused to resentment by it. By this technique we were able to get these intangible and elusive social phenomena into quantitative form so that they could be subjected to statistical investigation.

The mores are, of course, very many—hundreds upon hundreds. Societies have their attitudes toward each type of conduct that has social bearings, and of these types there is an almost endless number. It is obvious that no scientific study which undertakes to test thoroughly every generalization it announces could investigate the whole range of mores even in one society. It was necessary that we confine ourselves to a small sampling. Out of the dozens, therefore, that we should have liked to investigate and the hundreds that await investigation, we chose four elements that seem to play up largely in motion pictures: (1) aggressiveness of a girl in love-making; (2) kissing and caressing; (3) the treatment of children by parents; and (4) democratic attitudes and practices—that is, respect for the individuality of all sorts of persons and treatment of them on the basis of their intrinsic worth rather than on the basis of some artificial mark of prestige. This last covered only what is popularly called "social democracy"; it did not attempt to cover at all "political" or "industrial" democracy. Limited as this sampling is, it proved to be a bigger undertaking than we should have attempted. For when we got into the study we found these elements far from homogeneous; each broke up into a number of subdivisions, so that instead of four scales we were really dealing with fifty-four, and even these should have been subdivided considerably farther into qualitatively different elements. For each of these fifty-four elemental types of conduct we needed samples of various degrees of offense against taste, and needed these, too, with varying concomitants of mitigating circumstances.

Our first task was, therefore, to collect described bits of activity representing the various patterns of conduct under each of our four elements. The following conditions had to be fulfilled:

1. The items must extend, within each pattern, from the best that could be found to the worst, with intermediate stages reasonably equally spaced between the extremes at sufficiently short intervals to permit precise measurement.

2. The scenes must be written up briefly, so that the whole scale would not become too bulky, yet enough must be said to give the setting of the act described and to arouse a vivid picture in the mind of the reader.

3. Each scene must be quite homogeneous; the response aroused by it must be unmistakably attributable to one single fundamental factor.

4. The write-ups must be sufficiently varied and interesting that the raters will not be hopelessly bored by them.

5. All the patterns likely to be encountered in the movies must be included.

6. The total scale must not become so lengthy and complex that the rater will be hopelessly confused in using it.

Our first step was to collect, from the observation of motion pictures, from recollection of experiences, and from other sources, a large number of fragments of conduct for scenes. Having written these up we classified them by pattern and looked for missing patterns, or for missing quantitative stages within these, and filled the gaps with new scenes. With these items we constructed tentative scales and used them for several months in rating motion pictures. It soon became apparent, however, that we had missed many patterns; so we noted down every scene found in the pictures rated for which we had no scale element, against the time when we should revise the scales. At the time of revision we included all of these scenes and, in addition, undertook as complete analysis of our elements into basic patterns as the four of us working at the task were able to make. We tried to think of every possible variation that conduct in each of the elements in our area could take, then planned scale elements to provide each pattern in a number of degrees of "badness" reasonably equally spaced from one extreme to the other. Even after this revision it turns out that we have missed some basic patterns, especially in aggressiveness. If anybody thinks there is little originality in the movies—that the conduct follows a few endlessly recurring patterns—he should try to make a scale with all the patterns included for measuring aggressiveness of a girl in love-making. In our final set of scales we had 326 different scenes, distributed to the four scales as follows:

Aggressiveness of a girl in love-making.................. 89
Democratic attitudes and practices..................... 82

For the nature of these scenes the reader is referred to the appendix of this volume, pages 167–261, where the whole scale is printed.

Our purpose at this stage, it must be remembered, was to make a measuring stick by the use of which we could measure approvals on the one side and motion pictures on the other. In our four sets of elements, consisting of some eighty scenes each, we had the makings of such a measure. But we must calibrate it: we must get quantitative values for the "badness" of each of the scenes that is to appear on it. These values were to be derived from the extent to which the scenes shock the members of society as indicated by the proportion of readers in whom they arouse resentment or admiration. We chose not to derive these evaluations from a single group of persons but from a number of groups which, we believed, would jointly represent approximately a random sample of modern American society. For this purpose we used the following groups, with the indicated numbers from each:

1. STUDENTS. This group included 50 seniors in the School of Education at the Pennsylvania State College, of which number 25 were men and 25 were women.
2. FACULTY MEMBERS. In this group are 25 middle-aged members of the faculty of the Pennsylvania State College from all the different schools, and the wives of these 25 faculty members.
3. SOCIALLY ÉLITE YOUNG WOMEN. This group, numbering 42, consisted of young women between the ages of eighteen and twenty-five years who are of the wealthy, cultured class, living in New York City or in Baltimore.
4. FACTORY WORKING BOYS. This group was made up of 27 wage-earning boys, mostly working in factories in Bridgeville, Pa. Their ages were approximately eighteen to twenty-five.

5. FACTORY WORKING GIRLS. This group consisted of 18 girls of ages eighteen to twenty-five working in a factory in York, Pa.

To each of these persons we gave four three-pouch envelopes, each containing one of the four scales with the scenes mimeographed on slips of paper about two-and-a-half by eight-and-a-half inches in size. Each bore an identifying number which was wholly noncommittal as to the nature of the scene. To permit the rater to get the gist of the scene quickly, each paragraph was surmounted by a fairly long title that gave the theme of the paragraph. From these 187 raters were sought responses that we believed were in harmony with the psychology of the mores. The reader will recall that, in the functioning of the mores, the responses are emotional, impulsive, unratiocinated. In most cases the situation is taken as matter-of-course; the act is merely customary and passes without notice. But when the act is unconventional, it challenges attention; it arouses fear and resentment if it deviates from the customary in a direction that the group feels to be dangerous, or admiration if the deviation is in the direction in which the group aspires to move. The directions, quoted below, will give a clear picture of the procedure and permit the reader to judge whether it is in harmony with the principles of social psychology discussed above.

INSTRUCTIONS

In this package are a number of concretely described bits of conduct out of which we wish to make a "scale" for measuring goodness or badness of conduct. We get the values for this scale from the proportion of people who rank each specimen as "approved" or "disapproved." This is part of a very far-reaching study to determine social standards scientifically. It is very important that each helper should do the rating carefully; ratings made carelessly, or when one is too tired to do them attentively, are worse than useless to us, as they simply confuse our scale values. If you get fatigued while doing the rating so that you can no longer give keen attention to the work, drop it for awhile, then return to it after a rest.

Of some of the bits of conduct described on the cards you will disapprove; they are the kind that would more or less shock or pain you if you saw them happening in real life. You would feel "intuitively" that they are more or less wrong. Place on pile 1 all of the cards that describe such conduct. If you not only disapprove the conduct but disapprove very strongly, mark two minus signs (− −) on the card before placing it on pile 1.

Some of the cards may describe conduct that you not only approve but that you actually admire. Place these on pile 3. If you very strongly admire the bit of conduct, mark two pluses (+ +) on the card before placing it on pile 3.[3]

The remainder of the cards will describe conduct that you think O.K. but "nothing to brag about"—such conduct as you see so regularly that you take it as perfectly natural and matter-of-course. Place these on the middle pile—pile 2.

We have no idea that the three piles will be of equal size. Indeed you may not feel that any of the cards at all belong on the "admired" pile or on the "disapproved" pile. Be governed by your own actual feelings in the matter, not by what people are accustomed to say. A good test to apply if you are uncertain is to ask yourself whether you would feel at perfect ease if someone very dear to you would do the act in question under the conditions described on the card—sister, mother, daughter.

Now place the cards on pile 1 in the envelope marked "disapproved," those on pile 3 in the loose white envelope marked "admired," and those on the middle pile, pile 2, in the envelope marked "neutral." Place the white envelope with its contents inside either of the other two and slip the flap of the brown envelopes inside so as to prevent the contents from falling out. Do not seal the envelopes. Return the package to the person from whom you received it.

A concrete example will indicate how the returns were worked up. Item number 73 from the scale on Aggressiveness read as follows (from the scale with thrill as the motive):

GIRL SHOWS SPECIAL ATTENTION TO A MAN WHO ATTRACTS HER INTEREST

There were other fellows at the little party, but not for Jane; she had eyes only for Harry. At every opportunity she bestowed

[3] This request violated the psychology of the mores, and we paid the penalty by getting such inconsistent results that no statistical use could be made of the double minuses and the double pluses. The response of disapproval or of admiration is a naïve response. But when one undertakes to place a quantitative estimate on the amount of his disapproval or his admiration, his response ceases to be naïve and becomes speculative.

smiles upon him and managed more times than accident would account for to get engaged in conversation with him, or to be near him when a game was to start.

The following table shows the percentages of the persons in each group placing this scene in the indicated categories. In the column at the extreme right is shown the resultant "badness" value of the item for each group and for the groups combined, derived by a process described in our next chapter. This item has a mild negative value for all of the groups except one, consequently a mild negative value for the whole. The maximum badness value (where every member disapproves the act) is −3.00, while the maximum goodness value is +3.00.

TABLE I

PERCENTAGE OF APPROVALS AND DISAPPROVALS ON ABOVE ITEM AND RESULTING SIGMA-VALUE

Group	Per Cent Approving	Per Cent Neutral	Per Cent Disapproving	Sigma-Value
Wage girls	6	28	66	−.84
Faculty members	6	66	28	−.28
Students	10	65	25	−.19
Élite girls	20	56	24	−.05
Wage boys	15	78	7	+.10
Total	11	62	27	−.29

Having thus determined values for each of the scenes, our remaining task was to arrange these in hierarchical order, extending from the highest plus values through zero at neutral to the low minus values. Since each of the four scales contained in the neighborhood of eighty scenes, the whole of a series could not be conveniently printed on one strip as a single "ladder" of values. We therefore classified the scenes into sub-scales and arranged the scenes in descending order of values within each sub-scale. But most of these sub-scales contained within themselves subordinate phases. These we outlined at the top of the printed scale, indicating each by a letter which was then printed before each scene in the finished scale so that anyone employing the scale in rating motion pictures might readily find those scenes that belong to the pattern of conduct he is attempting to rate. An examination of the scales printed in the appendix of this volume will show what we mean. However, in this volume the scales are not printed on long strips, as they were in our use of them, but on ordinary book pages, so that the material of each of the sub-scales extends through several consecutive pages.

Our finished scales conformed to the following outline of phases:

I. Aggressiveness of a Girl in Love-Making

    A. Motive: Real love. Techniques: Direct approaches, I.
        a. Directly invites man to companionship by word or deed.
        b. Shows special solicitude for a particular man.
        c. "Pursues" a man.
        d. Resorts to physical manipulation.
    B. Motive: Real love. Techniques: Direct approaches, II.
        e. Takes the initiative in avowing love.
        f. Directly invites avowal.
        g. Indirectly avows love, as in a song.
        h. Argues for companionship or for marriage.
    C. Motive: Real love. Technique: Coquetry.
        a. Inveigles a man into situations calculated to bring love responses.
        b. Appeals for protection, or gives protection.
        c. Is attentive, solicitous, and purposively appreciative.
        d. Resorts to banter and flattery.
        e. Bestows smiles, and other coquetry, upon him.
        f. Invites pursuit by retreat.

D. Motive: Spontaneous expression or thrill. Technique: Coquetry.
  a. Inveigles a man into situations calculated to bring love responses.
  b. Appeals for protection, or gives protection.
  c. Is attentive, solicitous, and purposively appreciative.
  d. Resorts to banter and flattery.
  e. Bestows smiles, and other coquetry, upon him.
  f. Invites pursuit by retreat.

E. Motive: Spontaneous expression or thrill. Technique: Direct approaches.
  a. Directly invites a man to companionship by word or deed.
  b. Shows special solicitude for a particular man.
  c. "Pursues" a man.
  d. Resorts to physical manipulation.
  e. Takes the initiative in avowing love.
  f. Directly invites avowal.
  g. Indirectly avows love, as in a song or in an expression of solicitude.
  h. Argues for companionship or for marriage.

F. Motive: Material advantage.
  a. Get a job or promotion.
  b. Marriage or companionship for material advantage.
  c. Money or presents.
  d. Business for employer.

II. DEMOCRATIC ATTITUDES AND PRACTICES.

A. Social status.
  a. Attitude of those of "higher" social standing toward those of "lower" standing.

B. Social status.
  a. Attitude of those of "lower" status toward those of "higher" standing.

C. Treatment of employees and subordinates.

D. Race relations, general.

E. Race relations, Negroes.

III. Kissing and Caressing.
  A. By married people.
    a. In private.
    b. In public.
  B. Kissing in private.
    a. By serious lovers or betrothed persons.
    b. By casual lovers.
  C. In public, by casual lovers or slight acquaintances.
    a. Kissing.
    b. Caressing.
  D. In public, by serious lovers or betrothed persons.
    a. Kissing.
    b. Caressing.

IV. The Treatment of Children by Parents.
  A. Companionship with children.
    a. Delight in the presence of children.
    b. Expression of love for children.
    c. Participation in entertainment.
  B. Disciplining of children.
    a. Discipline through discussion, reason, or rewards.
    b. Impulsive *versus* purposive discipline.
    c. Coöperation of parents in discipline.
  C. Sacrifice by parents for children.
  D. Tolerance of the point of view of children.
    a. Appreciation of the child's love affairs.
    b. Bolstering the dignity and the morale of children.
    c. Sharing confidences.
    d. Willingness to forgive error.

When we employ a measuring instrument we always wish to know how reliable it is. If we repeat measurements of the same object with our device shall we always get the same results, or will our results fluctuate considerably? When such devices as meter sticks or balances are employed the problem of the reliability of the measurements is not a very serious one, although even here the meter stick may vary a little due to changes in temperature, the balances may be out of adjustment or may be affected by differing distances from the earth's center, and there may be small errors in reading the instruments. But in psychological and social research we are obliged to use much less stable measuring devices, so that here the question of the reliability of measurement becomes a question of major importance. In any good test of educational achievement the testmaker takes pains to ascertain the reliability of his test and announces an index of its reliability.

We investigated the reliability of our scale values by working up the indices separately for halves of each group and ascertaining the coefficient of correlation between the two halves. That gives us a basis for knowing how closely a second calculation of values, from a new sampling of data, may be expected to agree with the first calculation. If the correlation exceeds .90, and the means of the two halves are nearly alike, the reliability is high. Not many educational tests have reliability coefficients above .90, although occasionally a test is found in which the reliability runs as high as .97 or .98. The highest possible correlation is 1.00. Our reliabilities are given below for separate groups and for all the groups combined. It is the reliability of the combined groups that is of principal concern to us, since values derived from this whole group are the ones that stand as indices in our finished scales. As explained in the next chapter, we worked up our index values by two different methods, then chose for the permanent values in our scales the indices by the "median-man technique." Reliabilities by the former method are shown at the left in the table below, while those by the latter method are shown at the right. Our computed correlations had to be between the index values derived from a group half of the size of the one from which we had got responses and those derived from the other half. But the

TABLE II

RELIABILITY COEFFICIENTS OF THE SCALE VALUES

Group and Scale	Mid-Abscissa-Man Technique			Median-Man Technique		
	$r \frac{1}{2}$ vs. $\frac{1}{2}$	r Pred.	Means	$r \frac{1}{2}$ vs. $\frac{1}{2}$	r Pred.	Means
Kissing:						
Students	.925	.961	−.25, −.36	.975	.987	−.31, −.34
Faculty	.940	.969	−.64, −.62	.952	.975	−.59, −.56
Wage boys	.825	.904	−.76, −.62	.866	.928	−.52, −.53
Wage girls	.794	.885	+.28, −.50	.876	.933	+.22, −.45
Élite girls	.841	.914	−.11, −.36	.857	.922	−.15, −.28
ALL GROUPS	.975	.987	−.31, −.33	.975	.987	−.29, −.31
Democracy:						
Students	.945	.972	−.21, −.32	.940	.969	−.21, −.32
Faculty	.941	.970	−.51, −.48	.913	.954	−.54, −.52
Wage boys	.903	.949	−.64, −.75	.872	.931	−.51, −.63
Wage girls	.658	.794	+.22, −.19	.725	.840	+.18, −.20
Élite girls	.921	.959	−.37, −.30	.940	.969	−.29, −.16
ALL GROUPS	.98	.990	−.29, −.32	.989	.994	−.28, −.29
Parent-Child:						
Students	.836	.911	−.44, −.37	.940	.969	−.47, −.40
Faculty	.952	.975	−.54, −.52	.946	.972	−.64, −.61
Wage boys	.845	.916	−.54, −.46	.857	.922	−.58, −.43
Wage girls	.853	.921	−.02, −.18	.808	.893	−.12, −.19
Élite girls	.917	.957	−.45, −.57	.893	.943	−.44, −.54
ALL GROUPS	.972	.986	+.34, −.41	.981	.990	−.45, −.38
Aggressiveness:						
Students	.860	.930	−.91, −.96	.905	.950	−.64, −.72
Faculty	.796	.886	−1.16, −1.42	.898	.947	−.95, −1.08
Wage boys	.746	.855	−1.01, −1.02	.892	.942	−.60, −.65
Wage girls	.578	.733	−.50, −1.29	.662	.796	−.40, −1.20
Élite girls	.853	.921	−.98, −.59	.851	.919	−.85, −.92
ALL GROUPS	.928	.963	−.82, −.81	.968	.983	−.65, −.67

reliability from the whole number against another sampling of the same size would be higher than that of half against half. We applied the Spearman Prophecy Formula in order to predict this former correlation from our knowledge of the latter, indicating these stepped-up r's in a second column.

These correlations are extremely high. They indicate that responses from enough individuals were used in constructing the scales to stabilize the values in an entirely satisfactory manner. The technique of using these scales in getting a quantitative description of the mores of some thirteen different type groups of people is described in Chapter IV and their use in rating motion pictures in Chapter V. At those points reliabilities of measurements in those applications will be shown.

In this chapter we have explained the technique of making scales for measuring the mores on the one hand and the movies on the other. These scales consist of a series of briefly described bits of conduct arranged in hierarchical order, with a numerical index of "goodness" or "badness" attached to each. These numerical indices were derived from the percentages of 187 persons who placed the several items in the pile labeled "admired," "neutral," or "disapproved," the numerical values being in terms of the standard deviation of a hypothetical normal distribution. The scales are exhibited as Appendix A of this volume. In measuring scenes in motion pictures the scales are to be used in much the same manner as handwriting or composition scales have long been employed for measurement in their respective fields. Calculation of the coefficient of correlation between the scale values from random halves of the scale makers proved that the scales are very reliable measuring instruments.

We shall next discuss, in a more technical manner, the nature of our measuring unit.

CHAPTER III

OUR UNIT OF MEASUREMENT

THE basis of our measuring scheme is the proportion of persons who declared themselves as admiring, disapproving, or feeling neutral toward samples of conduct submitted to them in writing for their reaction. If a bit of conduct is sufficiently "good" everybody, or practically everybody, will admire it; if it is sufficiently "bad" everybody will disapprove it; if it is not very good and not very bad, many persons will be neutral toward it. If we start with a bit of conduct that is neutral and change it little by little in the direction of badness, very soon some of those observers who had been neutral will begin to dissent. As we move further toward badness we shall cause more and more of our observers to join the dissenters until, by the time we reach extreme degrees of badness, all or practically all will have done so. And a similar thing will be true as we move out from neutral toward goodness, only here the conversion will be from neutrality toward admiration. We can, therefore, fittingly construct a unit for measuring degrees of badness or goodness in terms of the proportion of observers who have been won from neutrality to disapproval or from neutrality to admiration at any given point. Somewhat analogous units have frequently been employed hitherto for measuring the difficulty of examination questions or the merit of handwriting or of composition.

But if approvals behave in this application in the same fashion as other phenomena do, the behavior is of a fascinatingly interesting type. Suppose we take as an illustration of this behavior the distribution of men as to size. Suppose, to make the matter concrete, a large tailoring firm is planning the number of suits of clothes it should make so as to match the proportions of sizes with the proportions of men of those sizes. First there would need to be considered the middle, the average, the modal sizes. Of these there would be a great many. Moving toward larger sizes, the proportion would not change so rapidly for a while, though it would decline a little. But after moderately large sizes

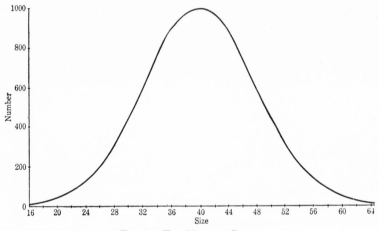

Fig. 1.—The Normal Curve

had been passed the number required would begin to drop sharply and continue to drop until it reached a rather small figure. Nevertheless, a few of the larger sizes would be required—fewer and fewer as the sizes became more extreme. And the same sort of behavior would characterize the demand as the sizes changed from average to small. If we lay off the sizes of the suits on a horizontal axis and the numbers required for each size on a vertical axis, and draw a line through

the ends of the uprights representing the number of each
size so as to close in the distribution under a curve, we shall
have a picture something like Figure 1. A distribution of
this shape is called a "normal distribution." The curve is,
you see, bell-shaped. It has remarkable mathematical properties. The shape of the curve is expressed by a formula
that has fascinated research workers for more than a century,
perhaps for two centuries. The formula is:

$$y = \frac{N}{\sigma\sqrt{2\,\pi}}\; e\; \frac{-\,x^2}{2\,\sigma^2}$$

It has been found that very many of the phenomena we
wish to measure conform to such distribution—the height
of corn stalks, the number of times heads turn up in many
throws of pennies, the scores pupils earn on an educational
test, the errors made in observations, etc. Techniques
turning on the properties of the normal curve are among
the most useful devices in psychological and sociological
research.

That some such behavior is characteristic of approvals
and disapprovals of items of conduct is easy enough to
discern. Suppose we start with treatment of children by
parents that is just what we are all accustomed to seeing—
just the ordinary, everyday mode of acting. The bulk of
people will think this treatment satisfactory but nothing to
praise and nothing to condemn. But let the parents manifest
a little cruelty toward their children. If this is very mild,
few people will resent it; but as the parents show more and
more selfishness their selfishness will begin to be noticed
by progressively more persons and, after a while, the number resenting it will increase at a precipitous rate; nevertheless a few unsympathetic ones will remain unresentful,
though fewer and fewer as the selfishness becomes extreme.

A converse thing happens as the conduct changes from neutral toward unselfishness: at first only a few will notice and admire the act; with greater increase in unselfishness more will notice it until, after a critical point has been passed, the proportion whose attention and admiration have been challenged will increase at a precipitous rate; but a few obtuse ones will remain unmoved, fewer and fewer as the conduct becomes more beautiful.

The unit we employ in this study for measuring degree of goodness or badness of conduct is put in terms of the distance we must go out from the neutral point in either

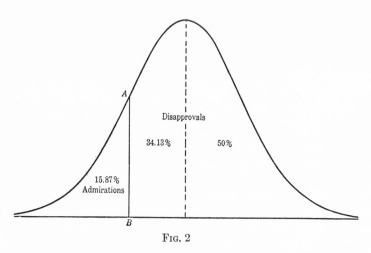

Fig. 2

direction in order to cause a given proportion of a group to shift from approval to disapproval or the reverse. Our unit is: *Such amount of change in badness as will produce sufficient shock to attract the attention of an excess of 34.13 per cent of a group when the point of origin is the mode (middle) of the distribution of evaluations, or an equivalent percentage if the origin is any other point in the distribution.* If this change is in the direction of disapprovals, we attach to the measures the minus sign; if in the direction of approvals, the plus sign.

Such unit has been extensively employed in research. It is called the "standard deviation" or, to employ the name of the Greek letter customarily used to symbolize it, *sigma*. Statistically trained readers will understand why we have set for its definition the peculiar 34.13 per cent; to attempt to explain this to others would lead us too far afield. The following two figures will illustrate the method of determining goodness or badness indices. For the sake of sim-

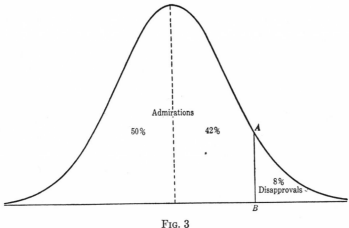

Admirations

50%   42%   A

8%
Disapprovals

B

FIG. 3

plicity a neutral belt has not been shown, only approvals and disapprovals. According to Fig. 2, 84.13 per cent of the judges indicated disapproval of the item, which was 50 per cent, constituting half of the distribution, and 34.13 per cent beyond the middle. That locates the line AB, which indicates the place of the item, at -1.00, a minus value because it has more disapprovals than approvals. In Fig. 3 the line AB, which locates the item, is placed so that 42 per cent of the judges lie between it and the mean. Its value is, therefore, somewhat more than +1.00 sigma, since only 34.13 per cent would have been required to make the distance 1.00. Reference to a table of sigma-values shows that the distance from the mean to include 42 per cent of the cases is 1.41 sigmas. Hence the value of the item in Fig. 3 is +1.41.

We did not, however, compel our respondents, in passing upon the bits of conduct placed before them, to choose between *disapproval* and *admiration;* we gave them as a third alternative, *neutral.* The reader will recall that, in our discussion of the nature of the mores, it was pointed out that the normal response is a matter-of-course attitude in the face of most goings-on in society. It is only those acts that markedly conflict with the mores that arouse an actively emotional response—fear and resentment if the deviation is in a direction that is felt to be dangerous, and admiration if the deviation is in the direction in which the group aspires to move. It was natural, therefore, that the response of any judge to many an item should be: "That is nothing to be alarmed about nor anything to praise," and that he should vote his attitude toward it as "neutral." In the distribution of judgments on any item we have, therefore, a certain percentage of *admirers* at one tail of the distribution, a certain percentage of *dissenters* at the other tail, and a broad belt of *neutrals* between these tails. We also permitted our respondents to express *great* admiration or *great* disapproval, but these responses did not prove of value and we made no statistical use of them. We located the value of an item at the *middle of the neutral belt* of the distribution of percentages of judgments on it. The following diagram will illustrate:

There were 68 per cent of admirers (50 plus 18), 10 per cent of disapprovers, and 22 per cent of neutrals—11 per cent on each side of the mid-point of the neutral belt. Hence the value of the item is that sigma which corresponds to the placement of an ordinate inclosing between itself and the

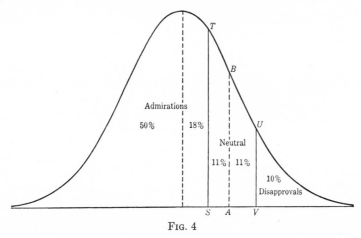

FIG. 4

mean 29 per cent of the cases. Reference to a table of sigma-values shows that to be +.81.

But what *is* the middle of the "trapazoidal" figure, *TSVU?* There are three possibilities:

1. The mean (average) position.

2. The median position—so placed that half of the judges in the neutral belt stand above the point and half below it.

3. The mid-abscissa position—halfway between the boundary lines of the neutral belt.

There was no particular reason for considering the first seriously, but each of the other two had strong claims. The mid-abscissa point has the advantage that it is just as far from the place where disapprovals begin as it is from the place where admirations leave off. Hence the judge who stands at the mid-abscissa point is like the proverbial ass placed midway between two haystacks—so completely poised between them that he died of starvation unable to decide which to reach for. The median man is closer to the inner boundary of the belt but exactly half of the persons in the belt stand to the left of him, and hence may be presumed to be slightly inclined toward admiration, while exactly the other half stand on the other side. After actually using the mid-abscissa point in our study for a while we changed all our machinery over to the median point, translating to the second system the ratings we so far had made. The further we went the more cumbersome the mid-abscissa technique became and the more we found the conditions of our problem driving us to the median-point technique. Besides, we found the latter far less erratic, so that the reliability coefficients of the values determined by it ran .01 or .02 higher than those by the other technique. Our rule, then, for locating the goodness or badness value of any item was to locate the ordinate at the median point in the neutral belt of our distribution and to express the degree of goodness or badness in terms of the distance of this median point from the mean, with the standard deviation as the unit of measure.

The standard deviation is, then, our unit of measure. But the standard deviation of *what?* About that we have as yet been too indefinite. Two alternatives confronted us between which we were obliged to choose:

(1) We might have the evaluations posited at equal, or at least at known, positions along a scale of badness objectively considered. Concretely speaking, we might have a group of judges sit before a series of ten or more boxes and, divorcing their own personal evaluations from the process, distribute to these ten positions descriptions of bits of con-

duct according to the degree to which the acts would gener-
ally be considered extreme. We might then find the median
position of each of these bits of conduct from all the rank-
ings and, to give relative positions a standard meaning,
put them in terms of distances from an arbitrary starting
point when the distances have all been expressed in terms
of the sigma of one of the distributions to which all the other
sigmas around the means of their own distributions have
been equated. In this case our measure would be in terms
of change in badness objectively considered. Our standard
deviation would be taken from distributions of bits of conduct posited on a scale according to estimates of such objective differences. This is the method so brilliantly developed by Dr. L. L. Thurstone and applied by him in the
making of his Attitude Scales.[1]

(2) We might take the evaluations as merely attraction
or repulsion without any effort on the part of the judges to
posit them on a quantitatively ordered scale, then get our
degrees of badness from the relative proportions of judges
reacting one way or the other. This would be a measure of
badness in terms of *shock* to observers. It would rest on
the assumption that the significant thing about conflict
with the mores is not the amount of "badness" intrinsically
involved in the act itself, if such "badness" could in any
way be determined, but the disturbance (annoyance) such
act causes to the persons who observe it or participate in it.
And it would assume that the amount of such disturbance
is truly evidenced by the proportion of observers or partici-
pants thus disturbed. The standard deviation by this technique would not be one taken from an empirical distribution
of serially posited units with empirically determined fre-

[1] Thurstone, L. L., and Chase, E. J., *The Measurement of Attitudes*, University
of Chicago Press, 1929, Chap. III.

quencies; it would be one taken from a generalized distribution that hypothetically represents the behavior of the evaluations in question. It would be the standard deviation of the series $(\frac{1}{2}+\frac{1}{2})^n$ as n approaches infinity, the $(\frac{1}{2}+\frac{1}{2})$ representing the total (unit) area of any distribution in which we are concerned merely with proportions and in which our data permit us to know how these proportions are divided between the two tails of the distribution.

The first method has some marked advantages, especially for certain kinds of applications. But it has the disadvantage of calling for a type of response that, in the case of our application, is entirely artificial. The mores rest upon direct impulsive responses. They are unratiocinated and often unreasonable. One's reaction is an immediate restlessness or fascination when there is conflict with a *mos*. While one can readily classify an act as admirable, neutral, or disturbing, he cannot assign to it a quantitative amount of goodness or badness without abandoning his naïveté and becoming psychologically speculative. This method provides, too, no meaningful zero point; such zero point would have to be superposed upon the ratings by a further artificial process. The scales resulting from the first method would be, therefore, wholly artificial; they would be the product of processes quite distinct from the processes they were intended to measure. The making of the scales would be one thing; their application to the determination of the mores a wholly different thing. This would not, however, be necessarily a fatal defect. A measuring instrument might appropriately enough be artificial if only it were known to consist of equal units that could be placed in one to one relation with the things to be measured.

The second method makes the process of constructing the

scales a normal part of the process of moral evaluation. It is oriented from a zero point that has a basic and sociologically significant meaning. And there is feasible a constant parallelism between the techniques of its construction and the techniques of its application in measuring the mores of various type-groups. We chose the second method. Either method would have done reasonably well. In fact the rank-order of our scale values would probably have differed very little when determined by the two techniques. We shall later see that the precision of measurement in the applications to which we must subject these scales is so crude that small defects in the unit of measurement are lost in the results. However, in order to avoid basing too much weight upon the supposed equality of our units of measurement, we avoided arithmetical averages and employed instead point measures as largely as possible.

It will be clear that our measuring unit rests on the assumption that, in respect to sensitiveness to increasing or decreasing badness in any particular type of conduct, the members of a group form a normal distribution. In the light of the fact that in power of reasoning, retention of information, and various other mental traits they are known to form a normal distribution, the assumption that in respect to sensitiveness to moral values they do so, does not seem to be a violent assumption. But the reader should carefully note that *to assume a normal distribution of members of a group in respect to sensitiveness to changes in conduct is a very different thing from assuming that the evaluations on conduct themselves make a normal distribution.* To assume normality in respect to sensitiveness is merely to assume that the successive members noticing the change follow one another with a given law of frequencies. It is to make no assumption whatever that the amounts of change objectively measured that call forth these conversions by the successive frequencies are equal or are normally distributed.

In fact we found plenty of evidence that moral evaluations on random samples of conduct distribute themselves in a manner that is very far from normal. It had often been observed that people are more prone to condemn than they are to commend. Where the guarding of the mores is at stake persons sensitive to the ever-present danger of lapsing from the levels attained take a "fine" deed calmly when it is done but look with fear and disapproval at anything that tends toward relaxation. Try as hard as we might we could not find or construct samples of described conduct on which large percentages of judges would vote admiration, but we could easily find samples on which they would nearly unanimously vote disapproval. So all of our distributions on aggregates of scenes tended to be skewed toward the negative end—very greatly on the scales on kissing and aggressiveness but also markedly on those on the relation of parents to children and on democracy.

Mathematically a normal curve is generated by developing the binomial $(\frac{1}{2}+\frac{1}{2})^n$, the height of the curve at any point being the value of the coefficient at that point in the binomial expansion. This curve is symmetrical because the two factors in the binomial are equal. But in our problem the weighting is unequal; people are *more* set to pronounce unfavorable judgments than favorable ones. The two factors in the binomial are, perhaps, something like $(\frac{1}{4}+\frac{3}{4})$, where the $\frac{1}{4}$ represents the chance of getting approval and the $\frac{3}{4}$ the chance of disapproval. If this unbalanced binomial is expanded to the nth power and the results graphed, a markedly skew curve of distribution results—similar to the ones we get from our data. Moreover our curves are likely

to be not only skew but also more narrowly pinched together at the top than the normal curve—leptokurtic,
the technical statistician would say. This is because in any
true group there is a high degree of "solidarity"—much
more than chance would provide. By reason of their association the members are pulled together and are made
like-minded, so that, as a bit of conduct moves toward
goodness or toward badness from the neutral point, the

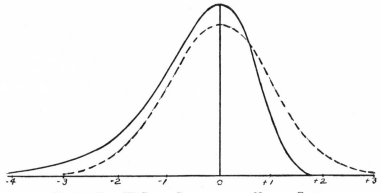

FIG. 5.—TYPE VI CURVE SUPERPOSED ON NORMAL CURVE

members change sides much more rapidly when the critical
point is reached than the normal curve would suggest. A
curve that correctly describes the distribution of these judgments within any true group would need, therefore, to be
a skew and leptokurtic one instead of the relatively flat
and symmetrical normal curve. Such a curve is provided
by the Type VI curve of the Pearson series, the formula of
which is:

$$y = y_0(x-a)^q x^{-q}$$

Fig. 5 will show the nature of the Type VI curve with a
normal curve superposed upon it.

At an expense of labor that only those can appreciate who have attempted the integration of such complex equations, we worked out the integrals of this distribution with such values for the constants as would best fit our data, expecting to be obliged to use them in our study. If we had adopted a unit that turned upon the distribution of evaluations rather than upon the distribution of persons with respect to sensitiveness to values, we should have been committed to the integrals of this complicated curve, changing with every area investigated, as measuring tools. Fortunately the choice of the second method, couched in terms of elements that presumably make normal distributions, freed us from that necessity.

For, regardless of differences in the external causes, as we move out toward badness we have gone one unit whenever we have moved far enough from the mode to cause 34.13 per cent to change from neutral to disapproval; when we have gone far enough to cause 47.72 per cent to change we have gone two units, etc. And in the same manner when we have moved far enough toward goodness to cause 34.13 per cent to change from neutral to admiration we have gone one unit and when we have gone far enough to cause 47.72 per cent to change we have gone two units. Thus the curve automatically becomes symmetrical when we define our units in terms of sensitiveness evidenced by the number whose attention has been attracted rather than in terms of objective changes in the stimulus. Whether it requires greater amounts of change in goodness, if we could measure this objectively, to shock this percentage into admiration than it does in badness to shock an equal percentage into disapproval, is of no concern to us. For us two units are equal when the shock occasioned is equal, and we count the shock equal when an equal proportion of judges have noticed it.

The distributions of actual evaluations involve, too, not only skew curves but also differing variabilities on the part of different groups and in the case of different items. Some groups are much more compact than others; the percentage of the group that will react to deviations of a certain size is much greater in the case of some groups than of others. Those that manifest a high degree of solidarity are

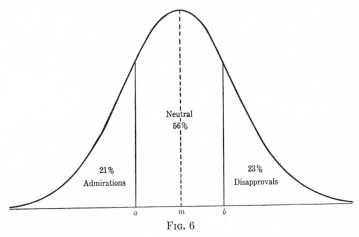

Neutral
56%

21%
Admirations

23%
Disapprovals

a *m* *b*

FIG. 6

(unless this phenomenon is due to accident in particular cases) true groups in the sociological sense; to the extent to which there is great diversity, to that extent we have mere aggregates of individuals instead of true groups. In Table IV of our next chapter we give measured evidences of the variabilities of our groups as well as the central tendencies of their evaluations. Variabilities of judgments on individual items of conduct also differ. Figures 6 and 7 are hypothetical distributions illustrating such differences.

We may compare the variabilities of these two distributions by comparing the distance between two or more pairs of similar points. We may take the distance between such pairs of points in the above distribution $a-b$ and $a'-b'$, each of which is the dividing point between neutral and admiration on the one side and disapproval on the other. The dotted line represents the mean of the distributions. Distance ma, mb, $m'a'$, $m'b'$, may all be put in terms of distances from the means expressed in sigma-values. Let us call these distances for convenience, x, y, x', and y' re-

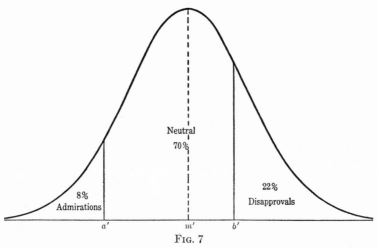

Fig. 7

spectively. Then, on the assumption that the span between the place where the admirations of a group leave off and that where the disapprovals begin is always a span of the same length if this distance could be measured in objective terms, $(x+y) = (x'+y')$. Therefore $\sigma(x+y) = \sigma'(x'+y')$ and

$$\frac{\sigma'}{\sigma} = \frac{x+y}{x'+y'}$$

In the case of the above samples the sigma-ratios are

$$\frac{.80+.74}{.58+1.40} = .78$$

The distribution on the right is, thus, only .78 as variable as the one on the left.

As long as the distributions remain reasonably symmetrical and normal such quantitative comparisons of variabilities would be an easy task. But as the distributions become skew and depart from the normal, the work becomes highly complicated; for the calculations need to turn on the integrals of curves with skewness and kurtosis indices that make a unique combination, and hence need to be separately calculated, for curves of every shape.

But to recognize that the evaluations as passed on actual items of conduct make distributions of unequal variabilities is again a very different thing from saying that there are unequal standard deviations in the distributions of judges according to sensitiveness. There may or there may not be. Consider first a group in which members freely and sympathetically intermingle but in which they differ in judgment in regard to the propriety of certain kinds of conduct. This sympathetic intermingling may make them tolerant of the point of view of the others even though they do not personally accept this point of view. Because of the habituation to other points of view and the consequent tolerance of them, there may be much greater shifts from the disapprovals of individual members without arousing violent emotional responses than would be the case in homogeneous groups. Thus differences in variability of evaluations would not parallel differences in variability of sensitiveness. When we turn to the cases where the members do not sympathetically intermingle and hence do not become accustomed to, and tolerant of, the points of view other than their own, we may find violently conflicting evaluations and emotional tensions to which wholly insufficient justice is done by the standard deviations taken from the proportion of the group indicated by the size of the majority vote. Here our unit becomes wholly unsatisfactory and psychologically indefensible. But that abnormality is due not so much to the nature of our unit as to the abnormality of the group with which we are operating. Our supposed group is not a true group at all in the sociological sense; it is a mere aggregate. The remedy is not the statistical one of attempting to correct mathematically for the abnormal variability but the sociological one of confining our operations to true groups. In our study we made a long and frantic effort to correct our sigma-values for differing variabilities by the technique indicated in the paragraph above, but we became convinced that we were introducing more error than we were correcting. So we let our variabilities stand undoctored. In this matter as in skewness we pay no attention to the nature of the conduct required to produce the shock; when we have moved far enough from the mode in either direction to shock 34.13 per cent of the group into change from neutrality to admiration or to disapproval we count one unit, and when we have caused 47.72 per cent to change we count two units, and corresponding proportions for other distances.

We have much use in our study for the curve of cumulative dissents or approvals, called the ogive curve. Suppose, starting at one extreme of a distribution, .1 per cent of the judges disapprove a certain item located at the beginning of our series; .8 per cent disapprove the second; 3 per cent the third; 9 per cent the fourth, etc. Then the second item would evidently be disapproved by .9 per cent of the judges, because both those against the second and those against the milder first would be against it, .1+.8=.9 per cent. The third would be disapproved by .1+.8+3=3.9 per cent; the fourth by .1+.8+3+9=12.9 per cent, etc. If we continue this process for all the items, representing at each stage the frequency at that stage plus all the preceding frequencies and "smooth" our graph, we shall have a curve like the following:

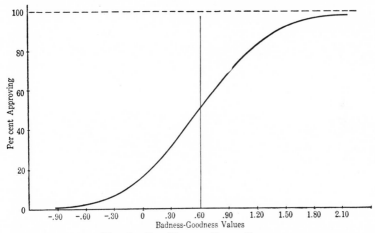

FIG. 8.—THE NORMAL OGIVE CURVE

This is called the "normal ogive curve," since it is produced by summing a normal distribution. Knowing the mathematical properties of a curve like this we are able to calculate at what point in badness values the curve of disapprovals of a group would cross the 25 per cent line, or the 50 per cent line, or any other line, by interpolation or by extrapolation from other known points in the curve. That is, we are able to compute the badness value of an item that exactly 25 per cent, or 50 per cent or any other per cent of the group would disapprove, even when that exact proportion was not found in the responses to any item but when smaller or larger percentages of disapprovals were known on near-by items.

This chapter has shown in some detail the nature of our measuring unit. This unit is couched in terms of the sensitiveness of the members of a group to changes in conduct in respect to approval or disapproval. One unit is such an amount of change in "badness" or in "goodness" as is required to shock 34.13 per cent of the members of the group into changing from assent to dissent or the reverse when the point of orientation is that of complete neutrality on the part of the group on the average. The unit is, thus, the standard deviation of a hypothetically perfect normal distribution. If the deviations from the neutral position are toward admirations, the values are called plus or "good"; if toward disapprovals, they are called minus or "bad." The value of an item is taken as the plus or minus sigma-distance from the mean of the distribution to the median position in the "neutral" belt, which lies between the lower limit of the admirations on the right and the upper limit of the disapprovals on the left. The numerical indices might be expected to range from +3.00 to −3.00 sigmas (though theoretically the range might be infinite). But in practice we did not find them extending above +1.23 nor below −2.26, which means that we were unable to construct any scenes for which 100 per cent of the judges would express admiration or 100 per cent express disapproval.

CHAPTER IV

MEASURING THE MORES OF
REPRESENTATIVE GROUPS

SOMETHING of a measure of moral standards was involved in the determination of the values for the elements of our scale, as far as the five groups were concerned who contributed toward its construction. But we needed to extend measures of approvals to many additional groups and to do so by a less cumbersome technique than that involved in the evaluations which had the construction of scales as their main objective and the measurement of standards of particular groups as only an incidental by-product. The scales, described in Chapter II, provided a tool for this. Not only did these scales permit us to measure the standards of such groups as we wished to use in this study but they also constitute a measuring instrument of fixed meaning which can be applied any time in the future, whether in making further studies of motion pictures, or in investigations of the relations of fiction or drama to morality, or in comparing the standards of one society with those of other societies in different parts of the world, or in determining the change of moral standards from one age to another.

A useful scale must ordinarily have its units arranged in ascending order. Thus the inches in a ruler are numbered serially and so are pounds on a balance, degrees on a thermometer, or amperes on an ammeter. In order to have a similarly systematic measuring instrument we arranged the items of conduct constituting any series in the order of values as determined by the procedure described in our preceding chapter, running from the highest plus values down through zero to the lowest minus values. There were nineteen such scales, each measuring a phase of the area of conduct we were investigating. However, as previously explained, each phase had sub-phases indicated by letter symbols, and one phase had so many scale elements that it had to be printed on two strips. Thus on each scale the items were arranged in order of badness according to the reaction of the 187 persons who had made the fundamental responses. But, although the numerical values of these scale elements were known to us as a condition necessary for the hierar- chical organization, these values were not printed on the strips lest they should prejudice the desired further ratings. The scales were then submitted to persons representing thirteen type-groups for the purpose of determining how far down each scale conduct could go and yet lie within the approvals of these several groups. The groups employed, and the number of persons responding from each, are as follows:

33 adult miners in western Pennsylvania, and their wives.
37 later-adolescent sons and daughters of the above class of miners.
39 graduate students at Pennsylvania State College attending Saturday classes or summer sessions.
39 Negro school teachers attending the summer session of Hampton Institute, Virginia.
25 ministers of the gospel in Lancaster, Pa.
21 ministers of the gospel scattered throughout the United States.
37 adult factory workers in western Pennsylvania.
25 male college seniors at Pennsylvania State College.
25 female college seniors at Pennsylvania State College.
25 business men around Reading, Pa., manufacturers and mer- chants.

23 rural male and female parents, members of a Brethren church community in Berks County, Pa.

31 later-adolescent sons and daughters of the above group of rural Brethren.

32 university professors of national reputation and leaders in social reform movements, called "Social Leaders" in our tables.

In addition to these groups we could draw upon the evaluations described in our preceding chapter from the following groups:

50 Penn. State faculty members and their wives; 42 young women of New York City and Baltimore belonging to the élite class; 27 young men working in factories around Bridgeville, Pa.; 18 young women working in factories in York, Pa., and an additional set of 25 male and 25 female seniors at Pennsylvania State College.

The instructions quoted below will show concretely the basis of responses.

DIRECTIONS FOR RATING

Each of the scales describes a number of bits of conduct ranging from good to bad. A certain theme runs through each scale, which you will find stated at the top of the scale. Some of the acts described you will probably admire, some you will disapprove, and others you will think neutral—O.K. but nothing to brag about. Those you admire you should mark with an X in the left margin; those you disapprove, with a —; and those you neither admire nor disapprove but merely think "ordinary" as life goes, with a O.

However, you may find it feasible to use a more economical system than marking each item. The items are arranged from good toward bad according to the judgment of about 175 persons. You may, therefore, find that nearly all the items of which you disapprove lie below a certain point and all those you admire, above a certain other point. In that case you may mark X, —, or O opposite the ones near those points and indicate your attitude toward the others by continuing a tail past them from your last mark. Perhaps it would be best to begin reading each scale somewhere near the middle of the page, passing out from there in each direction; then you can pass on the extreme cases by merely reading the titles, reading the paragraph as a whole only if the title suggests that you might want to mark it differently from its neighbors.

You may not, however, find the order of items in the strips to suit you at all. Good ones may be mixed among the bad ones and the reverse. Watch for these and mark them X, —, or O according to your own notion. Please be sure to mark the scales in such fashion that we could not possibly misunderstand your intention. Papers that we cannot interpret with certainty we cannot use.

Please mark these according to your *own* actual feeling, not according to what is customarily thought or said. You need have no fear that your markings will be shown to anyone. We shall have hundreds of these strips coming to us and we examine them only for the marks and report in terms of averages for the group, never in terms of the names of individuals.

In deciding how to mark the items a good test to put to yourself is this: Would I be proud, mortified, or satisfied if someone very dear to me should act as this item relates—a sister, mother, daughter, father, or son?

Please note that each strip is a separate scale. Mark each one. After marking them return them to the person from whom you received them.

To most of our groups the scales were carried by canvassers, usually college students or social workers. Those submitted to the group we called "Social Leaders," and a few others, were sent by mail. Although it was no small task to mark the scales, we got a most generous response and we have every reason to believe that practically all the respondents did the work carefully and honestly. Indeed some of them did it *too* carefully. It was our desire to have *naïve* responses, not ratiocinated ones, since *naïve* responses are characteristic of the mores in life. We hoped the reader would respond immediately and impulsively to the scenes just as he would to the acts if they occurred in real life. Some of our respondents, especially the more intellectual ones, spoiled their replies by too great conscientiousness. They speculated about whether this act would be right or wrong in this community or in that, if the circumstances were these or those, and the like. Particularly they debated with themselves whether such a scene ought to be depicted in motion pictures. In all such cases we failed to get the *mores*, which are characteristically emotional, impulsive, and confident, but got instead psychological and sociological speculations, which are rationalistic and halting. Indeed the intellectuals behaved less like a group than any other set from whom we got responses; the Q of the Social Leaders on aggressiveness was .65 while that of adult Brethren was only .31 and that of Factory Workers .44.

A serious problem now confronted us: how to work up statistically the returns from each group so as to express the status of its approvals in a form that would be adequate to the facts and yet sufficiently succinct to be manageable. The members of a group did not all extend their approvals the same distance down the scales so that we might point to a certain position where approvals ended and disapprovals began. Worse yet, very few respondents left off pluses and began zeros or minuses at a definite point; they mixed minuses among the pluses or the reverse, in spite of the fact that the scenes were supposed to be arranged in increasing order of badness. It was necessary for us to find some way of saying at just what point in badness half the members, or one fourth the members, or three fourths, or some other proportion of the members ceased to approve and began to disapprove. After trying without promise of success the idea of averaging the values of the scenes marked plus or minus, substituting pluses lower in the scale for minuses higher, empirically fitting a curve to the points and smoothing the curve mathematically, and fitting a straight line or an ogive curve by the Method of Least Squares, we finally settled upon an adaptation of a scheme Dr. Clifford Woody had used in connection with the scoring of some of his scales for measuring arithmetical abilities.[1] In order to explain this technique as applied to our problem we must first show the nature of our curves.

In the figure below we have laid off badness values along the horizontal axis and percentage of judges along the vertical axis. Each dot represents the placement of an element in one of the scales in respect to its badness (along

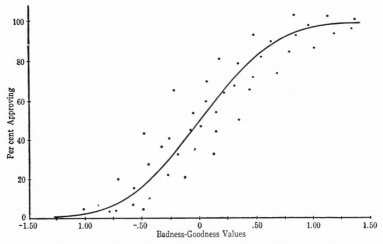

FIG. 9.—A Typical Ogive Curve Fitting a Set of Empirical Ratings

the x, horizontal, axis) and the percentage of judges approving it (along the y, vertical, axis). The percentage approving was taken to mean the percentage of those declaring admiration for the item plus half those marking the item neutral. It will be observed that the trend is a sort of S-shaped one. This S-shape is characteristic of these curves from all groups on all the scales. If the reader will turn

[1] Woody, Clifford, *Measurement of Some Achievements in Arithmetic*, Teachers College Bureau of Publications, Columbia University, 1916, pp. 14–19.

back to page 39 and compare the curve there with the one illustrated here, he will notice that the two are strikingly similar. Our curves are normal ogive curves.[2]

The percentage of persons disapproving (active disapprovals plus half the neutrals) at any point of badness is always shown, as indicated above, by the vertical distance from the base-line at that point to the curve, the y-distance. It will be seen that this percentage is very small at first but increases as we move to the right along the x-axis, at first slowly, then rapidly, then more slowly again. Our problem is to find how far we must move along the x-axis until our y-distance will be just half of its maximum. That will be the 50 per cent line, the point at which the percentage disapproving has reached just fifty. We shall be concerned, too, to find how far along the x-axis (how far down in badness) we must go in order to reach the 25 per cent line and the 75 per cent line. The former will be the point in badness at which a quarter of the respondents have come to be against the item and the latter the point at which three quarters of them are against it.

If we could be sufficiently fortunate always to find when we needed it an item on which the group split exactly 50-50, and could know that this even split was not a chance one, our task would be easy. But this very seldom happens. We find items on which 40 per cent, or 43 per cent, or 56 per cent express disapproval, but seldom exactly 50 per cent. But, since we know the mathematics of the normal ogive curve, it is possible to predict where the curve will cross the 50 per cent line when we know from our data where it crosses the 42 per cent line or any other line. If, for example, 42 per cent of the group disapprove an item in the scale

---

[2] That they should be so follows from the fact that we made up our scale values in terms of sigma-units from a hypothetical normal distribution.

that has a badness value of −.16 sigmas, we know that the item must be somewhat worse in order to draw 50 per cent of disapprovals. Tables of the integrals of the normal curve tell us that this added badness value required to bring us from the 42 per cent line to the 50 per cent line must be just .20 sigmas. From this calculation we determine that an item in the scale would need to have a badness value of −.16 plus −.20, which equals −.36, if it were to be disapproved by exactly half the group. But we dare not risk a final conclusion on the basis of a single determination, since there are some chance fluctuations in our data. We shall therefore make a number of determinations from other points at which our data give us the percentage of the group disapproving items of known values, then average these results. In our practice we took for the placement of the 50 per cent line in each of our curves as many determinations within its distribution as our data permitted without going more than a half sigma away, and tried to take as many from above the 50 per cent as from below it. This was an average of about eight for each sub-scale, or about thirty or forty for each whole scale. The calculated point at which the curve crossed the 50 per cent line was then taken as the average of these determinations. We located the 25 per cent and the 75 per cent lines in the same manner. From the fact that we were obliged thus to locate points for each of nineteen sub-scales for each of thirteen groups for three different methods of working up our scales, the reader may well believe that it was a tedious and time-consuming job.

For the benefit of others who may use our scales for similar measurements in the future, or employ the same sort of technique in some analogous problem, we shall give a table of corrections to be made in order to infer the point at which the ogive curve crosses the 25 per cent, the 50 per cent, and the 75 per cent lines from a knowledge of where it crosses some other percentile.

Table III

Table of Sigma Corrections

Per Cent	Q_1	Q_2	Q_3	Per Cent	Q_1	Q_2	Q_3
1	−1.65			32	+ .21	− .47	−1.14
2	−1.38			33	+ .23	− .44	−1.11
3	−1.21			34	+ .26	− .41	−1.09
4	−1.08			35	+ .29	− .39	−1.06
5	− .97			36	+ .32	− .36	−1.03
6	− .88			37	+ .34	− .33	−1.00
7	− .80			38	+ .37	− .31	− .97
8	− .73			39	+ .39	− .28	− .95
9	− .67			40	+ .42	− .25	− .93
10	− .61	−1.28		41	+ .45	− .23	− .90
11	− .55	−1.22		42	+ .47	− .20	− .87
12	− .50	−1.17		43	+ .49	− .18	− .85
13	− .45	−1.13		44	+ .52	− .15	− .82
14	− .41	−1.08		45	+ .54	− .13	− .80
15	− .36	−1.04		46	+ .57	− .10	− .77
16	− .32	− .99		47	+ .60	− .07	− .74
17	− .28	− .95		48	+ .62	− .05	− .72
18	− .24	− .92		49	+ .65	− .02	− .69
19	− .20	− .88		50	+ .67	− .00	− .67
20	− .17	− .84	−1.52	51	+ .69	+ .02	− .65
21	− .13	− .81	−1.48	52	+ .72	+ .05	− .62
22	− .10	− .77	−1.45	53	+ .74	+ .07	− .60
23	− .06	− .74	−1.41	54	+ .77	+ .10	− .57
24	− .03	− .71	−1.38	55	+ .80	+ .13	− .54
25	00	− .67	−1.35	56	+ .82	+ .15	− .52
26	+ .03	− .64	−1.32	57	+ .85	+ .18	− .49
27	+ .06	− .61	−1.29	58	+ .87	+ .20	− .47
28	+ .09	− .58	−1.26	59	+ .90	+ .23	− .45
29	+ .12	− .55	−1.23	60	+ .93	+ .25	− .43
30	+ .15	− .52	−1.20	61	+ .95	+ .28	− .39
31	+ .18	− .50	−1.17	62	+ .97	+ .31	− .37

Directions: Knowing the sigma-value for some particular per cent, add algebraically to this the amount standing opposite that per cent in the table—using the Q_1, Q_2, or Q_3 column according to your purpose. This table is oriented for increasing negative values with increasing percentages. If you want it oriented in the opposite direction, reverse all signs in the table.

Table III—*Continued*

Table of Sigma Corrections—*Continued*

Per Cent	Q_1	Q_2	Q_3	Per Cent	Q_1	Q_2	Q_3
63	+1.00	+ .33	− .34	82		+ .92	+ .24
64	+1.03	+ .36	− .33	83		+ .95	+ .28
65	+1.06	+ .39	− .29	84		+ .99	+ .32
66	+1.09	+ .41	− .26	85		+1.04	+ .36
67	+1.11	+ .44	− .23	86		+1.08	+ .41
68	+1.14	+ .47	− .21	87		+1.13	+ .45
69	+1.17	+ .50	− .18	88		+1.17	+ .50
70	+1.20	+ .52	− .15	89		+1.22	+ .55
71	+1.23	+ .55	− .12	90		+1.28	+ .61
72	+1.26	+ .58	− .09	91			+ .67
73	+1.29	+ .61	− .06	92			+ .73
74	+1.32	+ .64	− .03	93			+ .80
75	+1.35	+ .67	− .00	94			+ .88
76	+1.38	+ .71	+ .03	95			+ .97
77	+1.41	+ .74	+ .06	96			+1.08
78	+1.45	+ .77	+ .10	97			+1.21
79	+1.48	+ .81	+ .13	98			+1.38
80	+1.52	+ .84	+ .17	99			+1.65
81		+ .88	+ .20				

But we may use our table in this straightforward fashion only provided the variability of the group with whose ogive curve we are working is the same as that of the group from which the scale values were determined. For the sigma-units to be added or subtracted are standard deviations *of the group for which we are fitting the curve.* How many scale units make one of these standard deviations is another question. In our own problem the individual groups were not equal in variability to the group from which the scale values had been taken, chiefly because the former were real groups while the latter was a combination of five groups and hence rather heterogeneous. Our first job had, therefore, to be the finding of the relation of these two variabilities. This we did by spotting the values and corresponding

percentages on coördinate paper (badness values on the
x-axis and percentages on the y-axis), drawing through these
locations by hand what appeared to be the best-fitting curve
of the general ogive shape, and estimating the quartile
range (half the distance between the values at the 25 per
cent line and those at the 75 per cent line). From this
estimated Q, which we shall call Q_e, we got the approximate
ratio of the variability of our particular group to that of the
basic group from which the scale values had been made.
The addends standing in the table each had to be multiplied
by this ratio before using them as corrections. The quartile
range of the fundamental group was, of course, .6745, which
is the decimal that expresses the relation between the "Probable Error" and the "Standard Deviation" of any normal
distribution. If we let a represent the quantity standing
in the table as indicated to be added or subtracted, and b
the amount actually to be added or subtracted after taking
cognizance of the ratio of variabilities, then

$$b = \frac{Q_e}{.6745} \cdot a$$

A true Q can be found to replace the Q_e after the 25 per
cent and the 75 per cent lines have been located by the total
process described in the three preceding pages; it is half the
difference between the values computed for the 25 per cent
line and those computed for the 75 per cent line. We show
these Q's in connection with our various groups in order to
indicate how homogeneous or heterogeneous the groups are
in comparison with one another. If the determinations
that are averaged to get the true points, as described a
page or two back, are taken in about equal numbers from
the two sides and not too far away, little inaccuracy will
be involved even if it turns out that the Q_e was somewhat in

error. Nevertheless we discarded our estimated Q_e and repeated the calculations with the computed one as a new estimate if the difference turned out to exceed one tenth of a scale-sigma.

The three points of view from which we said awhile ago we worked up our curves were: (1) the "approval index"; (2) active disapprovals; and (3) admirations. By the "approval index" we mean the mid-point of the neutral belt for the successive elements of the scale. Thus in respect to the approval index the 50 per cent line is crossed at that point where the active dissenters plus half the neutrals equal exactly 50 per cent of the whole number of members of the group. The 25 per cent and the 75 per cent lines have analogous meanings. The curve of active dissenters is determined by the percentage marking the successive elements *minus,* and the curve of admirations from the percentages marking the elements *plus.* In the appendix, pages 262–275, a showing is made of the details of these computations by groups and by scales and sub-scales for each of the three types of reactions mentioned above. It will be sufficient to give at this point a table of the "approval indices" and the variabilities (Q's) of our several social groups on each of the scales as wholes. (See Table IV.)

In order to make concrete the meaning of such approval and disapproval indices we shall quote at this point two scenes from motion pictures, give their ratings, and interpret the ratings in terms of the proportion of certain of our groups that would approve or disapprove them. The first is a scene involving aggressiveness of a girl in love-making taken from the motion picture, *Young as You Feel.*

Lem Morehouse, a wealthy middle-aged meat-packer who has hitherto led a very conventional and highly regimented life, is

TABLE IV

POSITION OF APPROVAL INDICES OF OUR SOCIAL GROUPS, AND Q'S, ON
EACH OF THE FOUR MORES SCALES

Group	Aggressiveness		Kissing		Democracy		Parent-Child	
	App. Ind.	Q	App. Ind.	Q	App. Ind.	Q	App. Ind.	Q
Penn State faculty	+.03	.50	+.09	.53	+.16	.70	+.06	.73
Adult Brethren	−.03	.31	−.07	.29	−.13	.43	−.18	.53
Lancaster preachers	−.11	.47	−.23	.39	−.19	.41	−.23	.51
Preachers, U. S.	−.13	.39	−.19	.42	−.11	.47	−.16	.38
College senior boys	−.14	.47	−.19	.43	−.12	.42	+.09	.51
College senior girls	−.17	.46	−.25	.37	−.18	.49	−.16	.54
Young Brethren	−.21	.31	−.24	.43	−.21	.45	−.16	.55
New York élite	−.23	.64	−.22	.70	−.23	.64	+.03	.79
Hampton Negroes	−.24	.28	−.19	.32	−.21	.51	−.26	.47
Graduate students	−.36	.45	−.06	.37	−.12	.45	−.16	.49
Social leaders	−.37	.65	−.44	.52	−.28	.56	−.18	.45
Business men	−.38	.35	−.22	.43	−.24	.53	−.21	.44
Factory workers	−.55	.49	−.30	.40	−.18	.56	−.21	.57
Adult miners	−.65	.44	−.06	.44	−.14	.78	−.57	.49
Young miners, all	−.70	.43	−.28	.44	−.37	.75	−.59	.63
Young miners, male			−.30	.37	−.32	.63		
Young miners, female			−.37	.44	−.52	.97		

dancing with Fleurette, a French singer who is trying hard to
"vamp" him. As they dance, she snuggles down against his
chest and sings in a low voice to the accompaniment of the
orchestra:

> "No one else, no matter who
> But you could do the things you do—
> The cute little way you do—
> And the cute little things you do.
> No one else could be so shy
> And roll a naughty wicked eye—
> The cute little way you do
> And the cute little things you do.
>
> Out of sight is out of mind
> With others I have met—
> This I find, that you're the kind
> I never do forget.

No one else without a past
Could look so slow
And work so fast—
The cute little way you do
And the cute little things you do."

Lem is grinning ecstatically, and she puts her head down on his shoulder and declares, "Oh, you're doing much better, dear."

This scene falls into the category of spontaneous love-making for thrill and by the technique of coquetry. It was given an average rating of −1.37 by a committee of five members. This rating we shall interpret by the aid of our tables in Appendix B rather than from Table IV, since the former are much more detailed. The rating places the scene far below the approval of the population made up of all our social groups combined into one group, which stands at −.53 for this type of aggressiveness; and considerably below the approval index of even the most liberal group, which is at −1.03. We may explain its position in relation to admirations and active disapprovals, based on the tables in Appendix B. At −.78, 25 per cent of the combined group still cling to admiration for such a scene. This scene lies at .59 of the basic sigmas, or .81 of the combined-group sigmas, below that point. From this we estimate (on the basis of the mathematics of the normal ogive curve) that a scene of the level −1.37 would be admired by 7 per cent of the members of the combined group. The percentage of estimated admirers decreases to 1 in the case of our most conservative social group and increases to 23 in the most liberal of our groups. It is at the point in "badness" where it would be actively disapproved by 75 per cent of the combined group. The percentage disapproving it falls to 52 in the most liberal group and increases to 93 in the most conservative of our social groups.

Our next illustration is a kissing scene from *Young Man of Manhattan*. Toby and Ann, a young married couple, are both writers and a trifle jealous of each other's success. They have had a little quarrel and Toby has peevishly spent the night sleeping on a couch. Seeing him asleep there with no protection from the cold, Ann has covered him with a quilt. We find them now in the morning cautiously greeting each other.

"Hello!" Ann remarks quietly as she sees Toby's reflection in the dressing table mirror.

"Hello, Ann," he replies in a subdued tone of voice. "Working?" "Yes, I am trying to get a start on my first article for Dwight Knowles." She resumes her typing while Toby watches her in silence, then tells him, "The coffee's on the stove."

"Thanks," he says, then offers hesitantly, "Awfully sweet of you to put that cover over me."

Ann turns around and smiles. "I didn't want you to be cold." Toby, who has been looking dejectedly at the floor, brightens as he sees Ann's smile. She stands up, and he smiles in return, then they impulsively run to each other and embrace.

"Toby," Ann cries.

"Oh, Ann darling!" he exclaims, kissing her affectionately, and she returns the kiss.

"Mmm. Oh, Toby, I've been so unhappy."

He kisses her hair, then they both sit down, Toby keeping his arm about her. "Oh, what was it all about, for the love of Pete?" he demands. "Case of masculine egotism getting up on its ear because you're going to make more money than I can."

"Oh, silly, not more than you *can*," Ann protests. "Only more than you do right now."

This scene was given an average rating of +.74. The approval index for the groups combined on kissing by married people stands at +.10. The scene is, therefore, much above the approval index. The approval index for our most conservative group is at +.44, so that this scene is considerably above even that. This act would be disapproved by 6 per cent of the groups combined, by 10 per cent of the most conservative group, and by 4 per cent of the most liberal. Conversely it would be admired by 86 per cent of the combined group, by 83 per cent of the most conservative, and by 94 per cent of the most liberal.

These two scenes, one a rather low minus and the other a fairly high plus, will serve sufficiently to indicate what is meant by scenes arousing admiration or disapproval. In Appendix A many scenes are given, though more briefly narrated, showing concretely what is meant by plus or minus values at various levels. In Appendix B detailed tables are set up showing the standing of each of the groups on all phases of morality investigated by us. By referring to these appendices the reader may get as complete an impression as he wishes of the meaning of any "badness" value and of the relations of the groups to one another.

Table IV will bear some examination; it contains some interesting information about the standards of different groups. The groups are arranged in descending order of conservatism with respect to attitude on the item of the first column—aggressiveness of a girl in love-making. It will be seen that the fifty faculty members and wives at Pennsylvania State College are the most conservative of our groups in respect to all four of the elements of the moral code. Almost at the opposite end of the scale stand the university professors and leaders of social reform whom we have called "Social Leaders." In the second column this group of intellectuals is actually the most liberal. On the whole the most tolerant of the groups are the factory workers and miners, both adult and young. College students, who might be expected to be radical, are actually among the more conservative groups.

To a sociologist it is illuminating to observe the Q's in the table. They indicate the extent to which a group is homogeneous; the smaller the Q the more homogeneous the group. On the whole the most compact groups are the adult Brethren, the young Brethren and the Hampton Negroes. These are the most isolated and provincial groups, and isolation is highly favorable to the development of social solidarity. On the other hand the most heterogeneous groups are the Social Leaders, the New York élite girls, and the Pennsylvania State College Faculty. These are the intellectuals. They move about more. Hence they are less stampeded by local fashions of thought. Indeed they scarcely constitute social groups at all; they are little more than aggregates of persons. It will be noted from the table that the difference among the groups in variability is greatest in Democracy, and next greatest in the two love-making techniques. In these the mores are most in a state of transition.

The groups differ most from one another in approval indices in liberality toward aggressiveness of a girl in love-making, and next most in respect to kissing. The approval indices of the groups are remarkably alike in the other two, except for the drop in the case of the miners of both age groups.

In fact this close similarity among groups in their mean rating is one of our most surprising findings, especially when contrasted with the wide scatter within each of the groups. Differential Psychology has found consistently that the members of sex, racial, and geographical groups differ from one another within the group much more than the mean standing of one group differs from the mean of another. But sociologists have not suspected that that same thing may be true of group modes of thought and of feeling. The very foundation of sociology has traditionally been the doctrine of the solidarity of social groups. It looks as if a sociology that measures instead of speculating may find this central thesis of traditional social philosophy disproved and may be forced to accept a conclusion like that at which the psychologists have arrived. Even in the most extreme cases in our study as displayed in the table, no group as a whole differed from another group as a whole as much as the most conservative quarter of the group differed from the most liberal quarter of that same group. In other words, there is no case in which the difference between the means of two groups is as great as twice the quartile range of either of them. And, except for the case of factory workers and of miners, there is no instance in which the mean of one group differs from the mean of another by as much as the quartile range of either. Perhaps in this day of extreme mobility, the free interlacing of groups, and the ready matching of ideas through reading, motion-picture attendance, and the radio, groups in the sociological sense have almost ceased to exist and mores have lost their meaning as group phenomena.

The critical reader will observe that practically all of the variabilities shown above are less than that of the basic group from the responses of which the scale values were determined (.6745). There are several reasons for this. One is, doubtless, the fact that five groups were lumped to constitute the basic group. These differed considerably in their mean ratings, which differences would markedly flatten the distribution and thus increase the variability. Another important factor was the opposing effects of carelessness from the two techniques. In making the basic scales the respondents had all the paragraphs of a whole scale mixed together with no indication of relative badness. If a few raters read the slips hastily or carelessly and threw them into the wrong pile, that would have the effect of increasing the variability. But the raters by the second technique found the scales arranged in order of badness and they were advised to exploit these from the middle of the page. Carelessness in this work would manifest itself in an examination of only a few paragraphs near the middle, then a drawing of admiration or disapproval lines past the other items without giving them much attention. This would tend

TABLE V

COMPARISON OF SIGMA-VALUES DERIVED FROM DISTRIBUTION OF
INDIVIDUAL PARAGRAPHS WITH THOSE FROM RATINGS ON
HIERARCHICALLY ORDERED SCALES

Scale	Appproval Index			Disapprovals			Admirations		
	Q_1	Q_2	Q_3	Q_1	Q_2	Q_3	Q_1	Q_2	Q_3
Aggressiveness									
Ind. Par.	.35	−.09	− .68	−.22	−.62	−1.32	.75	.33	−.04
Scaled	.23	−.17	− .73	−.01	−.40	− .98	.48	.08	−.24
Kissing									
Ind. Par.	.53	−.22	−1.03	−.12	−.77	−1.64	1.54	.56	−.12
Scaled	.17	−.23	− .64	−.12	−.47	− .91	.38	.06	−.25
Democracy									
Ind. Par.	.47	−.07	− .56	−.14	−.58	− .92	.69	.39	.03
Scaled	.28	−.13	− .61	−.10	−.56	− .84	.46	.15	−.15
Parent-Child									
Ind. Par.	.51	.00	− .58	.03	−.53	−1.05	.84	.44	.03
Scaled	.49	−.04	− .62	.15	−.39	− .93	.67	.29	−.13

markedly to decrease the variability, thus having exactly the opposite effect from carelessness in the use of the first technique.

In order to learn how the results from the two techniques would compare, we got fifty college seniors to mark the scales according to the second technique who were apparently similar as a group to the fifty seniors who had used the first technique. The table above shows the comparison.

The table reveals that, on the approval index line which is our principal measure, the medians (Q_2) are practically identical by the two methods. The 25 per cent line and the 75 per cent line are, however, usually spread farther apart, which is the feature commented upon in the paragraph above. The disapproval lines lie lower, also, and the admiration lines higher by the first technique than by the second, which phenomenon is related to the greater variability. We may, therefore, safely compare the faculty group, the élite girls, and the working girls and boys (from whom we have responses only by the first technique) with the groups who used the second technique when working with the approval index 50 per cent line but may not compare them on the other lines without making adjustments to offset the differing variabilities.

Our technique, so far as we have yet described it, ascertained the declared approvals and disapprovals of our various groups. How do these approvals and disapprovals compare with the actual practices of those groups? Do people hold their own conduct within the limits of their approvals? Or does conduct lapse to lower levels than the members of the groups to which they belong approve? Or is conduct, perhaps, even more conservative than approvals? In order to get some data on this we asked a number of our groups, in sealed instructions to be read only after having done the rating already described, to make a second rating. This time each respondent was asked to mark a plus opposite each act described in the scales that, according to his observation, he believed the majority of the members of his "set" would do under circumstances like those related in the paragraph, a minus opposite those he believed the majority would not do, and a question mark if he did not know or if the item did not apply to his set. A colored pencil was provided for this second marking so as to distinguish it from the first. The reason we asked him to mark the conduct of the majority of the group rather than his own was that we hoped this would bring a more frank response. We believed, also, that he would be likely to use himself to a considerable extent as a criterion of what his set would do. How to work up these responses so as to get truly descriptive generalizations gave us some concern; but, on the assumption that prevailingly one's declaration of what the group does is a picture of what the responding individuals would do, we ran our lines by the same technique as that employed for declared approvals previously described. We took, that is, a declaration of 50 per cent of the group that the majority of the group would do an act of a certain degree of badness to indicate that probably 50 per cent of the group would fall to that level in their conduct. We located the 25 per cent line and the 75 per cent line on analogous assumptions. While these assumptions may not be strictly correct, they serve reasonably well for descriptive and comparative purposes.

In the table on page 62, the placement of the lines for these actual practices (from the point of view of "would not do it," that is, *restraints from doing*) is given immediately below the corresponding lines of disapproval for each of the groups from which we collected these data. Only the values on the scales as wholes are given; for the detailed showing on the sub-scales the reader should refer to the appendix, pages 262–275. The comparative standings of disapprovals and practices are shown for each quarter-point in turn for each of our four major scales.

How reliable are the ratings on the mores scales? If one sampling of members of a group mark the scales, will the results from this sampling agree at all closely with returns from a second sampling? Did we use large enough numbers of representatives from each group? These questions are answered by the calculation of reliability coefficients. Any

TABLE VI

COMPARISON OF DECLARED DISAPPROVALS AND RESTRAINTS FROM CORRESPONDING PRACTICES IN LIFE BY CERTAIN GROUPS IN OUR FOUR AREAS OF MORALITY

Groups	Aggressiveness			Kissing			Democracy			Parent-Child		
	Q_1	Q_2	Q_3	Q_1	Q_2	Q_3	Q_1	Q_2	Q_3	Q_1	Q_2	Q_3
Adult Brethren												
Disapp.	.14	−.16	−.53	.20	−.15	−.40	.14	−.37	.76	.10	−.35	−.81
Pract.	.16	−.06	−.67	.31	.17	.29	.38	−.39	.99	.50	−.20	−1.00
Young Brethren												
Disapp.	.00	−.36	−.62	.04	−.38	−.79	.15	−.26	−.72	.10	−.56	−.95
Pract.	.13	−.21	−.48	.09	−.39	−1.18	.32	−.75	−1.73	.14	−.80	−1.70
Hampton Negroes												
Disapp.	−.06	−.33	−.75	.11	−.22	−.64	.16	−.49	.97	.11	−.42	−.83
Pract.	−.13	−.31	−.65							.35	−.35	−1.25
Graduate students												
Disapp.	−.25	−.65	−1.15	.05	−.30	−.67	−.09	−.56	−.93	−.04	−.48	−.88
Pract.	−.14	−.55	−1.07	−.08	−.38	−1.12	.33	−.55	−1.49	.38	−.43	−1.24
College seniors												
Disapp.	−.01	−.40	−.98	−.12	−.40	−.91	−.10	−.56	−.84	.15	−.39	−.93
Pract.	−.15	−.59	−1.09	−.01	−.48	−1.33	.00	−.85	−1.77	.34	−.51	−1.32
Business men												
Disapp.	−.24	−.57	−.92	−.01	−.35	−.75	.12	−.52	−.96	.01	−.42	−.79
Pract.	−.26	−.68	−1.14	−.07	−.45	−1.18	.22	−.63	−1.30	.15	−.54	−1.16
Factory workers												
Disapp.	−.21	−.72	−1.26	−.09	−.44	−.86	.07	−.56	−1.02	.00	−.49	−1.00
Pract.	−.18	−.85	−1.50	−.21	−.51	−1.01	.36	−.41	−1.31	.15	−.57	−1.36
Adult miners												
Disapp.	−.38	−.82	−1.30	.23	−.18	−.65	.50	−.38	−1.14	.03	−.57	−.94
Pract.	−.53	−1.17	−1.89	−.20	−.94	−1.47				.12	−.93	−1.52
Young miners												
Disapp.	−.43	−.86	−1.23	−.03	−.51	−.86	.05	−.68	−1.27	−.35	−.92	−1.38
Pract.	−.54	−1.17	−1.55	−.20	−.65	−1.18				−.27	−1.21	−1.60

method will do that shows the consistency between a first sampling and a random second sampling. We got these two samplings by splitting our groups into two random halves for purposes of tabulation, computing coefficients of correlation between these two halves, then stepping up that correlation by the Spearman-Brown formula in order to predict the correlation that might be expected between our whole group and another equally large sample. Our correlations were between the array of percentages representing

Table VII

Coefficients of Reliability of the Ratings on the Mores Scales by Certain Groups

Group	Disapprovals Plus Half the Zeros				Restraints from Practice			
	Aggres.	Kissing	Democ.	Parent-Ch.	Aggres.	Kissing	Democ.	Parent-Ch.
Young Brethren	.965	.959	.989	.987	.880	.928	.940	.874
Factory workers	.961	.982	.978	.987	.926	.959	.934	.981
Hampton Negroes	.941	.958	.977	.985	.936	.917	.847	.888

the proportion of minus marks plus half the zeros to the total population of half the group and the array of paired percentages similarly computed from the other half of the group. The correlations in the second trial, on restraints from practices, were between the percentages of minuses on the several items for one half and the paired percentages for the other half. We found the correlations consistently so very high that it seemed useless to compute them for all of our groups.

We have not shown in the table the means for the correlated arrays, but they were also very close together. The correlations were a little lower for restraints from practice than they were for declared approvals, but satisfactorily high in both cases.

The chapter has shown how the mores of thirteen different groups were measured with the aid of our scales. When representative members from these groups (from 21 to 39 members from each) had marked *plus, zero,* or *minus* by each of the items in our hierarchically ordered scales, it was found that the curve representing the approvals or disapprovals of each group on the successive scale elements made a fairly normal ogive curve. We determined at what badness value the ogive curves for each of the groups crossed the point representing exactly 25 per cent, 50 per cent, and 75 per cent of the group. These places constitute points of orientation for comparing motion-picture scenes with approvals by various proportions of the several groups. We also secured measures, by means of our scales, on alleged practices within some of our groups, preparatory to comparing these with the status of approvals and of motion pictures. We found marked differences within each of our groups in regard to what conduct the members would approve—greater differences between the lowest quarter and the highest quarter than between the means of the different groups. The groups differed from one another, however, fairly widely in the limits of their approvals on aggressiveness of a girl in love-making and on kissing, but were markedly close together in respect to democracy and to treatment of children by parents.

In our next chapter we shall explain how these scales were employed in the study of the relation of motion pictures to standards of morality.

CHAPTER V

RATING MOTION PICTURES BY MEANS OF SCALES

WHAT technique should be chosen for measuring motion pictures in relation to morality is dependent upon one's hypothesis as to how motion pictures may affect morality. There are several possibilities:

1. It may be that incidents in the story, or the theme as a whole, sets for the observer a challenging problem upon which he may reflect after leaving the theater, perhaps meditating on it for hours or for days until he has clarified for himself a philosophy of life in respect to the issue raised by the problem-play. Although this sort of thing doubtless sometimes happens, it is probably very much the exception and pertains chiefly to a small percentage of persons of a highly reflective turn of mind.

2. It may be that the way in which the plot works out as a whole determines the lesson that is taught—whether the criminal is punished, whether the persons entering upon an unconventional marriage gain happiness or unhappiness, whether selfishness leads to success or to failure. Often people make generalizations about life that seem, even to the ones who make them, to come to formulation suddenly and without previous explicit reflection. Thus one may say: "Oh, the erring husband will after a while return to his wife; they always do"; or "Riches may satisfy a person for a while but ultimately he will be bored by them." Such generalizations are accretions from prolonged observations of "cases"

in life which the observer probably does not remember as particular cases but on which nevertheless his conclusions are grounded. Among the cases that contribute to people's concepts as to how life goes, it is more than probable that the movies contribute their share.

3. It may be that the particular scenes, without very much regard to how they fit into the plot as a whole, tend to be imitated as social techniques by people who take these acts as "the way people do." We have much evidence that techniques of burglary and modes of dress and speech are imitated by certain classes of attendants, and it is highly probable that other behavior patterns have like dynamic effects.

It was on the third of these hypotheses that our study proceeded. The bulk of the mores are specific fashions of conduct; integrated philosophies of life have a smaller place, especially in the case of the less reflective members of society. The things that "everybody" does, especially "everybody worth while," the rank and file of members of society do automatically, as they conform to all the mores automatically. Seeing players kiss under certain circumstances in the movies, or speak courteously to servants, or serve cocktails from a dainty pitcher, they are likely to pick up quite unconsciously the notion that these are the ways "people" act and to behave in the same manner themselves whenever the situation provides occasion. The studies of Thurstone and Blumer show this to be true. Mrs. Mitchell also found this fact frequently exemplified in the testimony she took from delinquent children.

"Lots of times I'd see boys and girls in movies smoking and with flasks. I'd come home and smoke a cigaret just for fun.". . . "Movies with drinking in them make me want to drink. Me and my girl friend after we saw a movie with lots of drinking in it, looked up a rooming house so we could get a drink and we did, believe me." . . . Others said that they would go home from a movie and blow smoke rings just as the actress had done, or tried to dance the latest steps they had seen in the show.[1]

Such acceptance of patterns is probably little affected by the manner in which these patterns fit into the theme of the drama as a whole, especially where the observers are persons of only moderate intelligence. And, of course, the adoption of what are supposed to be "the ways people do" is doubtless practiced by adults just as well as by children, particularly by those adults who are relatively unsophisticated.

It is likely, however, that the tendency to imitate the patterns set by characters played up in an attractive rôle is greater than the tendency to imitate those set by characters played in an unattractive rôle. Indeed it is probable that definite taboos tend to be built up *against* the patterns of conduct exemplified by unattractive characters. The observer gets the hunch that it is only disgusting people who are seen kissing on the street or talking impudently to hotel waiters, and he does not want himself to be seen in such disgusting light. But even apart from any question of ratiocination about the matter, the psychology of conditioning responses, first studied by Pavlov and now universally accepted as a part of psychological theory, would show it to be almost inevitable that there should be positive conditioning in respect to those responses that follow models set by attractive characters and negative conditioning in respect to those connected with unattractive characters. But, of course, to produce a negative conditioning effect the character must appear unattractive *to the particular observer in question*. Although the demarcation is found in practice

[1] Mitchell, Alice M., *Children and the Movies*, University of Chicago Press, 1929, pp. 136–137.

to be a fairly distinct one on which nearly all normal persons would agree, the mentally immature may make some eccentric reversals from the rule. But in spite of these difficulties arising out of eccentric interpretations by the very immature and requiring an estimate of attractiveness from these points of view as well as from that of normal persons, this distinction is an important one and on it some of the findings of our study definitely turn.

The hypothesis, then, that specific patterns of conduct tend to be accepted as "the thing" and to become a part of the mores, especially when set by attractive characters, seems sufficiently plausible to justify our investigation of motion pictures with respect to it. Our problem, then, is this: If the patterns of conduct exemplified in motion pictures tend to get imitated, how will their acceptance affect the mores? In which direction from the present standards do these patterns lie? How many of them are patterns that present members of our society would count it an asset to have imitated, and how many a liability? Undoubtedly it would also be worth while to study the problem with reference to the first two of our hypotheses, especially with reference to the second. But such studies would need to be made by techniques wholly different from ours, and our resources of time and money were not sufficient to cover all. Further reference will be made in Chapter XII to the outlook for these other studies.

Rating motion pictures with our scales is a process fairly similar to rating English composition with such an instrument as the Hillegas Scale. The picture, as indicated above, is rated by incidents, not as a whole. With a certain scene in mind the rater goes to the relevant scale and sub-scale, examines in succession paragraphs on this until he finds on the scale a sample nearly like the one he is attempting to rate, and then assigns to the scene the value attached to the comparable element of the scale. This he does with each scene from the movie that falls within the area he is investigating. If the element he finds in the scale is qualitatively like the one he is rating but somewhat more extreme, he adds to or subtracts from the scale rating somewhat so as to adjust for the difference. If, as sometimes happens, he cannot find the pattern he is attempting to rate represented in the scale at all, or finds it so far away from the value of his scene that it affords him little guidance, he assigns it such rating as he judges the makers of the scale would have given if it had been submitted to them, predicating his judgment upon the conservatism or liberality they displayed in this general sort of thing by the other ratings standing on the scale. Quotation of the printed directions given to the raters will make the procedure clear.

INSTRUCTIONS FOR RATING MOVIES

1. Feature reels and comics are to be rated but not news reels nor films that portray caricatures such as Krazy Kats.

2. We rate the movie for four different aspects: (1) kissing and other forms of caressing; (2) aggressiveness of a girl in love-making; (3) the relation of parents to children; and (4) democratic practices and attitudes. Note that the parent ratings involve only the one-way relation, the treatment of children by parents, not the treatment of parents by children. What is meant by each of these four aspects is best suggested by the items that constitute the scales. The raters should get familiar with the contents of the scales.

3. The movie is rated by scenes. Try to get all the scenes belonging under each of the four aspects, whether they are likely to call for a mild or an extreme rating. But those that call for an extreme rating are most important for our purpose.

4. Your greatest difficulty will be in deciding what constitutes a unit scene. *A scene is an act, or a series of acts, relating to the same theme, occurring in an essentially unchanged setting with regard to time, place, and circumstances.*

   a. A series of kisses or caresses under essentially the same environment would jointly constitute a scene.

b. A picture often breaks in order to show a contemporaneous action elsewhere, then returns to the original scene. Such a break is to be disregarded.

c. The fact that people walk along, or go from room to room, does not constitute a change of scene, unless the conditions change essentially by reason of the mobility. For example, if kissing had been private before the walk and public afterwards, two scenes would be rated; otherwise one.

d. There may be several phases to rate for the same time and place—referring to different themes on our scales (kissing, democracy, etc.).

5. The rating is made in the same manner that handwriting or English composition is rated by means of the scales long in use in those fields.

a. Go up and down the scales with each scene in mind and give it a rating guided by the values indicated on the scales. Note the theme indicated at the top of each scale. Do not expect to find a specimen exactly like the one you are rating in all respects but increase or diminish the rating you assign according to whether you think the item is more or less extreme than its nearest analog on the scale.

b. In some cases you may not find in the scales a pattern like the one you are rating, or the pattern in the scale may be placed so remote from the value of your own scene as not to be of much help to you. In such cases give the scene a rating governed by what you believe the persons who made the scale would have given if they had had this scene to evaluate. In this judgment draw your inference from the liberality or the conservatism of the makers of the scales as shown by the other paragraphs of the scale, especially those involving somewhat the same general motive. Do not distort your ratings by trying to follow a pattern that has a rating you *know* does not do justice to the real motives and merits of your particular scene.

c. Give to each scene a rating for the most extreme form it took during the scene—the worst instance of kissing or the best case of treatment of children by parents, or the reverse in either case.

d. Sometimes you will have both a good instance and a bad one in the same scene, especially where two different characters are involved. If the cases go on opposite sides of the zero of our scales, give a rating to each—a minus to the one and a plus to the other as the scales suggest. Be sure to indicate which goes with the attractive character and which with the unattractive.

e. The judges should do their rating independently. They should not compare ratings with one another.

6. Make your report on the note-book paper supplied to you, or on similarly punched paper.

a. Be sure to give the title of the picture rated. Rate each picture on a separate sheet, but put all four phases for the same picture on the same sheet.

b. Be sure to sign your name on each sheet.

c. Distinguish between attractive and unattractive characters in the report of each scene by attaching an *a* or a *u*. Call a character unattractive if, up to that point in the picture, he has been played up in general in such a way as to be more or less repulsive, so that observers would not likely be disposed to imitate his conduct. A character might change from unattractive to attractive within the same movie but a change in the other direction is not likely. But remember that a character is to be listed as unattractive *in general*, not in respect to the particular scene rated. In fact you should be very conservative about having any character change in your ratings from unattractive to attractive in the same picture. We list as attractive all the characters who are not definitely unattractive. That is, the neutral ones count among the attractive.

d. Every scene should contain two symbols besides the numerical rating—an *a* or *u* to indicate attractive or unattractive characters and a second symbol to indicate the sub-theme. These sub-theme symbols are as follows:

Kissing: c, by casual lovers; s, by very serious or betrothed lovers; m, by married people.

Aggressiveness: t, done for thrill only; l, done for real love; m, done for material advantage.

Parents: f, fellowship (companionship); d, discipline; t, tolerance; s, sacrifice.

Democracy: r, race (general or Negroes); e, employer; s, social status (whether higher to lower or the reverse).

Thus a scene under relation of parents to children that involves an unattractive parent and that has to do with discipline might be reported as follows:

$$Du - 1.43$$

e. Segregate your items in the report under the four phases. Be sure to affix before each rating its algebraic sign.

We had hoped to have represented on the scales every pattern of conduct that would ever be found in the realms we were covering by our ratings, and in sufficient numbers of quantitative stages to cover the whole scale at short intervals. But we found that impossible of achievement.

Certainly it would have required scales many times as long as the ones we used, and then these would have become so complicated that the raters would have been hopelessly confused in their use. They are complicated enough as they are. But even if much longer scales could be used without too much confusion, it would probably be impossible to catch all the patterns. It was our experience that new patterns would continue to appear no matter how hard we tried to complete the scheme. That same problem is, of course, encountered in the use of scales for the measurement of general merit in English compositions. There, as in our case, the problem is solved not by expecting to find scale elements with items like those being rated (except where the compositions have all been written on the same theme as that involved in the construction of the scales) but by seeking guidance through a comparison of the general level of merit of the composition with the general level of the scale.

The factor that gave most difficulty in rating, however, was not the absence of patterns from the scale but the difficulty of determining what is a scene and the difficulty of finding all relevant scenes. The definition of a scene, as given in the directions, helped considerably, but it did not produce perfect uniformity. Against the missing of scenes we found no adequate protection. It was the experience of all of us in rating that we could recognize scenes as perfectly pertinent when mentioned by another member of the committee which we had not recognized as such when observing the show and taking notes of it. This was much more true of such intangible features as democracy and aggressiveness than it was of the more overt conduct involved in kissing or in the treatment of children by parents.

Under such conditions ratings by a single individual would

be very unreliable. We therefore employed several raters and combined their ratings, first three, then five. In rating the first 121 pictures three judges attended the same motion picture, sat in different parts of the theater, took careful notes, in conference the next day agreed upon the designation of the scenes, and then rated them, the rating being done independently. Then each scene was given as its value the average of the three independent individual ratings. By this technique more scenes were found than any one rater would have discovered, since all could recall the scenes noted by each and could add the missing ones to his own list. As will be shown later, the ratings by this method were highly consistent and showed, by the Spearman Prophecy Formula, very high coefficients of reliability.

But we became suspicious that the high theoretical reliabilities, indicating how closely the results of one committee should be expected to agree with those of another like it, might not hold between two actual committees unless the two committees sat together and agreed jointly upon the scenes to be rated. We therefore set up two additional committees and had all three rate the same twenty-four pictures, each committee agreeing upon scenes as a unit but the three committees acting entirely independently of one another. In harmony with our fears we found lower agreement among the committees than we wanted. The ratings within each committee were highly consistent, but the different committees agreed less closely with one another. The statistical showing regarding this is made later in this chapter.

We then tried on sixty-one additional pictures a different technique of rating: we increased the number of judges from three to five and discontinued the conference. Each rated independently the scenes he had noted without any knowledge of what scenes others had noted. Moreover we gave the raters no other instructions than the printed sheet quoted above plus one conference at which a picture was rated for demonstration. We believed that this technique could be duplicated any time in the future, that it was a more feasible one for raters who might live in different parts of the country (for even the demonstration might be replaced by a paper one), and particularly that the average number of scenes found by five judges acting independently would be closer to the average found by another random selection of five raters than those by a single committee acting as a unit would be to those by another single committee similarly acting as a unit. We shall show below, by statistical methods, that this technique gives good reliabilities and that these are not vitiated by the assumption by which our previous technique was limited. The reliability of this method is amply high for a study of the general trend of motion pictures—that is, for what is true of motion pictures on the average. It does not give, perhaps, high enough reliabilities to enable individual pictures to be placed with sufficient accuracy. But we can get as high reliabilities as we please by increasing the number of judges.

It is altogether possible that a still better technique, from the standpoint of reliability and validity, would be a combination of our first and second procedure. We might have, say, fifteen raters form themselves into five committees of three members each, have each of the committees operate as a unit as we did in our first trial, then combine the average evaluations of these five committees as we combined the ratings of the five independent judges in our second trial. This technique would tend to find the maximum number of scenes and in addition would secure the statistical advantages accruing from an average of a number of independent judgments which has proved to be such an effective device for getting high reliabilities. But ratings so precise and so expensive to obtain are needed only if our problem requires the accurate placement of individual pictures; they are not needed for studying the trends, based on averages. It ought to be possible easily to reach reliability coefficients by this fifteen-member set of raters well up in the upper nineties.

Throughout the remainder of this chapter we shall discuss in technical form the reliability coefficients of our measurement of pictures by each of the techniques discussed above. Any reader not interested in those technical details may skip to the next chapter.

In a section of the appendix to this volume (pages 279–283) we show the development of the generalized Spearman Prophecy Formula and point out its assumptions and limitations. This formula is the basis for our study of the reliability of the ratings on motion pictures. In our particular application the formula predicts the coefficient of correlation that may be expected between the average of the evaluations made by any given number of judges on a series of motion pictures and the average of the evaluations that might be made by any other set of judges who constitute a sampling of the population similar on the whole to the first set, the prediction being based upon the amount of agreement among the first set of judges with one another. We desired to use the formula in two special ways: (1) We wished to predict the correlations that might be expected between the average of the estimates made by our five judges (in the final procedure) and that which would probably be secured from any second five. The formula for this is, if a represents the number of judges in each set, r_{aa} the coefficient of correlation to be predicted, and r_{11} the average intercorrelation among the first set of judges,

$$r_{aa} = \frac{ar_{11}}{1+(a-1)r_{11}}$$

(2) We wished to predict the extent to which the average of our five judges would correlate with the average from an indefinitely large number of judges—theoretically an infinite number. We may call the evaluation obtained from an infinite number of judges the "true" evaluation, and say that our second purpose was to measure the probable correlation between the evaluations of our committee and the true evaluations. The formula is:

$$r_{a\infty} = \frac{ar_{11}}{\sqrt{ar_{11}+(a^2-a)r_{11}^2}}$$

The average intercorrelations needed for these formulæ may be determined either by direct computation of all of them or by a certain scheme of summing across the a series. We used the latter method in our calculations for the original committees of three who sat together to decide upon scenes because the conditions there fulfilled the assumptions of that statistical method (that the means and the standard deviations of the several arrays be approximately equal), but used the former method with our later committees because those assumptions were not fulfilled. In the table below we shall give enough of these reliability coefficients to indicate the general trend of our findings. It must be understood that the scales carry scores that are either positive (for "good" scenes) or negative (for "bad" scenes), zeros representing the absence of scenes or neutral values on them. It will be remembered, too, that we counted separately the scores for attractive and those for unattractive characters. The legends in the table below refer to these separately aggregated scores, the "total net" being all the scores combined (algebraically), both positive and negative, for both attractive and unattractive characters. The table relates to our latest procedure, where we employed five judges and had them work completely independently of one another. We shall later show the reliabilities for our prior methods.

We encountered an unexpected obstacle in attempting to apply correlation techniques to this problem. From some points of view from which we rated there were many pictures with no scenes, or with scenes that had mostly zero ratings. This was especially true of the plus ratings and more particularly so of the plus ratings for unattractive characters. On the other hand most of the films had plenty of negative scenes to space out our ratings. When a considerable number of paired zero scores enter a correlation problem the resultant coefficient may be very misleading. Even if there were perfect agreement among the judges in giving to a series of pictures ratings of only zeros on a certain phase, the correlation among the judges might be only zero in spite of the perfect agreement which is ordinarily indicated by a coefficient of 1.00. To the extent to which there are many zero scores the technique of correlation is inadequate to describe the extent of agreement. In computing reliability coefficients we have, therefore, confined ourselves to situations to which the technique of correlation is applicable, and have given in the table a fair sampling of the results from these.

The showing for two committees in the table grows out of the fact that we had two committees rating motion pictures simultaneously, working on different films. One of these committees rated forty films and the other twenty-eight. There was also a third committee but it rated a smaller number. It will be seen from the table that all of the reliability coefficients are high enough to be satisfactory when we are concerned only to deal with trends based upon aver-

TABLE VIII

COEFFICIENTS OF RELIABILITY FOR THE RATING OF MOTION PICTURES BY COMMITTEES OF FIVE MEMBERS EACH

Scale	Committee One			Committee Two		
	Average Inter-Group Correlation	Expected Correlation with Another Similar Five	Expected Correlation with an Infinite Number	Average Inter-Group Correlation	Expected Correlation with Another Similar Five	Expected Correlation with an Infinite Number
AGGRESSIVENESS						
Attractive negative	.600	.883	.939	.517	.842	.914
Unattractive negative	.911	.980	.990	.563	.865	.930
Total net	.668	.909	.953	.520	.844	.921
KISSING						
Attractive negative	.394	.764	.874	.660	.906	.953
Unattractive negative				.667	.909	.955
Attractive positive	.772	.944	.971	.684	.915	.957
Net attractive				.737	.933	.965
Total net	.586	.876	.936	.756	.939	.969
PARENT-CHILDREN						
Unattractive negative				.717	.926	.962
Attractive positive	.675	.912	.955	.531	.849	.923
Net attractive				.421	.784	.886
Net unattractive				.643	.900	.949
Total net	.545	.856	.919	.502	.836	.919
DEMOCRACY						
Attractive positive	.309	.690	.831	.313	.694	.836
Net attractive				.277	.657	.814
Total net	.471	.816	.903	.245	.618	.787

ages for groups of pictures. The correlations are especially high for the scale on Kissing and the one on Treatment of Children by Parents. The conduct in respect to these matters was quite overt; there was little opportunity to miss scenes and little misunderstanding regarding the meaning of the scenes. But the correlations are somewhat lower on the scale for Aggressiveness of a Girl in Love-Making and much lower for the scale on Democratic Attitudes and Practices. Here the scenes were more subtle and their interpretation less certain and consequently more variable. Scenes that one rater would consider aggressive another rater might not apperceive as such, since he would differently interpret the motive. Also mild cases of aggressiveness would often be overlooked since there was no explicit sign to indicate them. Democracy was our most troublesome category. It was so many-sided and intangible in spite of the scales that we could not get different individuals to detect all the relevant scenes nor to interpret them in the same way. Hence all of our findings with respect to democracy are to be taken with less assurance than those on the other categories.

We shall next show the reliabilities by our first procedure. In this three judges did the rating, observing the pictures independently, but meeting in advance of the rating to agree upon the number and the designation of the scenes to be rated. Three different committees were involved, the first rating seventy-seven pictures and the other two twenty-four each—the same twenty-four, which were also included in the seventy-seven by the first committee. We call the principal committee, which rated the seventy-seven, committee "A" and the other two "boys" and "girls" respectively to describe their personnel. The findings are shown on page 80.

It will be seen that the average intercorrelations are considerably higher here than in our previous table, and the predicted correlations are also higher in spite of the smaller number of judges. *But these judges sat together* in planning the scenes, though not in rating them. The predicted

TABLE IX

AVERAGE INTERCORRELATIONS AMONG MEMBERS AND PREDICTED
CORRELATIONS BETWEEN WHOLE COMMITTEE AND OTHER
COMMITTEES FOR COMMITTTEES OF THREE MEM-
BERS SITTING TOGETHER

Committee	Scale	r_{11}	r with Com. of Three	r with Infinite Number
A	Aggressiveness	.684	.866	.931
A	Kissing	.885	.958	.979
A	Democracy	.812	.928	.963
A	Parent-child	.862	.949	.974
Boys	Aggressiveness	.870	.952	.977
Boys	Kissing	.860	.948	.977
Boys	Democracy	.950	.982	.977
Boys	Parent-child	.934	.976	.988
Girls	Aggressiveness	.880	.956	.981
Girls	Kissing	.752	.900	.949
Girls	Parent-child	.935	.977	.988

correlations would, therefore, hold only if the new set of
judges were to sit in with these and plan the scenes with
them. The chief value of the showing in the table is connected with the last column on the right, indicating the
probable correlations between the ratings of a committee
of three and those that might be expected from a committee
of infinite size. The high correlations shown in the column
indicate that three members make a sufficiently large committee to sit together and plan scenes preparatory to rating,
if that is a part of the technique to be employed.

It was to test the extent of agreement among different
actual committees, the members of which would sit together
to plan scenes but which would act independently of one
another as committees, that we had such different groups
rate the same twenty-four pictures. The obtained correlations are given below, first between the paired values of
scenes that could be identified as the same and second be-

tween the aggregate ratings regardless of identity of scenes. These results are given in Table X and Table XI.

Table X

INTER-COMMITTEE CORRELATIONS ON CORRESPONDING SCENES

Scale	A vs. Boys	A vs. Girls	Girls vs. Boys
Aggressiveness	.483	.727	.624
Kissing	.811	.725	.738
Parent-child	.767	.785	.673
Democracy	.926	.722	.911

Table XI

INTER-COMMITTEE CORRELATIONS ON AGGREGATE RATINGS ON TWENTY-FOUR MOTION PICTURES BY THREE COMMITTEES

Scale	A. vs. Boys	A. vs. Girls	Boys vs. Girls
Aggressiveness	.884	.877	.746
Kissing	.842	.631	.797
Democracy	.541	.245	.156
Parent-child	.778	.614	.583
All combined	.900	.909	.780

We concluded that these correlations were scarcely high enough, and certainly not high enough to permit placing individual pictures with justice. Besides, the task of assembling in committee for discussion of scenes is time-consuming and expensive. We therefore abandoned this scheme in the middle of our study and resorted to the policy of having five judges acting independently. The reliabilities for this latter technique were shown earlier in this chapter. An examination of ratings by two committees on a small number of pictures indicated that the inter-committee correlations would probably be as high as those predicted by the Spearman formula, all the assumptions of which are fulfilled by this technique.

But still better results could be obtained by combining our two techniques, having fifteen raters grouped into committees of three members each, the five committees acting independently. Such scheme of rating would be somewhat expensive but would give sufficiently valid and reliable returns to warrant complete confidence not only for studying trends in pictures as groups but for the placement of individual films. In Chapter XII we shall return to this point in connection with the proposal of a more objective and meaningful system of reporting on movies for the information of the public than the ones now in vogue.

Summarizing the chapter we may say that motion pictures were rated by particular scenes rather than as wholes. This was done on the hypothesis that such scenes set patterns which are likely to be taken by observers as "the way people do," and to be imitated as such. The mores seem to consist of such detailed patterns of conduct even more largely than of integrated philosophies of life. But the desirability of also evaluating motion pictures as wholes by some suitable technique is acknowledged. One hundred eighty-four pictures were rated by committees, consisting first of three members and later of five. In our first procedure the members of the committee sat together to agree upon the number and the designation of the scenes but assigned ratings to them independently. In our second procedure the members acted independently, both in the listing of scenes and in rating them. Our ratings from the first procedure proved to have fairly good reliabilities—sufficiently satisfactory for generalizing on trends of motion pictures based on averages. But from our second procedure the reliabilities were not only sufficiently high to justify generalizations based on averages but also high enough to permit the placement of individual pictures with justice.

Especially if the number of raters be increased to fifteen, and these work in five committees of three members each, thus combining our first and our second procedure, we have available a highly reliable means of measuring motion pictures with the aid of our scales. In our rating we also made a distinction between scenes enacted by attractive characters and those enacted by unattractive ones, on the hypothesis that the former tend to be imitated while the latter may build up taboos against the sort of conduct exhibited.

CHAPTER VI

THE DIVERGENCE OF THE MOVIES FROM THE MORES: AGGRESSIVENESS OF A GIRL IN LOVE-MAKING

In displaying our findings regarding the amount of conflict between motion pictures and standards of morality it is necessary for us to define certain points from which to orient our data. If all the members of a social group stopped approving and began disapproving at the same point in badness, and if a motion picture lay wholly on one or another side of this dividing point, our task would be easy. But neither of these conditions obtains. The members of a group differ rather widely in respect to what they will approve and many motion pictures contain scenes that run from very high to very low values. Until we adopt fixed points of orientation we cannot talk specifically and intelligibly about our findings.

What these points shall be, and how the scenes in motion pictures shall be displayed in relation to them, must be arbitrarily decided. We chose three points of orientation and two ways of showing the relation of motion pictures to each of them.

1. A point we called the "approval index" for each group.
2. The first, second, and third quarter-points in the distribution of disapprovals for each group.
·3. The first, second, and third quarter-points of admirations.

In relating motion pictures to each of these points we

show (1) the percentage of scenes lying above or below the point for each of the groups and for all the groups combined, and (2) the percentage of pictures having scenes lying beyond each point. Comedies are treated separately from feature pictures and a separate showing is made for scenes enacted by attractive characters and those by unattractive characters. Each of these categories will be explained as we proceed.

Our basic point of orientation is what we call the "approval index" of a group. The reader will recall the graphs of our distributions in Chapter II, where it was shown that, in the ratings on each specimen of conduct, there was a certain percentage of admirations at one end of the distribution, a certain percentage of disapprovals at the other end, and a band of neutrals between these. This held true also when the scales were marked by our social groups in the form of printed strips as explained in Chapter III. That position on the scale of increasing badness was taken as the "approval index" where the middle of the neutral belt stood exactly at the middle of the distribution. In other words, it is where the ogive curve of the disapprovals plus half the neutrals crosses the 50 per cent line. At this point approximately 37 per cent of the members of the group express admiration for the bit of conduct described in the scale, 37 per cent express disapproval, and 26 per cent are neutral—approve but do not admire. Thus 37 per cent are actively against the conduct and 63 per cent are mildly or aggressively for it. Of course the width of the neutral belt is not always the same, so that the percentages indicated in the sentence above are only approximate. This division of nearly two thirds for and one third against seems to be a reasonably exacting standard to apply. But those who think a more or less exacting standard should be used have our other two points of orientation in terms of which to think.

In this chapter we shall display our findings regarding the conflict of the movies with the mores in respect to Aggressiveness of a Girl in Love-Making. Of the four phases of morality explored in our study this is the one in which motion pictures most often conflict with present standards. We shall then show our findings on the other three phases, in successive chapters, in descending order of amount of offense against the mores.

In Table XII a showing is made of the percentage of aggressiveness scenes lying below the approval index, as defined above, for each of our social groups and for all the groups combined. In later tables we shall make a corresponding showing for active disapprovals and for admirations. In Table XII the groups are arranged in descending order of conservatism. The total number of aggressiveness scenes in the 142 feature pictures studied was 726 (when the number listed by the committees of five is divided by five so as to make it comparable with the numbers by the earlier committees). Of these 726 scenes 549 were by characters played up throughout the picture as a whole in attractive rôles, while 177 were by characters played in unattractive rôles. On these numbers the percentages of the table are based.

It will be seen from the table that 70 per cent of all the scenes listed on Aggressiveness of a Girl in Love-Making in the feature pictures lie below the approval index of the population constituted by all the groups combined, aggregating 484 persons. That is more than two thirds of the scenes. This percentage ranges from 53 in the case of the most liberal group, the adolescent sons and daughters of bituminous coal miners, to 94 in the case of the most conserv-

Table XII

Percentage of Aggressiveness Scenes in 142 Feature Films Lying
below the Approval Index for the Several Social Groups
and for All the Groups Combined

Groups	Attractive		Unattractive		Both	
	No.	Per Cent	No.	Per Cent	No.	Per Cent
Middle-aged college professors and their wives	508	92	175	98	683	94
Adult Brethren in Berks County, Pa. (men and women)	488	89	173	97	661	91
Ministers in Lancaster, Pa.	445	81	171	97	616	85
Ministers scattered throughout the United States	433	79	169	95	602	83
College seniors at Pennsylvania State College (men and women)	412	75	168	95	580	80
Young Brethren (adolescent sons and daughters of Group 2 above)	397	72	166	94	563	76
Young women, members élite society in New York City and Baltimore	389	71	168	95	556	77
Negro school teachers, Summer School, Hampton Institute, Va.	386	71	166	94	552	76
Graduate students, Pennsylvania State College (men and women)	332	61	158	90	490	67
Social workers and college professors in U. S. of national reputation	332	61	158	90	490	67
Business men in Berks and Lancaster counties, Pa.	319	58	158	90	477	66
Adult factory workers in western Pennsylvania	255	46	151	86	406	56
Adult miners and their wives, western Pennsylvania	251	46	149	84	400	55
Young miners, adolescent sons and daughters of group above	239	43	147	83	386	53
Total population—all the groups combined	349	63	161	91	510	70

ative group, middle-aged college professors and their wives at Pennsylvania State College. But it is worthy of note that a considerably higher percentage of scenes enacted by persons played up through the picture in unattractive rôles

Table XIII

Percentage of Feature Films Having One or More Aggressiveness Scenes Lying below the Approval Index for the Several Social Groups and for All the Groups Combined

Group	Pictures with Scenes below		With Scenes below by Attractive Characters	
	No.	Per Cent	No.	Per Cent
Faculty members and wives	127	89	116	82
Adult Brethren, male and female	126	89	114	80
Lancaster preachers	125	88	112	79
Preachers throughout U. S.	124	87	110	77
College seniors, male and female	122	86	109	77
Young Brethren, male and female	121	85	106	75
New York élite girls	121	85	107	75
Negro school teachers	121	85	105	74
Business men	117	82	99	70
Social workers and college professors	117	82	99	70
Graduate students	117	82	99	70
Adult factory workers	108	76	88	62
Adult miners and their wives	105	74	83	58
Young miners, male and female	105	74	81	57
Combined groups	118	83	101	71

lie below the approval indices than of those enacted by attractive characters.

But perhaps these aggressive scenes are concentrated largely in a few pictures. The data on the percentage of pictures having one or more scenes lying below the approval indices answer that question. These are again the feature pictures.

Eighty-three per cent of all the feature pictures had one or more aggressive scenes that lay below the approval index of the combined groups. This percentage ranged from 74 for the most liberal group to 89 for the most conservative. But the percentage of pictures that contained aggressive scenes enacted by attractive characters was less, though slightly less. It was 71 for the entire population and ranged from 57 per cent to 82 per cent.

We shall not display here the detailed tables for the comics. The divergence of the groups from one another is practically the same as in the case of the feature films. In the comics 87 per cent of all the aggressive scenes lay below the level of the index of approval of the combined groups. The percentage for attractive characters was 83 and for unattractive 96. Fifty per cent of all the comics contained scenes below the approval index and 45 per cent of them contained scenes below by attractive characters. Thus a smaller proportion of comics had offensively aggressive scenes, but when these scenes did occur they were more often of an extreme degree. Love-making techniques do not occur as frequently in comics as in feature pictures but when they do occur they are more often of a crude order (that is, an order that scores low on our scales). The average number of aggressiveness scenes listed for the 42 comics was 2.12 while the average for the 142 feature films was 5.11.

So far we have studied the matter from the point of view of the approval index. We turn now to active disapprovals and active admirations. What proportion of the scenes is such as to arouse the active disapproval of as much as 25 per cent of the group? Of 50 per cent of the group? Of 75 per cent? Conversely, what proportion of the scenes is such as to challenge the admiration of each of these percentages, so that these persons would feel it a social asset to have the patterns imitated? The data of Table XIV answer these questions for the feature pictures. Only the percentages of the scenes are given, not the numbers. The case of admirations is presented in the left half of the table and that of disapprovals in the right half. On the left the percentage of scenes *above* the respective points is given; on the right, the percentage of scenes *below*. Thus the 2 in the first column on the left means that 2 per cent of the scenes on aggressiveness enacted by attractive characters were such as to challenge the admiration of as many as 75 per cent of adult Brethren, the 1 in the second column means that 1 per cent of those enacted by unattractive characters challenged admiration from this 75 per cent, and the 2 in the third column gives the percentage for attractive and unattractive characters combined. The next set of three columns makes a similar showing for the percentage of aggressive scenes that were such as to challenge the admiration of 50 per cent of this group and the third set of three columns makes a showing for the most liberal 25 per cent of the group. The 55 in the column at the extreme right of the table means that 55 per cent of the aggressive scenes were such as to call forth the active disapproval of 75 per cent of the group of adult Brethren, and the 84 in the column next toward the left shows the percentage of scenes by unattractive characters that were such as to be disapproved by this 75 per cent. It will be recognized that scenes must be much worse to call forth disapproval by 75 per cent of a group than to call forth disapproval by 50 per cent or twenty-five per cent of the group.

The·table shows that 56 per cent of the scenes in aggressiveness were of such a nature as half the combined group would disapprove, offset by only 12 per cent that half the combined groups would admire. The former per cent ranged

TABLE XIV

Percentages of Aggressiveness Scenes in Feature Films Calling Forth Active Admirations or Active Disapprovals of Designated Proportions of Our Several Social Groups and of All the Groups Combined

Groups	Admirations									Disapprovals								
	75%			50%			25%			25%			50%			75%		
	Attractive	Unattractive	Both	Attractive	Unattractive	Both	Attractive	Unattractive	Both	Attractive	Unattractive	Both	Attractive	Unattractive	Both	Attractive	Unattractive	Both
Adult Brethren	2	1	2	5	1	4	22	5	18	94	99	95	77	95	82	46	84	55
Hampton Negroes	6	1	5	19	4	16	45	13	37	84	94	88	63	90	69	32	76	43
Young Brethren	4	1	3	13	2	10	42	11	34	90	98	92	60	89	67	45	84	55
Lancaster preachers	1	1	1	5	1	4	26	6	21	81	95	84	52	86	60	22	62	32
Preachers, U. S.	2	1	3	6	1	5	25	5	20	79	95	83	43	84	53	22	61	31
College seniors	2	1	2	7	1	7	30	6	24	79	95	83	43	84	53	22	61	31
Business men	7	1	6	28	6	22	51	15	42	70	94	76	44	84	54	24	68	35
Graduate students	4	1	3	19	4	16	44	14	38	69	94	75	39	82	49	13	46	21
Factory workers	7	1	6	39	10	32	73	28	62	69	94	78	35	81	47	11	38	17
Adult miners	14	2	11	37	13	31	73	29	48	58	89	66	29	75	40	9	35	16
Young miners	20	5	16	37	13	31	75	30	63	56	88	64	27	73	38	12	40	19
Social leaders	1	0	1	8	1	7	45	12	37	67	94	73	25	70	36	6	21	10
Groups combined	3	1	3	15	2	12	47	14	39	81	95	85	47	84	56	17	53	25

frọm 36 to 82 for the different groups while the latter ranged from 4 to 32. Eighty-five per cent of the aggressive scenes were of the kind that the most conservative quarter of the combined group would disapprove, while only 3 per cent were scenes that the most conservative quarter would admire. But the proportion of offenses was far greater with unattractive characters than with attractive characters.

We shall next show the proportion of feature films having one or more scenes on aggressiveness lying *above* each of the quarter-points of admirations for our several groups and, parallel to that, the proportion having one or more aggressiveness scenes lying *below* the quarter-points of disapprovals. The percentage of all the feature films will be indicated and also the percentage containing scenes by attractive characters.

Table XV shows that far larger proportions of pictures lie below the several points of reference of disapprovals than above the corresponding points of admirations. Seventy-six per cent of the feature films had scenes of such nature as to arouse the disapproval of half or more of the combined group, while only 41 per cent of them had scenes of a character to challenge the admiration of half the group. The percentages for attractive characters were 61 and 39 respectively. Nearly nine tenths of the pictures had scenes of the type to arouse the disapproval of a quarter of the population, and more than three fourths contained such scenes by attractive characters. But the range among the groups was great, especially in respect to the percentage of pictures containing scenes of the type to challenge admiration; the most conservative group found only 15 per cent (by both types of characters) above the 50 per cent line, while the most liberal group found 79 per cent. At the 50 per cent disapproval line the range was from 45 per cent of

TABLE XV

PERCENTAGE OF FEATURE FILMS HAVING ONE OR MORE SCENES
OF AGGRESSIVENESS LYING ABOVE THE THREE QUARTER-
POINTS OF ADMIRATIONS AND BELOW THE THREE QUARTER-
POINTS OF DISAPPROVALS FOR THE SEVERAL SOCIAL
GROUPS

Groups	Admirations						Disapprovals					
	75%		50%		25%		25%		50%		75%	
	All	Att.	All	Att.	All	Att.	All	Att.	All	Att.	All	Att.
Adult Brethren	6	5	15	13	51	48	89	81	86	77	75	61
Lancaster preachers	5	4	15	13	61	58	88	79	80	68	58	42
Preachers, U. S.	6	5	18	16	60	56	88	78	74	59	58	42
College seniors	5	4	21	19	67	63	89	80	82	69	58	41
Social leaders	6	0	25	23	79	73	84	73	62	45	31	18
Young Brethren	9	8	38	37	75	71	89	81	83	70	75	58
Graduate students	9	8	49	46	81	75	85	76	73	58	45	30
Hampton Negroes	18	16	60	56	79	73	89	80	83	72	68	51
Business men	20	18	57	54	82	76	85	74	74	60	62	44
Factory workers	21	19	73	70	88	81	85	74	71	54	41	26
Adult miners	37	36	79	73	88	81	82	69	65	49	38	23
Young miners	50	46	79	73	88	81	80	69	65	49	43	27
Combined groups	7	6	41	39	81	75	88	78	76	61	51	33

pictures to 77 per cent for attractive characters and from
62 per cent to 86 per cent for both types.

None of the comedies contained aggressive scenes challenging the admiration of 75 per cent of our combined group,
2 per cent contained scenes challenging admiration from

half the group, and 21 per cent contained scenes challenging the admiration of the most liberal quarter of the group. Conversely 33 per cent contained scenes of the character to arouse active disapproval of three quarters of the combined group, 50 per cent calling forth disapproval of half the group and 57 per cent engaging the disapproval of the most conservative quarter.

But if the movies defy social approvals in respect to Aggressiveness of a Girl in Love-Making, so also does conduct as reported by our respondents—and to just about the same degree. When having the mores scales marked we had some of our groups mark, as a second task, the prevailing *practice* of their set regarding the items of the scales. If, according to the observation of the respondents, half or more of their set would be likely to act as a scene in the scale related under the conditions described in the write-up, they were to mark a *plus* before the item with a colored pencil (so as to distinguish these markings from their first ones, which were made with a black pencil). If the majority of the members of their set would not do such a thing, they were to mark a *minus*. If they did not know how their set would act, or if the scene would not apply to their group, they were to mark a *question sign*. We constructed the ogive curves for the declarations of restraints from action and determined at what points in badness these crossed the values at the quarter-points of active disapprovals for the groups. We may reasonably assume that the values at these points suggest the proportion of the group that would be likely to indulge in conduct of the levels of badness indicated at those points in the scale. That is, if 25 per cent of the group say that their set would do acts down to a certain level, it is not a violent interpretation to hold that probably 25 per cent of the members of the group would engage in conduct as bad as that. Similarly if 50 per cent of the group say that their set would act as badly as a certain lower index value, we may take that to mean that 50 per cent of the group would go as far as that. And the same would hold for other percentages. With this interpretation we shall show, in Table XVI, the proportion of members of some of the groups that are said to practice acts beyond the indi-

TABLE XVI

COMPARISON OF THE PRACTICE IN CERTAIN SOCIAL GROUPS IN
AGGRESSIVENESS WITH CONDUCT IN FEATURE FILMS

| Groups | 25% | | | 50% | | | 75% | | |
| | Dis-approval | | Prac-tice | Dis-approval | | Prac-tice | Dis-approval | | Prac-tice |
	Att. Ch.	Both		Att. Ch.	Both		Att. Ch.	Both	
Young Brethren	81	89	71	70	83	58	58	75	48
Factory workers	74	85	74	54	71	55	26	41	33
Hampton Negroes	80	89	83	72	83	48	51	68	22
Young miners	69	80	81	49	65	66	27	43	41
Business men	74	85	76	60	74	57	44	62	37
Graduate students	76	85	81	58	73	54	30	45	46
College seniors	80	89	79	69	82	53	41	58	40

cated quarter-points in the disapprovals of these groups, in parallelism with the percentage of feature motion pictures that have scenes below these same levels. In the column under 25 per cent, opposite Young Brethren the 71 means that 71 per cent of this group would practice acts that one quarter of that same group would disapprove, while the 89 means that 89 per cent of the feature pictures have aggressive scenes that this same one quarter would disapprove. The 58 and the 83 have a corresponding meaning with reference to disapproval by half the group.

The table shows that in all groups except young miners a larger percentage of motion pictures fall below the various

levels of disapproval than of members of the groups alleged
to practice similar acts, when all pictures are considered.
If we consider only those films containing acts below the
various levels by attractive characters, motion pictures are
distinctly worse than practice in the group of young Brethren and Hampton Negroes, better than practice in the group
of young miners, and about parallel with practice in all
the other groups. It should scarcely be necessary to say that
paralleling practice gives no evidence of inherent "rightness."

It is, thus, clear from our presentation throughout this
chapter that motion pictures are vigorously opposing present
standards of value in respect to Aggressiveness of a Girl in
Love-Making. Practice, too, seems to be taking the reins,
but against a certain feeling of propriety yet persisting.
If practice were not falling below approvals, each percentage
in the practice column in the body of the table would be
exactly the complement of the 25 per cent, 50 per cent, or
75 per cent standing at the top of the respective columns,
whereas all but four of them are greater. But it is clear
that the mores (in the sense of *approved* customs) cannot
long lag behind practice, especially when the suggestions of
skillfully constructed drama tend constantly to give sanc-
tion to the deviating patterns and thus to win approval for
them. However uneasy people may be in the first stages
of the practice of conduct that deviates from established
modes of response, whether on the part of the offender
himself or on the part of those who react upon his response,
this feeling of emotional resistance tends to break down and
to be replaced by contentment or even by a sense of virtue
as soon as the new responses have been practiced long enough
to have become established habits. Those persons who still
cherish the traditional restraints against Aggressiveness of
a Girl in Love-Making will strongly resent as encouragement

to vulgarity that 76 per cent of pictures that set models of aggressiveness which half of our people disapprove (last line, Table XV), particularly the 61 per cent by attractive characters, or even the 88 per cent by attractive characters that the most conservative quarter of our population disapproves. They will claim that motion pictures are uniting their forces with the forces of human impulse to break down our moral code, and that it is not the function of art to parallel practice but instead to hold before us patterns of our better selves. But, on the other hand, the iconoclasts will answer them by lamenting the existence of the $100 - 76 = 24$ per cent of pictures that keep within the conventions of the conservative half of the population, and especially the 12 per cent that stay within the bounds of approval of the most conservative quarter, holding that these are lending the sanctions of art to the perpetuation of traditions which should be overturned.

CHAPTER VII

THE DIVERGENCE OF THE MOVIES FROM THE MORES: KISSING AND CARESSING

In this chapter we shall follow the same order of presentation as in our previous one on Aggressiveness of a Girl in Love-Making. The reader who needs a fuller definition of terms than this chapter provides, or a further explanation of the structure of the tables, should refer to the corresponding sections of our preceding chapter. We shall show first the percentage of scenes in the feature films that lie below the "approval index" of the several groups—the point at which the ogive curve of the active disapprovals plus half the neutrals crosses the 50 per cent line. At this point approximately 37 per cent are actively against the type of conduct involved, 37 per cent are actively for it, and 26 per cent think it acceptable but nothing to boast about. The groups are arranged in descending order of conservatism. The table shows only percentages below the approval indices, based upon a total of 741 kissing scenes in the 142 feature films, 653 of which were by attractive characters and 88 by unattractive. The distribution of these is shown to the three sub-types recognized in our ratings. These, with the number of scenes under each given in parentheses, are as follows:

1. By casual lovers (314+69).
2. By betrothed or serious lovers (194+6).
3. By married persons (144+13).

We consider the distinction, shown in the table, between scenes enacted by characters played up through the picture as a whole in unattractive rôles and those by characters played in attractive rôles to be a distinction of considerable importance. There is good psychological basis for believing that conduct exemplified by attractive characters is likely to be imitated by observers but that taboos are likely to be built up against modes of conduct that are shown in a disgusting light by reason of the fact that they are performed by disgusting personalities. In more technical terms, there may be expected to be positive conditioning with reference to the responses by attractive characters but negative conditioning with respect to those by unattractive characters. Perhaps we ought to consider the "bad" conduct of unattractive characters an asset rather than a liability for moral training. Perhaps motion pictures would be at their best as moral training factors if unattractive characters could never be shown doing anything but "bad" acts and attractive characters anything but "good" acts. The application of this principle is, however, considerably limited by the fact that immature or perverted observers may accept as attractive characters those who would be prevailingly taken in the reverse way. This ambiguity renders the effect of motion pictures on social control in heterogeneous audiences a somewhat uncertain one.

The relative numbers of scenes given above indicate that our raters were very conservative in calling a character unattractive. They were instructed to list a character as unattractive only if he was definitely so. Thus the attractive characters include also the neutral ones. The distinction, so far as normal observers were concerned, was not really very difficult for the raters to make, since the villains of a play are usually rather clearly marked off from the other characters.

Table XVII

Percentage of Kissing Scenes in 142 Feature Films Lying below the Approval Index for the Several Social Groups and for All the Groups Combined

Groups	Total			Casual Lovers			Betrothed			Married		
	Attractive Characters	Unattractive Characters	Both	Attractive Characters	Unattractive Characters	Both	Attractive Characters	Unattractive Characters	Both	Attractive Characters	Unattractive Characters	Both
Penn. State faculty	53	78	56	91	99	92	27	16	26	8	0	8
Graduate students	45	72	48	79	90	81	20	16	19	4	0	4
Adult miners	45	72	48	79	90	81	20	16	19	4	0	4
Adult Brethren	44	72	44	77	52	73	20	16	19	4	0	4
Hampton Negroes	34	64	37	61	80	64	13	16	13	3	0	3
Preachers, U. S.	34	64	37	61	80	64	13	16	13	3	0	3
Business men	34	62	37	61	78	64	12	16	12	3	0	3
New York élite	34	62	37	61	78	64	12	16	12	3	0	3
Lancaster preachers	34	62	37	61	78	64	12	16	12	3	0	3
College seniors	34	62	37	61	78	64	12	16	12	3	0	3
Young Brethren	32	62	36	58	78	62	12	16	12	2	0	2
Young miners	31	59	35	56	74	59	12	16	12	2	0	2
Factory workers	30	61	34	54	77	58	12	16	12	2	0	2
Social leaders, U. S.	25	55	29	46	68	50	9	16	9	1	0	1
Combined groups	35	64	38	62	80	65	14	16	14	3	0	3

The table shows that 38 per cent of the scenes lay below the approval index of the combined groups, 35 per cent by attractive characters and 64 per cent by unattractive characters. The range was from 29 per cent in the case of thirty-two ministers, university professors, and social workers throughout the United States, all of national reputation, who constituted our most liberal group, to 56 per cent in the case of fifty middle-aged faculty members at Pennsylvania State College and their wives, who constituted our most conservative group. By far the greatest amount of offense was by casual lovers and the least amount by married persons, in terms of the percentage of the scenes enacted by

Table XVIII

Percentage of Feature Pictures and of Comics Having Scenes Lying below the Approval Index for the Several Groups and for the Combined Groups

| Groups | Feature Films | | | | Comics | | | |
| | All Characters | | With Att. Ch. | | All Characters | | With Att. Ch. | |
	No.	Per Cent	No.	Per Cent	No.	Per Cent	No.	Per Cent
College faculty	119	84	105	74	16	38	14	33
Graduate students	108	76	94	66	16	38	14	33
Social leaders, U. S.	108	76	94	66	16	38	14	33
Adult Brethren	108	76	94	66	16	38	14	33
Hampton Negroes	101	71	85	60	13	31	11	26
U. S. preachers	101	71	85	60	12	29	11	26
Business men	100	70	84	59	12	29	10	24
New York élite	100	70	84	59	12	29	10	24
Lancaster preachers	99	70	83	58	12	29	10	24
College seniors	99	70	83	58	12	29	10	24
Young Brethren	99	70	83	59	12	29	10	24
Factory workers	98	69	83	59	12	29	10	24
Young miners	97	68	83	59	12	29	10	24
Social leaders, U. S.	93	66	77	54	11	26	9	21
Combined groups	101	71	85	60	13	31	11	26

them that lay below the approval index. Nearly twice as high percentage of the kissing scenes by unattractive characters lay below the approval index as by attractive characters.

Our next table shows the percentage of feature films that contain one or more kissing scenes lying below the approval index for the several groups and for the groups combined. We give in it, for each of the subdivisions of kissing and for all combined, the percentages of the 142 feature films containing such scenes and the percentages containing such scenes by attractive characters.

The table shows that 71 per cent of all the feature films contained kissing scenes below the approval index of the combined groups and 60 per cent contained such scenes by attractive characters. The former percentages ranged from 66 to 84 and the latter from 54 to 74. Not nearly so large a proportion of the comics contained offensive scenes, the percentages here being 31 and 26 and ranging from 26 to 38 in the case of all comics and 21 to 33 in the case of scenes by attractive characters. That is because the comics less often contain love-making scenes; the average number of kissing scenes listed for the 142 feature pictures was 5.22 while the average number listed for the 42 comics was only .9.

We turn now to a showing of the proportion of scenes in the feature pictures that lay above the three quarter-points for admirations and below the three quarter-points for disapprovals. The former are shown on the left and the latter on the right in the table below.

It appears from the table that 54 per cent of all the scenes in feature films were such as to arouse the active disapproval of one quarter of the combined groups; 31 per cent of half the combined groups; and 16 per cent of three quarters of them. These percentages ranged from 34 to 65, 20 to 39, and 8 to 30 respectively. But these scenes arousing disapproval were countered by 68 per cent that were such as to challenge the admiration of a quarter of the combined group; 44 per cent that challenged the admiration of half this group; and 26 per cent of three quarters of it. For attractive characters this rose as high as 64 per cent for half of one of the groups. Thus there were with respect to

TABLE XIX

PERCENTAGES OF KISSING SCENES IN FEATURE FILMS CALLING FORTH ACTIVE ADMIRATIONS AND ACTIVE DISAPPROVALS OF DESIGNATED PROPORTIONS OF OUR SEVERAL GROUPS

Groups	Admirations									Disapprovals								
	75%			50%			25%			25%			50%			75%		
	Attractive	Unattractive	Both	Attractive	Unattractive	Both	Attractive	Unattractive	Both	Attractive	Unattractive	Both	Attractive	Unattractive	Both	Attractive	Unattractive	Both
Adult Brethren	23	9	22	37	15	34	53	27	50	60	84	63	36	65	39	27	56	30
Graduate students	23	9	22	41	16	38	65	36	62	52	78	55	30	50	33	18	42	21
Preachers, U. S.	18	9	17	43	16	39	66	39	63	38	67	42	24	52	27	16	42	18
College seniors	27	.11	26	48	22	45	68	61	65	38	67	42	24	55	28	11	36	14
Lancaster preachers	23	9	22	48	22	45	69	39	65	34	64	38	24	52	27	11	35	14
Adult miners	32	13	30	48	23	45	71	42	67	63	85	65	34	68	38	18	42	21
Young Brethren	34	15	32	51	24	48	74	44	71	52	78	55	28	58	32	13	39	16
Business men	37	15	34	55	27	51	75	44	71	48	75	51	29	59	33	16	40	18
Social leaders	37	15	34	62	33	58	76	45	72	29	58	34	18	42	20	6	19	8
Factory workers	37	15	34	64	35	61	78	50	75	43	72	47	25	56	29	12	37	15
Hampton Negroes	28	11	26	51	24	48	70	39	66	54	81	57	34	61	37	18	44	21
Young miners	34	15	32	62	33	58	80	52	77	47	73	50	23	51	27	12	37	15
Combined groups	28	11	26	47	20	44	72	42	68	51	77	54	28	57	31	13	39	16

each point more scenes of such nature as to challenge admiration than of those likely to arouse disapproval. It will be also noticed that unattractive characters indulge in "bad" acts, and fall short of "good" ones, about twice as large proportion of times as attractive characters do. In this connection it should be recalled that the number of scenes by attractive characters was 652 for the feature films while the number by unattractive ones was only 88.

Of the scenes in the comics 63 per cent were such as to arouse active disapproval of a quarter of the combined groups, 47 per cent of half, and 34 per cent of three quarters of this population. Conversely 74 per cent of the scenes were patterns of the kind to arouse admiration of a quarter of the combined groups, 61 per cent of half, and 50 per cent of three quarters. But the total number of scenes was only 38.

We shall next show the proportion of feature films having one or more kissing scenes lying *above* each of the quarter points of admirations for our several groups and, parallel to that, the proportion having one or more kissing scenes lying *below* the quarter-points of disapprovals. The percentage of all the feature films will be indicated and also the percentage containing scenes by attractive characters.

Table XX tells essentially the same story as the preceding one; at every point of comparison the films containing scenes that challenge admiration slightly more than overbalance in number those containing scenes that arouse disapproval. Sixty-seven per cent of the feature pictures contained one or more scenes that were of such nature as to arouse the disapproval of half of the combined group while 57 per cent contained such scenes by attractive characters. The former percentage ranged from 52 to 72 and the latter from 42 to 61. With this may be compared the 75 per cent of pictures

TABLE XX

PERCENTAGE OF FEATURE FILMS HAVING ONE OR MORE SCENES LYING
ABOVE THE THREE QUARTER-POINTS OF ADMIRATIONS AND BELOW
THE THREE QUARTER-POINTS OF DISAPPROVALS

Groups	Admirations						Disapprovals					
	75%		50%		25%		25%		50%		75%	
	All	Attrac-tive	All	Attrac-tive	All	Attrac-tive	All	Attrac-tive	All	Attrac-tive	All	Attrac-tive
Adult Brethren	50	46	63	61	80	77	85	78	71	61	67	57
Graduate students	50	46	66	64	87	82	80	72	69	59	52	42
Preachers, U. S.	39	37	73	72	87	82	74	63	61	52	51	39
Lancaster preachers	50	46	74	73	87	83	72	61	61	52	42	30
College seniors	51	47	74	71	87	83	74	63	63	52	43	31
Adult miners	54	50	74	73	87	84	87	80	72	61	52	42
Young Brethren	58	56	77	68	87	84	79	71	66	56	55	36
Hampton Negroes	51	48	77	75	87	83	83	75	70	59	53	43
Business men	63	61	79	77	88	85	77	68	68	58	58	39
Social leaders	63	61	87	83	88	85	73	64	52	42	27	18
Young miners	58	56	87	83	89	87	77	69	61	52	44	32
Factory workers	63	61	87	82	89	86	75	67	65	55	44	32
Combined groups	51	47	75	73	87	84	80	71	67	57	44	32

that contained scenes of the type to challenge admiration
from half this same combined group, ranging from 63 per
cent to 87 per cent. Eighty per cent contained scenes disapproved by a quarter of the group, with a range from 72 per
cent to 85 per cent as against 87 per cent that challenged
admiration from a quarter of the group; and 44 per cent
contained scenes arousing disapproval of three quarters of
the group against 51 per cent containing scenes challenging
admiration from this same three quarters.

We shall next see how motion pictures compare with
current practice among some of our social groups in regard
to the number of films containing kissing scenes below the

several points. Under "Disapproval" we show the percentage of pictures containing scenes below the several
points of disapproval in the group's curve; under "Practice"
the percentage of persons reported as practicing acts below
the corresponding levels of badness. We show separately
the percentage of pictures containing scenes by attractive
characters (in the first column of each trio) and the percentage for all characters whether attractive or unattractive

TABLE XXI

COMPARISON OF THE PRACTICE OF CERTAIN SOCIAL GROUPS IN KISSING
WITH CONDUCT IN FEATURE FILMS

Group	Below 25% Line			Below 50% Line			Below 75% Line		
	Disap.		Prac-tice	Disap.		Prac-tice	Disap.		Prac-tice
	A.	B.		A.	B.		A.	B.	
Young Brethren	71	79	73	56	66	50	36	55	40
Business men	68	77	78	58	68	54	39	58	37
Factory workers	67	75	82	55	65	54	32	44	34
Graduate students	72	80	81	59	69	54	42	52	46
Young miners	69	77	83	61	61	58	44	44	41
College seniors	63	74	79	52	63	53	31	43	40

(in the second column of each trio). In our preceding chapter, and in Chapter IV, pages 60–61, an explanation was
given as to how information on practice was secured and
how it was worked up statistically.

Table XXI shows that life in these groups, as reported
to us, goes on almost exactly parallel with the conduct by
attractive characters in feature films as far as inhibitions
in kissing are concerned. Among young Brethren, for
example, 73 per cent of persons are reported as practicing
kissing acts below the level that the most conservative
quarter of their group would approve, while 71 per cent of
the pictures contained such scenes by attractive characters
and 79 per cent by either attractive or unattractive. Fifty

per cent of this group are reported to practice acts that the other half of the group would disapprove, while 56 per cent of the feature pictures contained scenes by attractive characters below this level. Forty per cent practice acts that three quarters of the group would condemn as against 36 per cent of pictures containing such acts by attractive characters and 56 per cent by either attractive or unattractive characters. A closely similar balance holds for the other groups. We may, therefore, say that the conduct in motion pictures, as far as kissing is concerned, is closely parallel to that of life in our six social groups so far as the conduct of attractive characters is concerned but that motion pictures are worse than life when we consider both kinds of characters. Even for attractive characters pictures tend to fall a trifle below practice, particularly at the 25 per cent and the 50 per cent lines.

The data of this chapter as a whole are to be interpreted to mean that conduct in the movies in respect to kissing almost precisely parallels life, from the standpoint of both approvals and of practices. There are large numbers of scenes that large sections of our social groups would disapprove, but at each stage the acts have about as large proportion of defenders as the proportion of the acts themselves constitutes. Indeed the conduct in movies reaches, in respect to some scenes, higher toward the "admiration" end of the scale than, in other scenes, it falls toward the "disapproval" end. Conversely, it reaches a little lower than practices do when all characters are considered. Whether the desirable patterns compensate for the nearly equal number of undesirable ones is an open question. The query may be raised, too, whether art is on a satisfactory basis when it merely parallels life, or whether it should have as one of its functions to set for us patterns of our better selves.

It must be clearly understood that *our findings have no bearing upon the propriety of showing kissing scenes on a screen in public.* That is a wholly separate question. It is entirely conceivable that it may be in perfect taste for a husband to kiss his wife in the privacy of their home, or for lovers to exchange an ardent kiss upon becoming betrothed, and yet in very bad taste for these acts to be exhibited on a motion-picture screen for the public to gaze at. Our study asked only whether the patterns of conduct were such as the people would be willing to have imitated under like conditions in life, whether the patterns were such that if imitated they would pull upward or downward on our scale of values. The good taste of exhibiting these things in public would need to be investigated by a different technique from ours. Possibly the same scales might be used but they would need to be re-marked by our several social groups with a different question in mind from the one we put to them.

CHAPTER VIII

THE DIVERGENCE OF THE MOVIES FROM THE MORES: DEMOCRATIC ATTITUDES AND PRACTICES

In the present chapter we abandon the field of love-making techniques and enter that of other social relations. In the two elements of which we have still to give an account motion pictures swing from predominantly negative divergence from the mores to predominantly positive divergence. That shift is made to a fair degree in the area of democratic attitudes and practices, discussed in this chapter, and to a marked degree in the area of treatment of children by parents, discussed in our next chapter.

In our section on democratic attitudes and practices we studied only what is customarily called "social democracy"; we did not enter the complementary areas, political and industrial democracy. What is included in our field is best indicated by the contents of our scales, published in the appendix to this volume, pages 212–238; to these pages the reader should refer. Our scenes under democracy were counted under three sub-phases. These are indicated below, with the number of scenes by attractive and the number by unattractive characters in the feature films indicated in parentheses after each.

1. Treatment of employees and subordinates (246 + 57).
2. Treatment of persons based on social or occupational status (187 + 63).
3. Treatment of persons based on racial discrimination (57 + 3).

Our first table will show the percentage of scenes in the 142 feature films lying below the approval index for the several groups, as defined in the opening of our chapter on aggressiveness. The percentages are based on the numbers

TABLE XXII

PERCENTAGE OF DEMOCRACY SCENES IN 142 FEATURE FILMS LYING BELOW THE APPROVAL INDEX FOR THE SEVERAL SOCIAL GROUPS AND FOR THE GROUPS COMBINED

Groups	Total			Employees			Social Status			Race		
	Attractive	Unattractive	Both	Attractive	Unattractive	Both	Attractive	Unattractive	Both	Attractive	Unattractive	Both
Penn. State faculty	38	82	47	32	80	40	48	84	57	37	100	40
Preachers, U. S.	34	81	43	27	79	37	44	81	54	30	100	33
Graduate students	34	81	43	27	79	36	44	81	54	30	100	33
Adult Brethren	34	81	43	27	79	36	44	81	54	30	100	33
College seniors	34	81	43	27	79	36	44	81	54	30	100	33
Adult miners	34	81	43	26	79	36	44	81	54	30	100	33
Factory workers	33	81	43	26	79	36	44	81	53	30	100	33
Lancaster preachers	33	80	43	26	77	36	44	81	53	30	100	33
Young Brethren	33	80	42	26	77	36	43	81	53	30	100	33
Hampton Negroes	33	80	42	26	77	36	43	81	53	30	100	33
New York élite	33	80	42	26	77	36	43	79	52	30	100	33
Social leaders	32	77	41	25	75	35	43	76	52	28	100	32
Young miners	31	76	39	24	75	33	41	75	50	28	100	32
Groups combined	33	81	43	26	79	36	44	81	53	30	100	33

of scenes given in our preceding paragraph. The distribution of the totals to the sub-phases is shown and the percentages given separately under each for attractive characters, for unattractive, and for both combined.

If conduct in the movies were an exact cross section of life, the percentages of scenes below the approval index would be in every case exactly 50. The table shows the percentage to be considerably less than that for scenes enacted by attractive characters and much more than that for scenes enacted by unattractive characters. Only a third of the scenes by attractive characters were below the approval index of the combined group while more than four fifths of those by unattractive characters fell below this point. That there is this vast difference between attractive characters and unattractive ones is a matter of great social significance, since the bad acts by disgusting characters make for taboos against undemocratic practices just as the good ones by attractive characters make for the idealization of desirable conduct. There is not much difference among the subphases of democracy, though social status shows up somewhat the worst and treatment of employees and subordinates the best. There is remarkable unanimity among the groups, as indicated by the small ranges; the approval indices of all of them fall at nearly the same place on the democracy scales. Evidently the American people have been forged into close agreement in their ideals of democracy.

We shall next show the percentage of pictures having one or more democracy scenes lying below the approval indices of the several groups, giving the findings for feature films on the left of the table and those for comics on the right.

Table XXIII indicates that 63 per cent of all the feature films contained democracy scenes below the approval index of the combined group but only 39 per cent contained such scenes by attractive characters. For the comics the percentages were much less, 24 and 19 respectively. But that is because the comics had a much smaller number of democracy scenes listed by the raters. The aggregate number of democracy scenes in the 142 feature films was 613, an average of 4.3 each, while the aggregate for the 42 comics

TABLE XXIII

PERCENTAGE OF FEATURE FILMS AND OF COMICS HAVING DEMOCRACY
SCENES LYING BELOW THE APPROVAL INDEX FOR THE SEVERAL
GROUPS AND FOR THE GROUPS COMBINED

Groups	Feature Films				Comics			
	All Characters		With Att. Ch.		All Characters		With Att. Ch.	
	No.	Per Cent	No.	Per Cent	No.	Per Cent	No.	Per Cent
Penn. State faculty	102	72	71	50	10	24	8	19
Preachers, U. S.	90	63	60	42	10	24	8	19
Graduate students	90	63	60	42	10	24	8	19
Adult Brethren	90	63	60	42	10	24	8	19
College seniors	90	63	60	42	10	24	8	19
Adult miners	90	63	60	42	10	24	8	19
Factory workers	90	63	61	43	10	24	8	19
Lancaster preachers	90	63	60	42	10	24	8	19
Young Brethren	90	63	60	42	10	24	8	19
Hampton Negroes	90	63	60	42	10	24	8	19
New York élite	89	62	59	41	10	24	8	19
Business men	90	63	60	42	10	24	8	19
Social leaders	87	61	56	39	10	24	8	19
Young miners	86	61	56	39	9	21	7	17
Groups combined	90	63	56	39	10	24	8	19

was only 36, an average of .9 per picture. Forty-two per cent of the scenes in comics enacted by attractive characters and 61 per cent of those by unattractive characters lay below the approval index of the combined groups. This is a larger per cent by attractive characters and a smaller per cent by unattractive ones than was the case with the feature films.

Table XXIV will show the proportion of democracy scenes in feature films lying above the three quarter-points for admirations and below the three quarter-points for active disapprovals of our several social groups, the former shown on the left side of the table and the latter on the right, the percentages for scenes enacted by attractive characters, unattractive, and both combined being separately indicated.

TABLE XXIV

Percentage of Democracy Scenes in Feature Films Calling Forth Admirations and Active Disapprovals of Designated Proportions of Our Several Groups and of the Groups Combined

Groups	Admirations									Disapprovals								
	75%			50%			25%			25%			50%			75%		
	Attractive	Unattractive	Both	Attractive	Unattractive	Both	Attractive	Unattractive	Both	Attractive	Unattractive	Both	Attractive	Unattractive	Both	Attractive	Unattractive	Both
Young Brethren	48	13	41	63	18	54	67	28	58	38	83	46	33	78	42	24	70	33
Adult Brethren	32	8	28	59	17	51	68	22	59	37	83	46	32	76	41	23	69	32
Adult miners	22	11	19	58	19	50	73	25	64	60	89	65	31	76	40	10	42	17
Preachers, U. S.	29	7	26	60	18	51	66	20	57	34	79	43	29	75	38	23	69	32
Hampton Negroes	26	13	39	65	19	56	73	25	63	38	83	46	29	75	38	18	58	26
Business men	39	11	33	65	18	55	71	25	62	37	83	46	28	75	37	18	58	26
Lancaster preachers	50	15	43	64	18	55	68	24	59	34	79	43	28	75	37	17	57	26
Factory workers	37	11	32	63	18	54	69	23	60	38	83	46	27	75	37	15	55	23
Graduate students	39	11	34	61	18	53	66	31	57	34	79	43	27	75	37	18	59	26
College seniors	44	13	38	62	18	54	66	20	57	34	79	43	57	75	37	21	64	30
Social leaders	37	11	32	62	18	54	70	25	60	34	79	43	25	70	34	14	46	20
Young miners	31	7	27	65	18	56	78	32	69	36	83	45	25	70	34	8	30	13
Combined groups	38	11	32	64	18	55	68	22	59	35	82	45	29	75	38	19	59	29

Twice as large proportion of the democracy scenes enacted by attractive characters are such as to be admired by 75 per cent of the combined group as are disapproved by this same percentage. Approximately the same relative standings hold for the other two pairs of corresponding points. At every point of comparison the percentage of "good" scenes enacted by attractive characters is about three times as great as the percentage of such scenes enacted by unattractive characters; and the reverse is true concerning the "bad" scenes, as shown by the larger percentages in the "unattractive" columns on the right side of the table. The groups differ little from one another at their 50 per cent lines but more at the two outlying quarter-points. This is true of both admirations and disapprovals.

The case of the comics is less favorable. No scenes by unattractive characters appeared above even the lowest quarter-point of admirations, but 58 per cent of the scenes by attractive characters rose above this level and 29 per cent above the 75 per cent line. Conversely all the scenes by unattractive characters fell below the first and second quarter-points of disapprovals and 33 per cent of them below the third quarter-point, while 42 per cent of the scenes by attractive characters lapsed below the 25 per cent line, 37 per cent below the 50 per cent line, and 21 per cent below the 75 per cent line of disapprovals. In regard to the placement of democracy scenes the comics are, therefore, distinctly below the feature films.

The next table will tell essentially the same story about the feature pictures as the one above, except that the data are put in terms of the percentage of films containing scenes calculated to arouse admiration or disapproval from indicated proportions of the members of our several social groups.

TABLE XXV

PERCENTAGE OF FEATURE FILMS HAVING ONE OR MORE DEMOCRACY SCENES LYING ABOVE THE THREE QUARTER-POINTS OF ADMIRATIONS AND BELOW THE THREE QUARTER-POINTS OF DISAPPROVALS FOR OUR SEVERAL GROUPS

Groups	Admirations						Disapprovals					
	75%		50%		25%		25%		50%		75%	
	All	Attractive	All	Attractive	All	Attractive	All	Attractive	All	Attractive	All	Attractive
Young Brethren	63	61	73	69	77	72	69	49	63	42	56	34
Adult Brethren	51	49	72	68	77	73	68	48	61	39	55	34
Adult miners	38	37	72	68	80	75	75	68	61	39	36	17
Preachers, U. S.	46	44	72	68	75	70	65	43	61	39	55	34
Hampton Negroes	62	59	73	70	80	75	69	49	60	38	46	27
Business men	56	54	73	69	80	75	68	48	58	37	46	27
Lancaster preachers	65	62	73	69	80	75	63	43	59	38	45	26
Factory workers	54	51	73	69	80	75	68	46	58	37	40	25
Graduate students	58	55	72	68	73	70	65	43	58	37	46	27
College seniors	60	57	73	69	75	70	65	43	58	37	51	32
Social leaders	55	51	73	69	80	75	63	43	58	35	42	22
Young miners	48	45	73	69	80	75	67	46	58	38	27	14
Combined groups	55	51	73	69	77	72	66	45	60	39	46	28

It will be seen, by observing the table, that more than half the feature films contain democracy scenes of such nature as to challenge the admiration of three fourths of the combined group, and nearly three quarters of the films have such scenes appealing thus to half the group. Conversely two thirds of the films have democracy scenes of the nature to arouse disapproval from a quarter of the group, 60 per cent have such scenes disturbing half the group, and 46 per cent three quarters of the group. But the percentage of pictures having such scenes enacted by attractive characters is substantially less, being for the three quarter-points respectively 45, 39, and 28.

In evaluating the relation of the movies to the mores it is illuminating to compare scenes in motion pictures not only with verbally declared approvals and disapprovals but also with habitual practice within the groups. As explained in our chapter on aggressiveness, we collected information on this point and shall present in Table XXVI the comparison as it involves democratic attitudes and practices. The

TABLE XXVI

COMPARISON OF THE PRACTICE OF CERTAIN SOCIAL GROUPS IN DEMOCRACY WITH CONDUCT IN FEATURE FILMS

Groups	Below 25% Line			Below 50% Line			Below 75% Line		
	Disap.		Practice	Disap.		Practice	Disap.		Practice
	All	Attractive		All	Attractive		All	Attractive	
Young Brethren	69	49	71	63	42	62	56	34	50
Adult Brethren	68	48	66	61	39	47	55	34	33
Business men	68	48	72	58	37	54	46	27	35
Graduate students	65	43	64	58	37	50	46	27	40
Factory workers	68	46	67	58	37	45	40	25	33
College students	65	43	72	58	37	59	51	32	53

table shows, in the third column under each of the three quarter-points, the percentage of members of the several groups alleged to practice acts lying below the indicated levels of disapproval of their groups. In the first column is displayed the percentage of feature films having scenes lying below these same disapproval points, and in the second column the percentage of feature pictures containing such scenes by attractive characters. If the movies were just like life, the percentage of practice falling below each point would be exactly equal to the percentage of pictures having scenes below the corresponding level; if the percentage under practice is larger, that means that conduct in life is worse than that in the movies.

The table indicates that democratic practices, as determined by our technique, stand just a trifle above conduct in motion pictures when all scenes are considered. But the conduct in movies in which attractive characters participate stands well above that of outside life. On the whole, therefore, motion pictures are setting patterns of democratic conduct that are somewhat better than those to which people are accustomed in their daily lives, and are making these patterns attractive by associating them with persons whom observers would be disposed to emulate.

The findings displayed in this chapter as a whole have indicated that motion pictures stand rather above the mores in respect to democratic attitudes and practices—in the sense that the scenes fall somewhat more largely toward the plus ends of our scales than approvals by the various groups would demand or than current practices attain, and also in the sense that the "good" acts are done largely by attractive characters and the "bad" ones by unattractive characters. There are some members of society who would consider this fact a social liability. They would fear that the movies tend to make the rank and file of common people dissatisfied with their station in life, less disposed to respect their "betters," and less reverent toward the wealthy and the élite. Others, on the contrary, count it "good" to have the ideal stressed that worth is found among the lowly as well as among the great, that courtesy and respect are due to all regardless of occupation or social status, and that human values are more fundamental and lasting than material ones.

CHAPTER IX

THE DIVERGENCE OF THE MOVIES FROM THE MORES: THE TREATMENT OF CHILDREN BY PARENTS

In this final chapter presenting our findings of the divergence of the movies from the mores we find motion pictures offending the least of the four phases we studied. While there is some divergence "downward," there is a much greater amount of divergence "upward."

The topic we discuss here includes only the one-way relation, the treatment of children by parents; it does not include the reciprocal relation, treatment of parents by children; that ought to be made a separate study. What is included under treatment of children by parents is best shown by the contents of the scales, published in the appendix to this volume. We counted the scenes separately for three major divisions, which we herewith list together with the number of motion-picture scenes found on each in the 142 feature films rated. The scenes by attractive characters are indicated first in the parentheses after the titles and those by unattractive characters second.

1. Discipline of children (71 +26).
2. Companionship with, and tolerance of the point of view of, children (322 +25).
3. Self-sacrifice of parents for children (54 +24).

In Table XXVII we shall show the percentage of parent-child scenes below the approval index, as defined in Chapter VI, for our several groups and for the groups combined,

a separate showing being made for scenes by attractive
characters and those by unattractive ones and for the two

Table XXVII

Percentage of Parent-Child Scenes in 142 Feature Films Lying
below the Approval Index for the Several Social Groups and
for the Groups Combined

Groups	Total			Discipline			Companion-ship			Sacrifice		
	Attractive	Unattractive	Both	Attractive	Unattractive	Both	Attractive	Unattractive	Both	Attractive	Unattractive	Both
New York élite	21	77	29	73	92	78	7	52	10	33	87	49
Penn. State faculty	21	77	29	75	92	79	7	52	10	33	87	49
College seniors	21	77	29	72	92	77	7	52	10	33	87	49
Preachers, U. S.	20	71	27	66	85	71	7	44	10	33	83	48
Graduate students	20	71	27	62	85	68	7	44	9	33	63	48
Young Brethren	20	71	27	66	85	71	7	44	10	33	83	47
Adult Brethren	16	69	24	66	85	71	7	44	10	33	83	48
Social leaders	20	71	27	66	85	71	7	44	10	33	83	48
Business men	19	71	26	61	85	67	7	44	10	33	83	48
Factory workers	19	71	26	61	85	67	7	44	10	33	83	48
Lancaster preachers	18	71	25	58	85	65	6	44	9	33	83	48
Hampton Negroes	18	69	25	56	81	63	6	44	9	33	83	48
Adult miners	12	67	20	28	73	40	5	44	8	33	83	48
Young miners	12	65	19	25	69	37	5	44	8	33	83	48
Groups combined	17	69	25	56	81	63	6	44	9	33	83	44

combined.   The total for all phases is shown and also the
distribution of these to the three sub-phases.

The most remarkable thing about the showing in
Table XXVII is the great difference between attractive and

unattractive characters in respect to the proportion of "bad" scenes. In the column of totals the proportion is four times as great for unattractive as for attractive characters. This same phenomenon holds for all of the sub-scales, though in one of them the proportion for unattractive characters is only one and a half times as high while in another it is more than seven times as high. From the standpoint of social training this is a significant condition; it tends to make "good" patterns attractive and "bad" ones unattractive both by reason of the fact that attractive people refrain from "bad" practices and that unattractive ones do them and thus make them seem disgusting. The fact that 17 per cent of the scenes by attractive characters lie below the approval index must be interpreted in the light of the fact that approximately 37 per cent of the members of a group not only approve but admire scenes lying as "low" as the group's approval index. Another notable thing about the table is the evidence of close agreement among the social groups as manifested by the small ranges. Attention should be given to the fact that a very large percentage of the scenes having to do with techniques of discipline fall below the approval index while an extremely small percentage of the scenes by attractive characters having to do with fellowship (companionship) fall low. Self-sacrifice comes between these two extremes.

We shall next show the percentage of pictures having one or more parent-child scenes lying below the approval index for the several groups. Separate showings will be made for the feature films and for the comics. We shall show also the percentage of pictures having scenes by attractive characters below the approval indices, as well as the percentage by both types combined. We shall give findings only for parent-child relations as a whole; the distributions to the sub-phases are balanced in the same proportion as indicated in Table XXVII.

Table XXVIII

Percentage of Feature Films and of Comics Having Parent-Child Scenes Lying below the Approval Index for the Several Groups and for the Combined Group

Groups	Feature Films				Comics			
	All Characters		With Att. Ch.		All Characters		With Att. Ch.	
	No.	Per Cent	No.	Per Cent	No.	Per Cent	No.	Per Cent
New York élite	58	41	41	29	7	17	5	12
Penn. State faculty	58	41	41	29	7	17	5	12
College seniors	56	39	39	27	7	17	5	12
Preachers, U. S.	54	38	37	26	6	14	4	10
Graduate students	54	38	37	26	6	14	4	10
Young Brethren	54	38	37	26	6	14	4	10
Social leaders	54	38	37	26	6	14	4	10
Business men	52	37	35	25	6	14	4	10
Factory workers	52	37	35	25	6	14	4	10
Lancaster preachers	52	37	35	25	6	14	4	10
Hampton Negroes	50	35	33	23	6	14	4	10
Adult miners	41	29	25	18	3	7	1	2
Young miners	40	28	24	17	3	7	1	2
Combined group	50	35	33	23	6	14	4	10

The table shows that about a third of the feature films contained parent-child scenes below the approval index of the combined group, and about a fourth contained such scenes by attractive characters. The range of percentages from the most conservative to the most liberal group was rather small. A much lower percentage of the comics have parent-child scenes below the approval indices than the feature films; but that is because the comics as a whole have a much smaller number of such scenes, not because the scenes are prevailingly better. The 42 comics contained an aggregate of only 29 parent-child scenes, an average of .7 each, while the 142 feature films contained an aggregate of 523, an average of 3.7. Fifty-seven per cent of the scenes enacted by the unattractive characters in the comics lay below the approval index of the combined group, 18 per cent of those by attractive characters, 28 per cent for both types. That places such parent-child scenes as did occur in the comics a little lower in quality than those in the feature pictures.

Our next table will show the proportion of scenes in the feature pictures that lay above the three quarter-points for admirations and below the three quarter-points for disapprovals. The former are shown on the left and the latter on the right, the percentages for attractive, for unattractive, and for both types of characters being shown separately at each of the quarter-points.

It will be observed, from Table XXIX, that 70 per cent of all the parent-child scenes were such as to challenge the admiration of half the combined group, while this percentage rose to 78 for the scenes enacted by attractive characters. Eighty-five per cent of all the scenes enacted by attractive characters were of the level to draw admiration from a fourth of the combined group, while 41 per cent of such scenes moved to admiration three fourths of the group. On the other hand a much smaller percentage of scenes by attractive characters were of the kind to arouse active disapproval. Only 12 per cent of such scenes were such as to arouse disapproval from half the combined group, 21 per cent from the most exacting quarter, and 7 per cent from three quarters. But again there is a vast difference between the scenes by attractive characters and those by unattractive characters. Only a small percentage of the latter were of the "good" type while the vast majority were "bad."

TABLE XXIX

PERCENTAGES OF PARENT-CHILD SCENES IN FEATURE FILMS CALLING FORTH ACTIVE ADMIRATIONS AND ACTIVE DISAPPROVALS OF DESIGNATED PROPORTIONS OF OUR SEVERAL GROUPS AND OF THE COMBINED GROUP

Groups	Admirations									Disapprovals								
	75%			50%			25%			25%			50%			75%		
	Attractive	Unattractive	Both	Attractive	Unattractive	Both	Attractive	Unattractive	Both	Attractive	Unattractive	Both	Attractive	Unattractive	Both	Attractive	Unattractive	Both
Adult Brethren	42	9	63	65	19	59	82	29	74	22	77	30	15	67	22	11	64	18
College seniors	28	7	25	67	19	60	80	29	73	23	77	31	15	67	22	8	63	16
Graduate students	41	9	36	77	23	69	83	31	75	20	77	28	13	67	21	9	64	17
Young Brethren	36	7	32	77	24	70	81	32	77	22	77	30	12	65	20	8	63	16
Social leaders	49	13	44	77	23	70	83	29	75	20	76	28	12	65	19	7	60	15
Factory workers	38	8	34	78	24	71	85	33	78	20	77	28	13	67	20	7	60	15
Preachers, U. S.	68	19	69	79	23	71	83	29	75	20	76	28	15	67	22	9	64	17
Business men	39	8	35	79	23	71	84	31	76	21	77	29	14	67	22	11	64	18
Lancaster preachers	46	12	41	79	24	71	85	33	78	20	71	27	12	65	20	7	61	15
Hampton Negroes	48	13	43	79	23	71	85	38	78	22	77	30	13	67	21	10	64	17
Young miners	65	19	59	80	31	73	92	37	84	15	68	22	9	64	17	4	56	11
Adult miners	65	19	59	83	33	76	89	36	72	15	68	22	11	64	18	5	56	12
Combined groups	41	9	36	78	32	70	85	33	78	21	77	29	12	65	19	7	60	15

From either point of view that is a fortunate condition, for it associates bad conduct with disgusting characters and thus contributes toward making it taboo, while it does not to any great degree contribute toward the negative conditioning of good acts by connecting them with unattractive personalities.

In the comics no scenes by unattractive characters were sufficiently high to be admired by three fourths of the combined group, but three of the seven scenes reached this level for both half and three quarters. However, 14 per cent of the scenes by attractive characters in the comics were in the admiration list for three fourths of the combined group, 73 per cent for half the group, and 96 per cent for the most liberal quarter. In respect to disapprovals the figures for unattractive characters were, for the successive quarters, 57 per cent, 57 per cent, and 14 per cent, while those for attractive characters were respectively 23 per cent, 5 per cent, and 5 per cent. In general, then, the comics conform reasonably well to the interpretation already made for the feature pictures in respect to the treatment of children by parents.

Next we show the proportion of feature films having one or more parent-child scenes lying above the several quarter-points of admirations for our groups and, parallel to that, the proportion having one or more parent-child scenes lying below the quarter-points for disapprovals, showing first for each quarter-point the proportion for all feature pictures and then the proportion containing scenes by attractive characters.

The table shows that approximately two thirds of the feature films contained parent-child scenes of such character as to challenge the admiration of 50 per cent of the combined groups, and more than half of them contained such

TABLE XXX

PERCENTAGE OF FEATURE FILMS HAVING ONE OR MORE PARENT-CHILD
SCENES LYING ABOVE THE THREE QUARTER-POINTS OF ADMIRATIONS
AND BELOW THE THREE QUARTER-POINTS OF DISAPPROVALS FOR
THE SEVERAL GROUPS

Groups	Admirations						Disapprovals					
	75%		50%		25%		25%		50%		75%	
	All	Attrac-tive	All	Attrac-tive	All	Attrac-tive	All	Attrac-tive	All	Attrac-tive	All	Attrac-tive
Adult Brethren	53	49	60	57	65	60	40	33	34	26	27	15
College seniors	42	39	62	59	64	60	41	34	34	26	25	13
Graduate students	50	46	63	60	66	60	39	31	32	24	26	15
Young Brethren	46	44	64	60	67	61	39	31	32	24	26	15
Social leaders	55	51	64	60	66	61	39	30	28	21	23	12
Factory workers	48	46	64	60	67	61	39	32	30	23	24	13
Preachers, U. S.	62	59	64	60	66	61	39	30	34	26	26	15
Business men	48	45	64	60	66	61	39	32	32	25	27	16
Lancaster preachers	53	50	64	60	67	61	38	30	30	22	23	12
Hampton Negroes	54	51	64	60	66	61	40	33	31	23	26	15
Young miners	60	57	64	60	68	63	34	27	25	18	19	7
Adult miners	60	57	66	61	68	61	34	27	28	21	22	10
Combined groups	52	49	64	60	66	60	39	32	29	22	24	13

scenes appealing thus to three fourths of this population. On the other hand, about half as many of them contained scenes disapproved by the corresponding proportions of the group. Evidently motion pictures set patterns of conduct in respect to treatment of children by parents that we should wish to have imitated, much more frequently than they set those of the opposite type. This is especially true of scenes having to do with companionship between parents and children and tolerance of the point of view of children.

How do motion pictures compare with practice in our groups in respect to the treatment of children by parents? This is answered in Table XXXI, practice having been ascertained by the techniques described in the chapter on aggressiveness. According to our returns practice follows approvals fairly closely for our groups, though the former tends to drop just a little below where corresponding proportions of the group begin disapproving the acts. But the members of groups are more diverse in respect to practice than they are in respect to disapprovals; that is, the highest quarter of practice stands somewhat above the highest quarter of disapprovals, while the lowest quarter of practice falls considerably below the lowest quarter of disapprovals. We do not show this directly in the accompanying table but it may be inferred from the percentage of practice lying below the several quarter-points. If restraints from practice precisely paralleled disapprovals, the percentages of practice below the three quarter-points for each of the groups would be, respectively, 75, 50, and 25. If conduct for a given proportion of a group extends further down than the approvals of a corresponding proportion of the group, the percentages for practice will be greater than the ones indicated in the preceding sentence. The table's direct showing relates to the parallelism between motion pictures and reported practice. It shows the percentage of feature pictures having scenes lying below the various quarter-points of disapproval and, parallel to that, the percentage of members of the group practicing acts below the corresponding levels of badness.

From the table it will be seen that the movies practice restraints from "bad" parent-child scenes to a much larger degree than the people of our several social groups practice restraints from corresponding acts. At all three quarter-points the percentage of people reported as practicing acts below the level in question is more than twice as great as the percentage of pictures having scenes of corresponding

TABLE XXXI

COMPARISON OF THE PRACTICE OF CERTAIN SOCIAL GROUPS IN PARENT-
CHILD RELATIONS WITH CONDUCT IN FEATURE FILMS

Groups	Below 25% Line			Below 50% Line			Below 75% Line		
	Disap.		Prac-tice	Disap.		Prac-tice	Disap.		Prac-tice
	Attrac-tive	Both		Attrac-tive	Both		Attrac-tive	Both	
Adult Brethren	33	40	62	26	34	45	15	27	31
Hampton Negroes	33	40	66	23	31	47	15	26	37
Graduate students	31	39	63	24	32	48	15	26	35
Factory workers	32	39	70	23	30	53	13	24	36
College seniors	34	41	69	26	34	54	13	25	33
Business men	32	39	70	25	32	55	16	27	38
Young Brethren	33	40	74	22	30	56	13	25	44
Adult miners	27	34	73	21	28	62	10	22	42
Young miners	27	34	72	18	25	62	7	19	32

"badness" by attractive characters and nearly twice as great as the percentage of pictures having such scenes by any kind of character. This means that, in respect to the treatment of children by parents, the movies are distinctly "better" than life (in the sense of deviating toward the plus end of our scales more largely than toward the minus end), and consequently set patterns that pull "upward" much more largely than patterns that pull "downward" as compared with the situation to which people are accustomed in daily life.

Throughout this chapter we have found that motion pictures diverge from the mores "upward" more than "downward," in the matter of treatment of children by parents; they set patterns that challenge admiration more often than patterns that elicit condemnation; and they stand prevailingly "above" current practice. Furthermore, the "good" things are done principally by attractive characters and the "bad" things by unattractive ones. Of course here, as in each of the other three phases of morality covered by our study, there still remain at least three important questions. The first is: In which direction are deviations toward *better*, when they are toward the plus end of our scales or toward the minus end? Although in the matter of treatment of children by parents there would be considerable agreement on this point, there are many people in the aggregate who would hold that a sound ethics demands less sacrifice by parents for children, and more drastic methods of punishment, rather than the opposite. The second question is: Do 78 per cent of "good" scenes compensate for 12 per cent of "bad" ones? How large must the proportion be before the situation is a satisfactory one? Similarly, how far above "practice" must "art" stand before it is fulfilling its ideals as art and its functions in social control? A third question is: What is the effect of the number of scenes of a given type upon their potency? We do not know the relative dynamic effect of an example that stays within convention, of one that lies in the direction of aspiration, and of one that swings in the direction of the forbidden. Nor do we know the effect of frequency of occurrence of a type of scene. Possibly the dynamic effect increases with constant acceleration; possibly the law of diminishing returns operates, so that each successive scene decreases in potency; or possibly the curve of effect declines beyond a certain point because of surfeit. Our study stops with pointing out the extent of balance or of unbalance among the numbers of scenes; it leaves open for speculation, and for scientific study, the question as to what constitutes a satisfactory balance.

CHAPTER X

THE MOTIVES TO WHICH APPEAL IS MADE IN ADVERTISING MOTION PICTURES

THE arguments a business man employs in attempting to sell his goods furnish clear evidence of his conceptions of the intelligence and the desires of his customers. Perhaps, too, these arguments show what sort of goods he would deliver if economic and statute laws permitted him to do so. If the expressions employed by exhibitors, the posters displayed by them, and the glimpses of coming pictures flashed on the screen as advertisements, do thus express the business manager's conception of the level of the public's intelligence and of its tastes, that conception is certainly not very flattering to the genus that calls itself *homo sapiens*.

In order to ascertain on a factual basis to what motives, and on what intellectual level, exhibitors appeal to the public we studied a large number of advertisements of movies in newspapers and on billboards.[1] The following sources were used, some of them for advertisements and some for criticisms.

New York Times (Daily and Sunday), November 1930–September 1931

Philadelphia Public Ledger (Daily and Sunday), November 1930–September 1931

Pittsburgh Press (Daily), November 1930–May 1931

[1] This study was made by Sylvester P. Koelle, Supervising Principal of the Granville Township Schools, Claysburg, Pa. Besides the material shown in this chapter it included a study of the features commended or condemned in critical reviews. The report of the investigation is filed as a master's thesis in the Library of Pennsylvania State College. In the thesis the entire tables are given from which we take in this chapter only the top frequencies.

Altoona Mirror (Daily), November 1930–September 1931
Altoona Tribune (Daily), November 1930–September 1931
The Film Daily, September 1920–November 1930
Billboard, November 1930
Variety, November 1930
Motion Picture News, September 1920–December 1929
Exhibitor's Herald World, October 1929–March 1930
Motion Picture Herald, April, May, June 1931
Film Daily Yearbook, 1927–1928–1929
Harrison's Reports, August 1929–December 1930
Director's Annual and Production Guide for 1930
Fox's *Standard of Business in the Realm of Entertainment*
Metro-Goldwyn's *Talk of the Industry* for 1925–1926
The Motion Picture Monthly, year 1931
Liberty, January 1931–September 1931
Billboards from January to May 1931

We shall first show what sort of adjectives are used in the advertisements of motion pictures to convince the critical public that here is a picture it should not miss. Only those occurring ten times or more are given here. The complete list constitutes a dictionary of propagandist terms. The total number of different adjectives found in the study was 1540. These ranged in frequency from 1 to 410.

TABLE XXXII

ADJECTIVES FOUND IN MOTION–PICTURE ADVERTISEMENTS

Adjective	Frequency	Adjective	Frequency
great	410	talking	114
big	212	best	106
sensational	166	famous	102
box-office	160	tremendous	99
dramatic	149	fine	96
new	144	thrilling	93
beautiful	121	funny	90

Table XXXII—*Continued*

Adjectives Found in Motion-Picture Advertisements—*Continued*

Adjective	Frequency	Adjective	Frequency
comedy	87	different	35
outstanding	85	lovely	35
amazing	85	stirring	33
brilliant	82	unusual	33
musical	66	charming	32
glorious	65	exciting	31
modern	63	strange	31
human	62	high	31
marvelous	60	smash	31
real	59	wild	30
daring	58	glamorous	30
powerful	58	important	29
mighty	58	original	29
good	58	terrific	29
gorgeous	57	lavish	28
romantic	56	fast	28
first	55	supreme	27
gay	54	strong	27
smart	50	mad	27
smashing	50	dancing	27
perfect	49	delightful	26
startling	49	handsome	26
magnificent	46	merry	26
grand	43	vivid	25
excellent	42	breath-taking	25
fascinating	41	dazzling	24
spectacular	41	exploitation	24
splendid	41	happy	24
colorful	40	stupendous	23
singing	40	remarkable	23
hilarious	39	clever	23
sure-fire	37	hair-raising	22
sparkling	36	mystery	22
gripping	36	superb	21
		sophisticated	21
		laugh	21
		amusing	20

TABLE XXXII—*Continued*

ADJECTIVES FOUND IN MOTION–PICTURE ADVERTISEMENTS—*Continued*

Adjective	Frequency	Adjective	Frequency
flaming	20	laughing	13
leading	20	lovable	13
better	19	nation-wide	13
immortal	19	thrill	13
rich	19	convincing	12
alluring	18	emotional	12
best-selling	18	epic	12
capacity	18	gala	12
entertaining	18	inimitable	12
tuneful	18	pretty	12
exquisite	17	roaring	12
interesting	17	successful	12
outdoor	17	surprise	12
record-breaking	17	vibrant	12
snappy	17	vital	12
young	17	whirlwind	12
intimate	16	dark	11
absorbing	15	delicious	11
astounding	15	effective	11
dynamic	15	fiery	11
gigantic	15	fighting	11
irresistible	15	intelligent	11
realistic	15	passionate	11
refreshing	15	red-blooded	11
super	15	special	11
swell	15	unforgettable	11
tense	15	absolute	10
appealing	14	big-time	10
dashing	14	bright	10
exceptional	14	complete	10
glittering	14	enthusiastic	10
golden	14	fabulous	10
love	14	joyous	10
natural	14	latest	10
riotous	14	rare	10
rollicking	14	reckless	10
tender	14	side-splitting	10
distinguished	13	spicy	10
exotic	13	superior	10
heart	13	sweeping	10
		wonder	10

The list of adjectives suggests that motion-picture exhibitors have harmonized their efforts with those of certain other advertisers in conducting a program of ballyhoo. The adjectives do not indicate any very profound appeal to the intellect. The typical ones are such as: "great," "sensational," "marvelous," "startling," "glamorous," "breathtaking." More moderate terms, like "funny," "natural," "tender," have a small place. But we do not find a single adjective suggesting that the picture may be informative, or ethically inspiring, or sobering.

In order to show in more general terms the types of motives appealed to, we classified the adjectives into a comparatively small number of categories. Three judges were asked to classify the 1540 words into the indicated groups, then the number belonging in each category was taken as an average from the three classifications. Table XXXIII shows the distribution of those that could be thus classified, arranged according to frequency.

TABLE XXXIII

TYPES OF ADJECTIVES USED IN MOTION-PICTURE ADVERTISEMENTS,
WITH FREQUENCIES OF EACH TYPE

| | Average |
Categories	Classification
Adjectives suggesting energy and action	145
Adjectives appealing to baser emotions	110
Adjectives denoting high praise	89
Adjectives denoting amusement or fun	81
Adjectives denoting condemnation or disapproval	78
Adjectives denoting power or great strength	74
Adjectives denoting undifferentiated praise	61
Adjectives exciting fear or terror	58
Adjectives referring to large scope	57
Adjectives referring to music or sound	51
Adjectives challenging thrills	40
Adjectives suggesting admiration	37
Adjectives denoting lasting quality or permanency	34
Adjectives suggesting love-stirring emotions	34

Table XXXIII—*Continued*

Types of Adjectives Used in Motion–Picture Advertisements,
with Frequencies of Each Type—*Continued*

	Average
Categories	*Classification*
Adjectives challenging attention	31
Adjectives denoting great size	31
Adjectives challenging pathos	31
Adjectives referring to color	27
Adjectives referring to beauty	25
Adjectives exciting wonder	25
Adjectives denoting mild praise	24
Adjectives designating success or fame	24
Adjectives appealing to finer or ennobling emotions	23
Adjectives denoting weakness	23
Adjectives denoting the extraordinary	22
Adjectives referring to progressiveness	22
Adjectives denoting the ordinary	21
Adjectives denoting courage	19
Adjectives denoting diminutiveness	19
Adjectives denoting high talent	16
Adjectives challenging friendliness	13
Adjectives denoting last word or finality	12
Adjectives denoting realism	11

Our final showing from this study relates to the type of
pictures employed in advertising motion pictures, in newspapers and on billboards. The table may speak for itself.

Table XXXIV

Pictures in Advertising of Motion Pictures

Picture	*Frequency*
Pictures showing man and woman embracing	275
Pictures depicting facial expressions of joy, fear, sorrow, anguish, remorse, doubt, hate, deep thought, anger, etc.	273
Pictures of pretty girl	246
Pictures too multiple in character to classify	237
Pictures depicting nudity	164
Pictures showing handsome man	163
Pictures showing dancing	71
Pictures of man and woman conversing	64
Pictures depicting something weird or eerie	61
Pictures showing children	60

Table XXXIV—*Continued*

Pictures in Advertising of Motion Pictures—*Continued*

Picture	Frequency
Pictures showing crowds	49
Pictures of men fighting	42
Pictures of western life	36
Pictures of war	26
Pictures of some sport	25
Pictures showing man and woman fighting	25
Pictures of man protecting woman	25
Pictures showing man and woman in compromising positions	23
Pictures of airplanes	20
Pictures showing jungle scenes	16
Pictures showing impossible feats	14
Pictures depicting family scenes	13
Pictures of ships	12
Pictures of animals	12
Pictures of jail scenes	11
Pictures depicting underworld	10
Pictures of oriental scenes	9
Pictures depicting mother and son embracing	7
Pictures of men conversing	7
Pictures of court-room scenes	6
Pictures of trains	6
Pictures of historic scenes	6
Pictures of beach scenes	4
Pictures of night-club scenes	4
Pictures of radio	3
Pictures showing religious scenes	3
Pictures showing women conversing	3
Pictures of hospital scenes	2
Pictures of business conferences	2
Pictures showing luxurious settings	2
Pictures of marriage scenes	2
Pictures of rustic scenes	2
Pictures showing women embracing	2
Pictures showing women fighting	2
Pictures of persons weeping or mourning	1
Pictures of stock exchange	1
Pictures showing woman protecting man	1
Pictures showing woman and man singing to each other	1

The type of pictures with greatest frequency in the table indicates the same general level of appeal as do the adjectives in the advertisements. The appeal is grandiose, erotic, and suggestive of passion or of sin. Producers and exhibitors probably have their own reasons for intimating through their advertisements that motion pictures are very naughty, but if the revelations of our next chapter showing negative correlations between moral offense and the appeal of pictures are significant, it is difficult to believe that business managers are correct in ascribing to the public the low motives that the advertising suggests.

CHAPTER XI

RELATION OF THE MORALITY TO THE SUCCESS OF A MOTION PICTURE

In this chapter we shall set forth, and give some evidence in defense of, certain hypotheses having to do with the question whether "naughtiness" contributes toward the success of a motion picture. This is a most important practical problem. For, unless the state stands ready to subsidize the industry for contributions to educational service, we can scarcely expect motion-picture producers to refrain from introducing *risqué* elements into their shows if doing so increases their profits or in any other way contributes more to the success of the pictures than it detracts from success. If, on the contrary, both the producers and society lose by reason of offense against morality, a knowledge of this fact is of supreme importance. We shall ask first how offense against the mores is related to the success of a motion picture as a work of art. Thereafter we shall inquire how such offense is related to commercial success through increasing or decreasing the popular appeal of the picture and thus affecting box-office receipts. On the latter of these questions we have, fortunately, some statistical evidence resulting from our study; on the former we have hypotheses well defended by certain factors in the theory of art and on which hypotheses we invite scientific test.

I

There are at least three fundamental principles about the nature of art which have pertinency to the problem of the relation of art to conflict with the mores:

1. *Art must call forth responses that are free from jarring conflict*, unless indeed this conflict constitutes a part of the challenge of the work. If a symbolic representation provides a setting in which an observer may let himself go and experience a full satisfaction of his suppressed yearnings, this representation performs a function of art so long as self-consciousness is not aroused by the process or by its technique. But just so soon as the observer begins to have pricks of conscience about the matter, just so soon as he begins to question or resist or to feel a little abashed or even to have his attention at all attracted by the technique of what is happening, so soon that element of conflict and of strain is introduced that is fatal to art. A statue with the sex organs exposed may, on account of its complete naturalness, make better art for him who does not notice this detail except as a part of an æsthetically complete whole; but this feature may ruin the statue as art for the person whose attention is morbidly attracted thereby. Shakespeare's poem, *Venus and Adonis*, may be high art for the reader whose only reaction is thrill from the vividness of the portrayals; but it drops from the level of art to the level of forbidden adventure for anyone who is morbidly conscious of the frankly erotic element in its narrative. And the same thing is doubtless true of a motion picture that, as a whole or in some detail, conflicts negatively with the mores. There will be many members in the audience who will become conscious of the "naughtiness," whose attention will be withdrawn from the synthetic unity of the drama as a whole and centered upon this detail; who will be subject to a certain restlessness and questioning and embarrassment because of the intrusion of the conflicting element; and for these persons the resultant strain will be fatal to the value of the drama as a work of art. For all those other persons whose

self-consciousness and resistance are not aroused the play may still remain high art—may even be stronger art because it permits release in directions so seldom experienced. But to the extent to which there is conflict with the mores of those present, to that extent the artistic appeal will be limited to only a part of the audience. On the contrary (our hypothesis runs), when the presentation reënforces the mores, and is otherwise equally stirring, it brings that high joy which comes with success in attaining those ends to which at heart we all dynamically and idealistically aspire. That is to say, art alienates nobody by leading him in vicarious success through a world that gives expression to his "higher" ideals and aspirations, for all can thrill to these with no morbid self-consciousness; but it may alienate some when it exploits experiences that are likely to arouse in them a sense of impropriety.

2. *Art must call forth an active response, and high art is differentiated from low largely by differences in the complexity, and the consequent challenge, of this response.*[1] The dramatic art that attempts in heterogeneous audiences to call forth responses in opposition to the mores is likely to stop with no very profound challenge. For the most part moral values have to do with restraints. Organized society requires inhibitions on practices to which individual impulses prompt but which have been found to be antagonistic to group welfare. The most pronounced valuations are placed upon those customs that are felt by the group to be in the most precarious danger of losing in the battle with individual

[1] For an effective development of the idea that art must bring a complex multiplicity into unity see Santayana, George, *The Sense of Beauty*, Charles Scribner's Sons, 1896, pp. 95–110. For some good experimental evidence bearing upon it see the article by A. R. Gilliland and H. T. Moore, "The Immediate and Long Time Effects of Classical and Popular Phonograph Selections," in the *Journal of Applied Psychology*, VIII, 309–323. For further experimental evidence on both the points see Valentine, C. W., *The Experimental Psychology of Beauty*, Dodge Publishing Company, New York, especially Chaps. IV–V.

impulse. Mild resentment may, it is true, be felt in the presence of violation of any of the customs, but fierce resentment is directed chiefly or wholly to transgressions in dangerous directions. When, therefore, release is provided through art for vicarious living in forbidden ways it is most likely to have to do with certain elemental human impulses of rather narrow scope. Perhaps the impulse may be that of revenge or cruelty or vagrancy. Most likely, however, it will be some elemental form of the sex impulse. In any case, the response is likely to involve a small fraction of one's personality, a very narrow range of his interests and aspirations. He may enjoy giving vent to these limited impulses for a little while, but they constitute a toy of which he soon tires. They are like the simple mechanism of rag-time music. The art that caters to them cannot call itself high art. But our aspirations that reach upward toward service, toward idealism, toward honor, and toward the uplift of mankind are complex aspirations the realization of which challenges the organization of thought and of effort through realms of vast scope. The art that calls forth, leads forward, and satisfies these longings is in a position to become high art.

This does not, of course, mean that motion-picture plots should be doctored artificially to translate all scenes into morally impeccable ones. To do such artificial doctoring would ruin the artistic value of the production since it would draw attention to the awkwardness of its technique. If a play with an "immoral" theme is to be put on, the canons of art require that the theme be worked out through all the scenes demanded by its logic. It does mean, however, according to our hypothesis, that "immoral" themes have less potentialities as materials for effective art than those which accord with the idealistic aspirations of mankind.

And it does mean that deliberately to select "immoral" themes, or to go out of the way to introduce into the development of a play some "naughty" elements, is deliberately to sacrifice art of wide appeal. To fulfill the conditions of wide appeal is to make art democratic.

3. *Great art lays bare the vital truths of nature in fresh and original ways which give vivid articulation to the insight of the creative artist without regard to defiance of any sort of convention.* We distinguish here between "good" art and "great" art after the manner in which Nietzsche distinguished between a good man and a noble one. "The noble one," he says, speaking through the mouth of Zarathustra, "wisheth to create something new and a new virtue. The good one willeth that old things should be preserved." And he goes on to add about this noble one: "Thou compellest many to relearn about thee; that is sternly set down unto thine account by them." Perhaps society needs some great cinematic art that will boldly challenge the conventional mores— art so powerful in the handling of its theme, so fundamentally right in its message, and so far-reaching in its implications that it will compel the attention and the consent and the ecstatic Yea of at least some members of the crowd, setting them to profound reflection and to the reformulation of their philosophy of life. But such art would not be democratic; it would make its appeal to a few heroic spirits while alienating the vast herd. And, of course, it would have no interest in being unconventional for the sake of unconventionality, much less in being "nasty"; it would well proclaim fearlessly the truth about life—whether relating to economic adjustments, to marital relations, or what not. It can perform its function as such art only when it is addressed to those who are able to receive it. It is, therefore, our further hypothesis that motion pictures can render

satisfying social service as art only when they come to be created for differentiated audiences: art that appeals to child nature for children, æsthetically and morally "safe" art for the masses, and art that boldly analyzes pressing though delicate social problems for thinkers and reformers. If such differentiation is made, the advertising should indicate clearly and truthfully to which class each picture belongs, whereas now one can get almost no dependable concept of the nature of a picture from the statements advertising it.

All of the three hypotheses set forth in this section—that conflict with the mores produces a morbid self-consciousness on the part of many members of a heterogeneous audience and thus loses its appeal as democratic art, that violation of standards merely for the sake of the thrill which comes from unconventionality involves appeal to impulses of such narrow scope as to afford only feeble and transient æsthetic satisfactions, and that great cinematic art can flourish only when motion pictures are produced for differentiated audiences—could all be subjected to scientific test. Their validation would greatly clarify the social function of the motion picture as dramatic art.

II

We raise next the question: Does conflict with the mores give personal appeal to a picture? Do people like better to attend motion pictures that are "naughty"? It has often been alleged that they do and on this principle producers are believed to put into their pictures as much of the *risqué* as can pass censorship.

In order to get some evidence on the relation of the appeal of motion pictures to conflict with the mores, we had several groups of persons whom we could reach fill out the following type of report on sixty-one feature films they had attended and we had rated, the reports being filled out soon after attending each show.

TITLE OF MOTION PICTURE.................................

Please give us your evaluation of the motion picture named above. We want this to use in an extensive study of the Social Value of Motion Pictures in which a number of universities throughout the country are participating.

Please mark an x alongside the number before the proper one of the following alternatives to indicate how good you thought the picture. By "good" we mean a picture you enjoyed—the kind of picture like which you hope there will be many more. By "poor" we mean a picture that disgusted you—the kind of picture like which you wish there might be few, if any, more.

6. Very excellent—among the best 1 per cent of pictures you have ever seen.

5. Excellent—among the best 7 per cent, but not in the "very excellent" class above.

4. Good—among the best third of the pictures you have seen, but not in either of the classes above.

3. Average.

2. Rather poor—in the lowest third of the pictures you have seen, but not in either of the two classes below.

1. Poor—among the lowest 7 per cent but not in the "extremely poor" class below.

0. Extremely poor—among the worst 1 per cent of pictures you have ever seen.

Underscore for your sex: MALE   FEMALE

What is your age? —————   Your occupation? —————————

It was our hope to distribute these to people as they left the theater, apportioning them to type-groups according to a systematic plan. However, the owners of the house where we did our rating would not permit this. We, therefore, collected them through college and high school classes, offering pay to those who secured them for us. This was not a very systematic way of collecting the reports, but it was all we could do under the circumstances. The reports per picture per group varied from ten or twelve up to nearly a hundred. Returns were received from the following groups: college boys, juniors and seniors; college girls, juniors and seniors; high school students; and parents of high school students. An index of appeal for each picture for each group was then obtained by averaging the moments indicated by the numbers prefacing the seven stages in the scale above. These values were correlated with certain of our measures of conflict with the mores. We also made index numbers from the committee ratings reported in each issue of *The Educational Screen* by preparing as a guide for this purpose numerical equivalents from 0 to 6 for the differential verbal expressions of commendation or condemnation and assigning each of our pictures a score in terms of these numerical equivalents. These ratings also were correlated with our measures of conflict with the mores. We used *The Educational Screen* ratings only for intelligent adults. Some of these correlations are given in Table XXXV.[2]

During this part of our study three different committees were rating pictures for us, one rating forty and the other two combined twenty-eight. We could not safely throw all of these ratings into the same correlation problem because the three committees might be sufficiently unlike in ratings to wreck our correlation. We, therefore, depend chiefly upon the coefficients computed from the committee that rated the largest number (called "Committee 1" in the table), but show results (under "Com. 2") for the other two committees combined, for whatever little confirmatory value they may have. This second set of ratings is less dependable than the first both because the number of pictures rated is

---

[2] Mr. F. L. Cropp, instructor in the high school at State College, Pa., participated in this part of the study as a master's thesis.

less and because the raters consist of two sets combined. Our number of cases is in each case too small to give very reliable coefficients, but they will serve the purpose of illustrating a technique and will give considerable hint of the trend.

The layman may be disposed to criticize the showings in Table XXXV on the ground that the coefficients of correlation are not perfectly consistent. But anyone acquainted with statistics knows that coefficients of correlation computed from a relatively small number of cases are normally rather erratic, especially when low. Indeed a set of r's that were perfectly consistent when computed from a small number of cases would be subject to the charge of doctoring. Coefficients of correlation taken from a succession of samples of a population theoretically make a normal distribution around the "true" r having a standard deviation equal to $\dfrac{1-r^2}{\sqrt{n}}.$ The stability of a coefficient of correlation thus depends upon its size and upon the number of cases, and is rather flighty when n is as low as twenty or thirty. In our case we must depend upon prevailing tendencies among the correlations, rather than upon small probable errors.

On the whole our table shows some unmistakable trends. The correlation between the appeal of pictures and the delicate type of kissing rated plus in our scales is consistently positive, with only one small exception. Conversely the r's with the offensive type of kissing, which our scales rate minus, is consistently negative. It is thus clear that, as far as these samples show, motion-picture producers are wrong if they suppose that they must have in their pictures as much kissing as the law allows; the very opposite is true. Aggressiveness tells the same story, only here the correlations are prevailingly negative for plus as well as for minus

TABLE XXXV

COEFFICIENTS OF CORRELATION BETWEEN CERTAIN MEASURES OF APPEAL OF MOTION PICTURES AND CERTAIN MEASURES OF CONFLICT WITH THE MORES

Scale	College Boys		College Girls		High School		Parents		Screen Com.	
	Com. 1	Com. 2	Com. 1	Com. 2	Com. 1	Com. 2	Com. 1	Com. 2	Set 1	Set 2
Kissing										
Aggregate plus	.336	.339	.270	.346	−.101	.195	.305	.245	.399	.124
Aggregate minus	−.395	−.067	−.142	.049	−.113	.140	−.248	−.029	−.286	−.229
Aggressiveness										
Aggregate plus	−.059	−.312	−.294	−.175	−.051	−.119	−.040	.059	−.326	−.217
Aggregate minus	−.126	.226	−.204	−.024	−.213	.230	−.040	.094	−.217	−.344
Democracy										
Aggregate plus	.236	−.178	.169	.205	.220	.098	.271	.286	.205	.233
Aggregate minus	.061	.041	.415	−.030	−.222	−.072	−.137	.248	.249	.008
Parent-Child										
Aggregate plus	.076	.212	.100	.275	.082	−.257	.105	−.160	.252	.260
Aggregate minus	.117	.324	.346	.477	.404	.281	.113	.203	.256	.166

forms. But the r's are somewhat smaller than in the case of kissing.

In democracy and parent-child relations there is a less clear case. The correlations are prevailingly positive for both plus and minus scenes. (The r's in the table are plus unless preceded by a minus sign.) This has a very plausible explanation. Scenes rated negatively in parent-child relations often are brought into the plot in the form of a setting for the success of the child-hero. He has hard conditions to combat in the form of harsh or unsympathetic parents, yet comes to glory in spite of these obstacles. Thus it is the "badness" of the treatment by parents that lends challenge and zest to the drama. On the other hand tender treatment of children by parents, together with the whole atmosphere of the play that goes with this, often makes other motion pictures attractive, so that a positive correlation goes also with the plus ratings. In fact our groups all seemed to be appealed to by the presence of those dramatic situations that the presence of children in a play involves, for the correlations between *appeal* and *number of parent-child scenes* (not shown in the table) were substantially positive ones. On the contrary, the correlations with number of aggressiveness scenes were prevailingly rather high negative ones and with number of kissing scenes were prevailingly negative but low. What was said above by way of interpretation of the parent-child correlations, and the correlations with number of scenes, applies also to democracy, though in a less systematic way.

Perhaps it would be well before proceeding further to say something more about the meaning of such correlations as those shown in Table XXXV. Our coefficients of correlation between *number* of aggressiveness scenes and the appeal of the pictures to our various groups in the two samples of pictures ran as follows (not shown in the table): −.149, −.024, −.361, −.269, −.311, +.084, −.132, −.021. These average −.147. Of course the true correlations would differ somewhat from group to group and from place to place, so that we could not properly speak of the correlation between number of aggressiveness scenes and appeal of the picture as being any one particular coefficient. But for illustrative purposes let us suppose that −.14 represents the r between these two factors. That means that the appeal of the picture is appreciably affected by the number of aggressiveness scenes, that the appeal decreases as the number of such scenes increases, and that aggressiveness together with the elements correlated with it accounts for 14 per cent of the variance in appeal. The variance in appeal! What does that mean? This: Perhaps all pictures have some appeal; but between the minimum and the maximum there is considerable room for fluctuation. This is the variance. It is most convenient to measure this variance in terms of plus and minus deviations from the mean for all pictures and to divide these deviations by the standard deviation of the whole set. We then have "standard measures," which may be regarded as equal to one another just as all meter sticks are equal. We measure the variance in the other variable in the same manner. When we say that, if the correlation between number of aggressiveness scenes and appeal is −.14 the aggressiveness accounts for 14 per cent of the variance, we mean that if the amount of aggressiveness in a large number of motion pictures is increased or decreased by any number of standard units the average appeal will be decreased or increased 14 per cent as many of these units.[3]

---

[3] The statistically trained reader will at once recognize this as merely a verbal statement of the simple regression equation when put in terms of standard measures: $z_y = r z_x$.

Suppose, to use a more concrete illustration, we should find that the box-office returns as well as the "appeal" of pictures were correlated −.14 with number of aggressiveness scenes. That would mean that the box-office returns would decrease as the aggressiveness increases and that the box-office receipts would tend to move down 14 per cent as fast as the aggressiveness increased. Of course it would not be true that any one picture would stand low in appeal or in profit because it contained much aggressiveness, for there are many other factors making for its success which may offset and cover up this one factor. But the average success from enough films to balance up all these other factors would decrease as the aggressiveness increases, by r times the amount. Apart from statistical manipulation of the data onlookers are likely to be misled by exceptional individual cases; the data are too complex to permit isolation of subtle trends by inspection. But if enough cases are treated to reveal a dependable trend of connection no matter how small, the technique of correlation will discover it however much it may be overlaid with confusing elements.

When we say that aggressiveness is correlated −.14 with appeal, we must not ascribe to aggressiveness as such and alone this relation. Many other factors probably go normally along with aggressiveness: a certain kind of story, much cheap love-making technique, dependence upon erotic appeal rather than upon dramatic art for effects, etc. A more technical way of saying that these other factors tend to go along with aggressiveness is to say that they are correlated with it. It is, then, in our problem, aggressiveness and all the factors that are correlated with it that correlate −.14 with the appeal of the picture.

As far as we have measured the several factors separately which may be expected to correlate with our factor and have determined their correlation with it and with one another, we can remove this overlapping feature by resorting to the rather involved technique of partial correlation. Regression weights in terms of standard measures serve essentially the same purpose and are much easier to compute. In fact partial regression coefficients from standard measures ("weights") are the same thing as partial correlations except for an inequality between the partial standard devia-

Table XXXVI

Weights (Partial B's) of Certain Factors in Accounting for the Appeal of Motion Pictures to Various Groups

Groups	Kissing		Aggressiveness		Parent-Child		Democracy	
	+	−	+	−	+	−	+	−
College boys	.2657	−.3937	−.0494	.0609	.0409	.0483	.2273	.0596
College girls	.2079	−.0504	−.2767	−.2120	.0469	.1843	.1559	.3631
High school	−.1337	−.0518	−.1134	−.1981	−.0197	.3372	.1742	.1267
Parents	.2667	−.2486	−.0040	.0788	.0457	.1160	.2372	−.1611
Screen com.	.2956	−.2160	−.3029	−.1474	.2165	.0865	.1950	.2377

tions, which is likely to be small.[4] We have applied this partial regression technique to our problem for the ratings by our main committee and give the results above. Because kissing and aggressiveness were largely uncorrelated with parent-child and democracy measures, we did not put all four elements into the same regression equation but treated the two sets as independent of each other. The partial regression coefficients indicate the weights of the four factors (plus and minus values in aggressiveness, plus and minus values in kissing, and same for the other sets), in accounting for appeal, the plus ones indicating help and the negative ones hindrance.

[4] For an account of this technique and work-sheets for using it, see the articles by Peters and Wykes in *Journal of Educational Research*, XXIII, 383–393, and XXIV, 44–52 (May and June 1931).

The partial regression technique can be safely applied only if the number of cases from which the r's are computed is sufficiently large to yield highly reliable and valid zero-order correlations. Our number was by no means large enough, so that the figures given in the table are not to be taken too seriously. But we have been concerned here only to illustrate a technique and to show probable trends, with the hope that others interested in the problem will apply this technique on a scale sufficiently large to insure reliable findings.

Another criterion of success we employed was selection by Mordaunt Hall for *The New York Times* of the best ten films for the preceding year. We had rated eight of the twenty films selected by him for the two-year period 1930 and 1931. Comparing these eight with the whole 142 feature films studied by us we found the following: The eight "best" had an average of 3.37 kissing scenes per picture while the average number of kissing scenes for all feature films was 5.22. The average moral "goodness" value of the kissing scenes in the selected eight was +.115, while that of the kissing scenes in all feature pictures was −.168. The average number of aggressiveness scenes for Hall's eight was 3.5 while that for the 142 feature films was 5.11. The morality score for the aggressiveness scenes in the blue ribbon set averaged −.58 while that of all feature films was −.72. This comparison, while of small scope, points in the same direction as the other findings set forth in this section.

III

It was our hope to apply the technique illustrated in the preceding section to measuring the effect of conflict with the mores upon the commercial success of pictures as directly indicated by box-office receipts, applying this to the whole 142 films we had rated. We have good reason for believing that the correlation with this criterion would also be negative, and that motion-picture producers lose money, instead of making it, by moral offenses. The discovery as to whether this hypothesis is true or false would be a matter of supreme importance both to producers and to society at large. But we could not get dependable data on the commercial success of motion pictures. Producers guard information about this matter as carefully as if they were trying to shield some black crime from the public. We hoped at first to use the figures published in *Variety*, but were shown that these are only estimates which greatly miss the facts. We spent three months negotiating with the Hays organization to get the data from the Motion-Picture Producers and Distributors of America, only to find in the end that the secretary of that organization could not furnish the information except in a form so vague as to be worth little in a correlation problem. The local manager of the theater in which we rated our pictures prepared for us an accurate statement of the relative earnings of all the pictures we had rated, but the Warner Brothers, who own the theater, forbade him to give us any figures on financial matters no matter how much disguised. A letter addressed by us to an independent exhibitor fell into the hands of a producer-exhibitor who had bought the chain of theaters and we received the reply: "I am sorry the policies of our company do not make it possible to give you the information requested in your letter of Feb. 1st." The attempt to get the data on any large scale from independent exhibitors failed, not because of unwillingness on their part to give it but on account of the work involved and the shortness of the time remaining. One independent exhibitor has offered us such data as he has, but too late to get results in this volume and too meager to give more than a hint of the trend. But we hope that even yet some producer-exhibitors may avail themselves of the ratings we have collected on 142 feature pictures to make a statistical study of this problem.

The author gets the impression that the procedures of the motion-picture producers in respect to meeting social needs and desires are primitive and naïve—incredibly so in an age of scientific research. They are still in the stage of magic and of haphazard trial and error. They follow the pattern of the people who, in Lamb's essay, first discovered the taste of roast pig from the accidental burning of a hut, then, unable to isolate the roasting from the total situation, continued to burn a hut containing a pig every time they wanted that delicacy. When some producer, "by dumb luck," succeeds in producing a film that pays, other producers rush in and make pictures like it until the public gets disgusted with that particular pattern.

The theory upon which this whimsicality of production is grounded is set forth by Pitkin and Marston in a book on the art of sound pictures.[5] They hold that there are vogues which come from environmental factors and last a while and that a run of pictures to meet this demand when accidentally discovered is the proper thing. They claim that this taste for a particular kind of picture is not only transient but wholly unpredictable.

There is no scientific evidence available to defend such a theory; it is based only upon uncontrolled observation of situations which combine very mixed variables. It conflicts with the findings of science in every area where science has been applied. It smacks of the magic that has character-

[5] Pitkin, W. B., and Marston, W. M., *The Art of Sound Pictures*, D. Appleton and Co., 1930, pp. 25–30.

ized the pre-science stage in every field. In primitive times good crops, the behavior of the weather, disease, the activities of inanimate objects, were all supposed to be unpredictable and subject only to the whims of the gods. Magical incantation was the only means of control. But scientific study has shown the physical world to be not whimsical in its behavior but characterized by uniformities in terms of which we can predict. The whimsicalities that appear to the superficial observer are due merely to combinations of forces acting in accord with law, but combinations which he does not understand. The social scientist has found similar uniformities in the world of human behavior, although the compositions of factors here are somewhat harder to untangle into their component variables. In the million years or more that man has lived upon this earth his basic activities have become pretty well stabilized. To assume that human nature is made and remade with kaleidoscopic rapidity, so that it demands one kind of motion picture one month and another kind the next month in a way that only happy chance can discover, is so implausible as to seem absurd.

We would have an analogy to this sort of thing if restaurant keepers, observing a certain variety in appetite, were to conclude that at a certain month in the world's history people had chanced upon that stage in their evolution when they wanted deviled eggs and therefore served up nothing but deviled eggs until a noticeable falling off of attendance at restaurants indicated that the age in world history had passed when men happened to want deviled eggs; if then, on the accidental discovery by some waiter that the age of hot tamales had arrived, they would serve only hot tamales as long as people would tolerate them; and so on. As a matter of fact human appetite has been pretty well stabilized in man's million-year history. He wants a certain variety, to be sure, and some fashions in menus may influence his desires to a certain extent, but the combinations of basic food elements he needs, and consequently in the long run craves, are knowable, are not subject to whimsical change, and can be definitely and systematically planned for.

A scientific analysis of the fundamental services wanted by men and women from art throughout the ages, of the factors and their combinations that have been present in successful art, and of the rise of social changes which might react upon the sorts of recreations and informations people are likely to need, should place the production of motion pictures on an equally intelligent basis. It is the author's belief that a few good social-science research men could render as important service in improving motion-picture production as research in agriculture has rendered to scientific farming or research in physics to the improvement of the radio and of refrigeration. That motion-picture producers have so far failed to take cognizance of this possibility is equally pathetic from the point of view of their own interests and of those of the public. It has been repeatedly found that in the long run (though not necessarily through a short span) the interests of society and those of a group attempting to do business with society rise and fall together. There is every reason to believe that this same principle holds of the motion-picture industry, and that whatever research pointed the way to pictures more useful to society would also point the way to a sounder business policy for the producers.

CHAPTER XII

THE POSSIBILITIES OF FURTHER RESEARCH
FOR THE IMPROVEMENT OF MOTION
PICTURES

In this chapter we shall suggest certain further desirable
and feasible studies concerned with the improvement of motion pictures in meeting their social functions and oppor-
tunities.

I

The availability of our scales makes possible a more
objective form of evaluating motion pictures for the information of the public than the individual or committee
estimates now employed. A profile of each picture could be
shown visually which would indicate in concrete imagery
the character of the picture in respect to the phases covered
by the report. Our own scales provide for rating on only
four phases, but the number of phases could be extended
to as many additional ones as desired by the construction
of further scales. We shall give as illustrations the profiles
of two widely contrasted pictures, *Bad Girl* and *Murder
by the Clock*. The heavy line down the middle of the chart
indicates the approval index 50 per cent line for our combined groups (which constitute a pretty fair sample of our
whole population), while the lighter lines on either side
locate the 25 per cent line and the 75 per cent line respectively. The scenes located to the left of the mid-line are
below the approval index of our population and those beyond

the light line on the left are below the point where 75 per cent of society would be against them if they occurred in real life; that is, the dissenters plus half the neutrals amount

MORAL PROFILE OF BAD GIRL

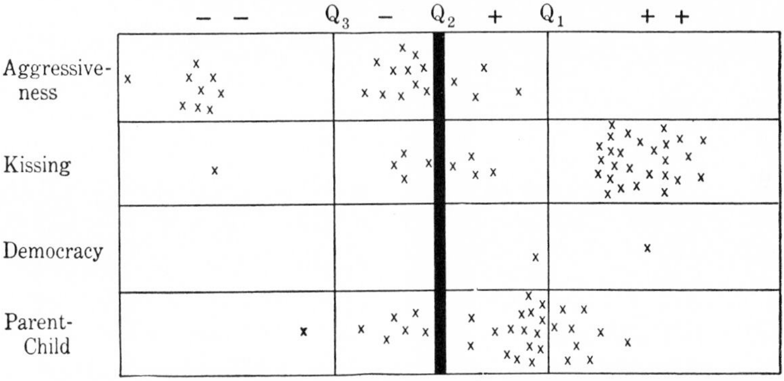

	− −	Q_3 −	Q_2 +	Q_1	+ +

Aggressiveness

Kissing

Democracy

Parent-Child

MORAL PROFILE OF MURDER BY THE CLOCK

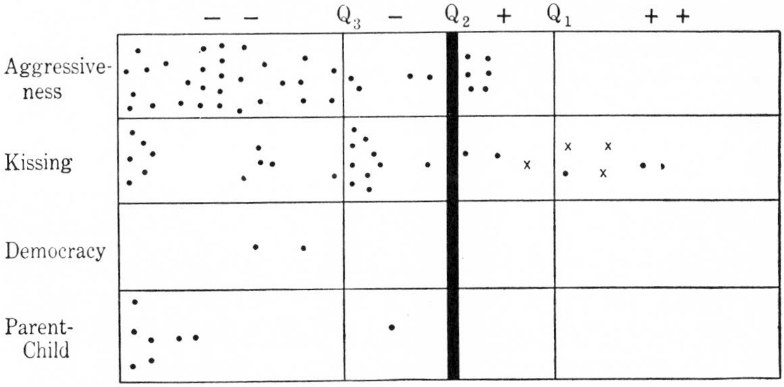

	− −	Q_3 −	Q_2 +	Q_1	+ +

Aggressiveness

Kissing

Democracy

Parent-Child

Fig. 10

to three fourths of the whole population we sampled. The light line on the right has a similar meaning with reference to the 25 per cent line. Scenes by attractive characters are indicated by × and those by unattractive characters by • Since there are five raters, each rated scene is duplicated on the profile five times. Besides being inevitable in our scheme of rating, this gives greater density to the chart so that a visual impression of the general distribution of scenes can be got without any effort at counting them.

If high reliability is desired for the rating of individual pictures, it is suggested that five committees be employed instead of five individuals, each committee to consist of three persons who, after seeing the picture to be rated, will sit together to agree upon the identity of the scenes but assign ratings to them independently. The five committees should act wholly independently of one another, or the five individual raters if only five instead of fifteen are employed. The technique is described in Chapter V. The cost of rating each picture by five committees of three each would probably approximate twenty-five dollars. This would need to be done only once, however, so that the cost would be insignificant compared with the capital invested in a picture. Motion-picture producers might well make it a practice, either voluntarily or by legislative requirement, to flash on the screen a moral-profile of each picture in connection with the advertisement of it.

II

A number of additional elements of civism and morality might profitably be studied by essentially the same technique as we used on our sample of four. Among these are the following: the use of vulgar jokes, the treatment of officers of the law, extravagance, courtesy and kindness to others, the treatment of parents by children, conduct between brothers and sisters, rational consideration *versus* romance in betrothal, drinking and smoking, forgiveness *versus* revenge, nudeness, treatment of husbands by wives and the reverse, industriousness, and kindness to animals.

The author believes that a simplification of technique would give nearly as good results as our elaborate one. It was scarcely necessary to employ five different groups in getting our basic scale values, since the groups turned out to be·correlated so highly with one another.[1] One hundred persons from a rather heterogeneous population would have done satisfactorily. It would be an improvement to submit to this smaller set of scale makers a much larger number of samples of conduct than was wanted in the finished scales, so that out of the whole number could be selected a set that would have values spaced at more regular intervals than ours. In view of the close agreement we found among our groups, a smaller number of groups might be used for marking the scales. Four or five well-selected groups, instead of thirteen, would give a sufficiently dependable sampling of the whole population. And, finally, we believe that a much simpler method of marking the scales than we employed would give satisfactory results. We had the respondents mark each paragraph. We might have instructed them instead to find a point in the hierarchically ordered scale below which they did not feel it proper for people to go in conduct and draw a line across the page there. Of course the respondents would have claimed that they could find no point which completely satisfied them—that at any point they would find some paragraphs above which they would wish to condemn and some below which they would approve. Nevertheless if they had been forced to choose *some* point as best they could, the marks for any group would probably have arranged themselves in a normal distribution around approximately the same point as that at which our approval ogive curve crossed the 50 per cent position. If this technique could be successfully employed it would save

[1] See page 276 for these correlation coefficients.

the respondent some time and trouble and would elimi-
nate the immense task of running the ogive curves which
consumed for us hundreds of hours.

These methods are, however, less exact than the ones
we employed. We did not risk using them because in this
pioneer study we desired the maximum precision.

III

Now that we have available an instrument for measuring
the mores and for making possible quantitative comparisons
of them, it would be immensely illuminating and interesting
to compare the mores of the people of our country with
those of other nations, and those of diverse groups with one
another within nations. It will also be of great interest
and importance to see how the mores change from genera-
ation to generation by resubmitting the scales for marking
at periods twenty-five years or so apart. It is to facilitate
such comparisons of peoples and of ages that we are publishing (in the appendix) analytic tables showing the status
of the approvals, disapprovals, and practices of each of our
social groups. In studies where comparisons are to be made
with ours the same techniques must be employed as those
used by us. The suggestions of the previous section about
simplified techniques would apply, therefore, only to the
making of a new series of scales, not to comparisons on the
basis of ours.

Our scales, as well as further new ones of a similar sort,
might also be used for measuring the legitimate drama,
fiction, and even social life itself from observation. A
comparison with the findings from rating these other areas
would throw useful light on the standing of the movies as
educational agencies.

IV

In our study we have measured only detailed patterns of conduct in the movies, on the ground that they set models which might be imitated by observers. But through such detailed patterns is not the only way in which motion pictures may influence morality. Perhaps the manner in which the theme as a whole works out influences people's notions about life. Perhaps seeing that sin brought unfortunate consequences, that a reformed criminal was quickly taken back into respectable society, that affection for an abandoned wife persisted and finally triumphed over the transient appeal of free love, persons add concepts and convictions to their philosophy of life which come to be determining factors in their conduct. Whether or not this does happen to any great extent from movie attendance is difficult to say, but the work of Dr. Thurstone, at least, has shown that observation of certain motion pictures has significantly changed attitudes of the observers. We should have a thorough investigation of this problem with regard to the effect of the commercial movies in their normal social setting, including both the question of the actual extent of such influence and its nature and direction. The technique of such a study would probably need to be very different from ours. It is conceivable that a scale somewhat like ours but of pictures as wholes could be devised having as its elements reasonably brief accounts of the handling of the themes, and having these organized in hierarchical order with numerical "anti-social" indices for each; and that these scales might be used for the quantitative rating of motion pictures. But the author has serious fears that the complexity of pictures as wholes would be too great to permit much headway with such a device. What we need is actual measurement of changes in a sampling of people by reason of having attended the exhibition of particular pictures rather than estimates of the probable effects. We may have the instruments for making these measurements in such devices as Thurstone's Attitude Scales. But the difficulties of doing this sort of thing with sufficient accuracy, under conditions that would permit isolating the effect of an individual picture from other factors, and of achieving this not merely illustratively but for all of the thousand films produced per year so as to get a morality rating for each, seem almost insurmountable.

Perhaps reasonably useful findings could be secured from *estimates of probable moral effects.* We might have judges sit through the showing thinking all the time how the picture as shown would be likely to affect the ideals and practices of different classes of attendants, then at the end assigning it a rating on a scale of minus ten to plus ten according to the extent to which it was judged to make a negative or a positive contribution to healthy social attitudes.[2] Such ratings should be as analytic as feasible; they should be on particular phases of morality rather than on morality as a whole, since any picture is likely to be "good" in some respects and "bad" in others. And an average of estimates should be taken from a number of judges, since the reliability of ratings has been shown to rise rapidly with the use of an increasing number of judges. It is altogether possible that some such technique might give very useful results.

V

A fifth desirable type of study is controlled experimentation. This does not mean merely trying something new and concluding on the basis of general observation that it is good

[2] For an example of this see Peters, C. C., *Foundations of Educational Sociology,* Rev. Ed., The Macmillan Co., 1930, pp. 327–329.

or bad.   It means experimenting under careful scientific
controls with the aid of the techniques now available for
isolating and controlling the variables, for measuring them
singly, and for attributing to each the effects due to it.
No type of research in psychology and education has been
more refined in technique than that of the controlled ex-
periment. Scientific experimentation involves pitting against
each other pairs of contrasted procedures, keeping all factors
constant in the two situations except the experimental
factor, and precisely measuring comparative outcomes.

There should be such experimentation to determine the
relative effects of different types of advertisements, of de-
signing motion pictures for classified audiences instead of
for people in general, of what constitutes effective techniques
for appealing to different types of people, of what are the
most effective combinations of pictures, of the effect of the
presence or absence of each of many features in pictures, etc.

Where situations cannot be controlled, as scientific experimentation demands, the partial correlation technique,
illustrated slightly in Chapter XI, can be employed. This
scheme furnishes a method of holding all factors constant by
statistical manipulation except the one the behavior of which
is to be studied in relation to a criterion. The method is,
therefore, a sort of substitute for controlled experimentation.

VI

The most fruitful of all types of study would, the author
believes, be a constructive study of what is required to
constitute a "good" picture. "Good" is here our criterion
and it may be of a multiple character; it may include commercial success, ability to appeal to and interest people, and
the rendering of valuable educational service in society.
Many techniques suggest themselves as possibilities.

a. Investigations of what values, at various stages throughout history, people sought through art and through play, and in what forms they found the values that satisfied them.

b. Study of what factors have tended to be more or less common in the works of art (literature, drama, music, pictorial art) that have lived through time because they satisfied cravings fundamental in all human nature.

c. In a large sampling of motion pictures investigation of what are the elements that correlate positively, and what are those that correlate negatively, with commercial success and with other criteria of success. All sorts of factors should be tried: pictorial art, dramatic art, accompanying music, novelty, revelation of how the other half lives, intricacy of theme, etc. We could get along pretty well with bi-serial r's, which demand as ratings only classification of the pictures into those above and those below average in respect to the feature under investigation. With large numbers of pictures these simple correlation measures would serve almost as well as the more elaborate Pearson product-moment ones.

d. Similar correlations with other evidences of the appeal of the pictures than box-office receipts, and with the approval or condemnation of leaders of thought.

e. An analysis of the components of goodness from each of several points of view by the techniques employed by the author in analyzing citizenship, personal culture, etc., and described in his *Foundations of Educational Sociology*, Revised Edition, Chapter V.

f. The building of a score card for motion pictures after the analogy of the score cards developed by Strayer and others for measuring merit of school buildings.

g. The study of emotional responses to various types of factors in motion pictures by different type groups with the aid of such instruments as the galvanometer, the plethysmograph, and the pneumograph. Such study might become a routine part of the examination of each film before it is released and while conditions still permit changes, as well as a basis for the derivation of principles which would guide future production.

h. A psychological and sociological analysis of the functions needed by society from art and from play, the manner in which these differ for different situations in which various types of people live, and deductions therefrom as to what kinds of residual services are needed from motion pictures to meet these needs.

The above suggestions are some that occur at random to the author; when the field is entered many more possibilities will open up. It has been our experience in general that when scientific research got a toe hold in any field and pressed on from that point, it found possibilities enlarged with every achievement until our mastery of our world under the leadership of scientific research surpassed anything that even the most daring could have dreamed at the beginning. There is this same promise in this area. We therefore conclude by repeating, what we said in an earlier chapter, that it is our conviction that a small group of highly competent social-science research workers, at an expense of not exceeding a hundred thousand dollars a year, could do as much to set up the motion-picture industry on a high plane as agricultural research has done for scientific farming or research in engineering for the improvement of the radio and the refrigerator.

APPENDIX A

THE MORES SCALES

AGGRESSIVENESS OF A GIRL IN LOVE–MAKING

MOTIVE: Real Love.

TECHNIQUES: Coquetry.

a. Inveigles man into situations calculated to bring love responses.

b. Appeals for protection, or gives protection.

c. Is attentive, solicitous, and purposively appreciative.

d. Resorts to banter and flattery.

e. Bestows smiles, and other coquetry, upon him.

f. Invites pursuit by retreat.

b.   GIRL DEFENDS MAN FROM DANGER

+0.62   Louise and Don have only recently met when Don's life is threatened by a jealous lover. Louise immediately comes to his aid as she tries to dissuade the persecutor from his purpose.

b.   GIVES HINT OF HER PREFERENCE FOR A MAN BY SEEKING PROTECTION

Helen secretly adores Jack Benton and on this occasion is with him at a party. During the course of the merri-

+0.16   ment, Helen is frightened by approaches from a man she dislikes, and, turning to Jack, she takes hold of his arm saying: "I'd rather not talk to that man; let's get out of here."

c.   A GIRL SMILES AND TALKS PLEASANTLY WITH A MAN SHE HAS JUST MET IN THE HOPES OF "INTERESTING" HIM

Nordine is introduced to Mr. Brady, a rising young lawyer, who has just won an important case. With the

+0.08 secret hope of "catching" him, she makes an unusual effort to be agreeable. They talk conventionally about the weather, discuss a show that had been running recently, and other topics of minor importance. She smiles and laughs very winningly at his somewhat trite witticisms.

b. A Girl Goes into a Man's Arms for Protection

+0.02 Cora is a Chinese girl whose wedding with the egotistical, affected, polygamous Charlie Young, an Americanized Chinaman, is being arranged by her guardian. Unexpectedly Tom Gray, a Yankee whom she secretly loves dearly, calls on her. Charlie at once boasts his intentions and claims her. As he would take her into his arms she avoids him, slips into Tom's instead, pleading as she clings to him, "You won't let him marry me, will you?"

c. A Woman, Secretly Adoring a Man, Gives a Hint of Her Love by Stroking His Shoulder

−0.13 Kate, a none-too-handsome middle-aged lady, has long served as secretary to the elderly bachelor, Mr. Fellows. She is secretly in love with him but has hitherto expressed her love only by her solicitous care for his welfare, and by her faithfulness to duty. But tonight as she remarks that he needs a new suit, that his old one is getting shiny on the back, she strokes his shoulder very lightly and caressingly for an instant, then as quickly draws her hand away as if frightened by her act of familiarity.

e. Shows Special Attention to a Man Who Attracts Her Interest

−0.24 There were other fellows at the little party, but not for Jane; she had eyes only for Harry. At every opportunity she bestowed smiles upon him and managed more times than accident would account for to get engaged in conversation with him, or to be near him when a game was to start.

a. A Girl Maneuvers a Man Whom She Loves into a Situation Calculated to Invite Love-Making

Frank and Sarah have been going together for a number of months, but he has never made any love approaches to her. He is somewhat bashful although he has given Sarah reasons to believe that he loves her. On this night, she suggests that they drive over to Coulter's Point, a small, lightly wooded promontory jutting out into the sea. Seating herself upon a grassy knob, she pulls him down beside her, saying, with a pleading tone of voice: "Come, Frank, tell me what the sea is saying to us."

−0.30

d. Girl Flatters Lover in Private in Order to Hasten Proposal

It was not that Jessie was a "gold-digger" or "flirt," but she did ardently hope that Jacob would soon "propose" to her. So she resorted to some "taffying" when they were alone with each other, partly because she really meant the compliments and partly because this was her way of drawing him on with the hope of hastening their bethrothal.

−0.38

c. Girl Seizes Opportunity to Speak Endearingly to a Man

Evelyn would like to receive more attention from Dick and tries to be nice to him. Her father has an unusually difficult task that he wants Dick to perform for him, but which he at first refuses to do. After some persuasion from both Evelyn and her father, he reconsiders the proposition and when he announces that he will do the task, Evelyn greets the announcement by falling on his neck as she says, "You are a darling."

−0.53

d. A Girl Tells a Man How Wonderful He Is and Flatters Him

George Longwell is a good-looking fellow and really quite a capable young lawyer. Blanche feels that George is the man for her and that she must secure more of his

attention. When he asks her, on rare occasions, to have
−0.57 a date with him she is quite free to tell him what a
popular and successful lawyer people think he is, and
how she thinks he is the most brilliant person she has
ever known. She frequently addresses him with, "How
is the handsome boy tonight?"

d. Sweetheart Says Flattering Things to Her Lover in Public

Joe, a famed aviator, is being banqueted by his admirers. They insist upon hearing some of his war experiences, whereupon, in his most oratorical manner, he
−0.76 tells of the thrilling air combats in which he took part.
As he turns to sit down, his sweetheart rises from her
seat beside him, clasps his hand in hers and exclaims:
"You're almost as good a speaker as you are an aviator.
What a dear you are, my hero!"

a, b, c. A Girl Repeatedly Attempts to Flirt with a Man She Secretly Loves in the Hope That He Will Be Interested in Her

All through the investigation of the murder, Miss
Morgan, the maid, has been very attentive to Mr. Dugan,
the detective. While he is sipping the coffee she has
made for him, she smiles beguilingly at him over the rim
of her cup, tells him he looks tired and that he ought
to rest or get some recreation, and mentions several
good shows she would like to see. After the murder has
been solved, Miss Morgan remains in his office. Dugan
−0.92 tells her that her faith has helped a great deal. She
replies that she will never forget him. A phone call
interrupts, Dugan tells her that he must leave. "I'll be
here when you return," she said. "What do you mean?"
She goes over, smoothes his coat lapels and replies,
"It shouldn't take a detective to know what I mean."

e. Mildly Flirts with Man to Get Him as Partner in Dance or Tête-a-Tête

Pauline is "crazy" to have Mr. Flanders as partner
for a dance or talk this evening and she does not hesitate

-0.99 to show it by signs that he ought to be able to understand. As they pass in the dance she bestows upon him her most inviting smile. When this is not enough she takes a seat by a vacant chair and, as he comes along alone, begins to talk with him. When he pauses for conversation she grasps his hand and draws him into the vacant chair beside her.

b. Woman Feigns Danger in Order to Provoke Attention from a Man

-1.14 Lucille Evans is very desirous of securing attention from Tom Howard and hopes to induce him to marry her. When they chance to be together at the beach one day, Lucille struggles and pretends to drown while bathing. This of course has the desired effect of drawing the attention of Tom. When he goes to save her she appears very helpless and allows him to help her from the water and to try to revive her.

AGGRESSIVENESS OF A GIRL IN LOVE–MAKING

Motive: Spontaneous Expression or Thrill.
Techniques: Coquetry.
  a. Inveigles a man into situations calculated to bring love responses.
  b. Appeals for protection, or gives protection.
  c. Is attentive, solicitous, and purposively appreciative.
  d. Resorts to banter and flattery.
  e. Bestows smiles, and other coquetry, upon him.
  f. Invites pursuit by retreat.

c. Girl Smiles and Clasps the Hand of a Man She Has Just Met to Express Her Appreciation of Kindness

+0.03 Mary is without money in a strange city. A friend introduces her to Joe Brooks, who discovers her plight and tactfully thrusts money into her hand as a "loan."

Assured of his intentions, she clasps his hand, smiles
with renewed determination, and says, "I can't thank
you enough."

c. GIRL SYMPATHIZES WITH A MAN IN HIS TROUBLE

To Virginia Bickett, Tom Morrow is a very much
admired and publicly worshiped hero,—which makes
him a much-to-be-desired boy friend. Tom has the
−0.01 unfortunate knack of getting into embarrassing situations. After one of his embarrassing moments, Virginia
comes to him and tries to console him as she says, "You
poor boy," etc.

c. GIRL PLACES HER ARMS AROUND MAN AS SHE
THANKS HIM FOR A FAVOR

Because she was lonesome, Mary particularly appreci-
ated the confidence and help of a friend. Such a friend
−0.23 was Joe Brown. In showing her appreciation of what he
had done for her, she places her arms on his shoulder as
she tells him of her gratitude.

d.   A GIRL "KIDS" AND JOKES WITH A MAN

Lucille Downey believes that one way to get a beau
is to "kid him into it." She would like to have some
attention from Bill Welsh and so we find her giving
−0.30 him such a greeting as "Hello, Big Boy; how is the
world's hero this morning?" If they happen to talk
together she mixes their general conversation with jests
about his golf, or the "swell" necktie he is wearing.

d, e. GIRL COQUETTISHLY SMILES AT, AND BANTERS
WITH, DANCING PARTNER

At the beginning of the next dance Paul exchanged
dances with his friend. Paul's new partner put her
left hand on his arm in the accustomed position as
they began to dance. Suddenly the quick time of the
−0.64 music changed to a slower waltz rhythm. As they slowed
their steps Ethel looked up into his face, said, "I love
waltzes," slipped her left hand around his neck, and

smiled continuously up into his face as she engaged in mild banter.

f. GIRL INVITES APPROACHES BY PRETENDING TO AVOID THEM

Young Johnston's rocking chair had the troublesome habit of "walking" as he rocked, or at least Miss Shultz pretended to think that it did. From time to time she would move her chair an inch or two farther away. −0.77   But in spite of this care to keep her chair at a distance she would frequently lean toward him with a playful pout of protest at something he had said, projecting her lips suggestively. But if he would approach her face, whether intentionally or accidentally and as little as you please, she would quickly draw away in feigned alarm.

c. GIRL SHOWS SYMPATHY AND COMFORT TO A MAN TO GAIN HIS ATTENTION

Like many of her sex, Helen is continually alert for new "conquests." While in the company of one of her −0.78   latest admirers, who is slightly injured in a fall, Helen goes to him, puts her arms around him and holds him close to her as she utters words of sympathy and condolence.

b. GIRL THROWS HERSELF FOR PROTECTION INTO THE ARMS OF A MAN SHE KNOWS ONLY SLIGHTLY

Clarissa had never met Archie before the party. They had just finished a dance and were standing near an exit talking quite conventionally about nonimportant −0.80   things when there was a sudden crashing noise caused by the overturning of a piece of furniture. "Oh, what is that?" ejaculated Clarissa, as she threw herself into Archie's arms and hid her face against his shoulder.

a. A GIRL DELIBERATELY MANEUVERS A MAN INTO A SITUATION CALCULATED TO INVITE LOVE-MAKING MERELY FOR THE THRILL

Ruth wants a new thrill and sees the possibility of one in Steve. On the second night of the house party, she schedules him for two successive dances on her program. When they have danced only part of one, she suggests −0.87 that they go for a walk. Ruth takes his arm, and leads him to a little seat beside the fountain. She sighs, comments on the beauty of the night, the dance, and the fragrance of the air. She says that she wished nights such as this could last forever.

f. A Girl Invites Pursuit by Retreat

Gladys and young Mr. Roe are summer boarders at the mountain hotel. As Roe wanders leisurely about the −0.92 grounds Gladys peeps at him through the bushes. When Roe spys her she hastily turns and runs away. The sophisticated Roe rightly interprets her retreat as an invitation to follow.

e. Girl Coquettishly Smiles at, and Cuddles Against, Man while Dancing

At the first strains of the waltz, Earl Patterson makes his way across the dance floor to his sister's group where he claims the dance with her college classmate, Marjorie, who is spending the holidays with the Pattersons. As they start to dance she places her left hand on his arm −1.05 in the accustomed way but she smiles and holds his gaze all the while they exchange a few words. As the lights are turned low and the music softens, Marjorie slips her left hand around Earl's neck, clings closer to him, lays her head against his so that their cheeks touch, and with a sigh closes her eyes.

b. A Girl Pretends to Drown in Order to Attract Attention from a Man

"What a good-looking fellow that is with Tom Manning, and wouldn't I like to be the first to meet him." That was secretly the sentiment of each of the −1.09 girls in the bathing party. Della, more resourceful than the others, was swimming when she suddenly feigned cramps and drowning, which had the desired effect of attracting Tom's friend, who carried her from the pool.

e. A GIRL REPEATEDLY ATTEMPTS TO FLIRT WITH A MAN IN THE HOPE THAT HE WILL COME AND TALK WITH HER

Carlotta is introduced to Pablo at a dance. Pablo is the son of a wealthy ranch owner and considered quite a "fast" young man. Throughout the entire evening, Carlotta seldom takes her eyes from him. At times −1.17 their glances meet, and she smiles very engagingly at him. She dances with rather an elderly man, and when she passes Pablo and his partner, she winks at him, apparently inviting him to "cut-in." During the intermission she drapes herself rather carelessly over a settee on the veranda where he is smoking.

e. A GIRL TALKS RATHER FAMILIARLY AND CASTS COQUETTISH GLANCES AT A MAN SHE HAS JUST MET

A "house-to-house" salesman has called at Nordine's home to interest her mother in a vacuum cleaner. In the absence of her mother, Nordine assumes the responsibility of interviewing the man. He is young, good-looking, and a brilliant conversationalist. Nordine frequently −1.22 interrupts his sales talks in order to ask him whether he knows certain people about the town; whether he attended this or that dance, and whether Caroline Newman's mother bought a sweeper—"You know Caroline, don't you?" She smiles very coquettishly at him during the conversation, apparently trying hard to "vamp" him.

a. BY NATURE OF HER SUGGESTIONS INVITES KISSES AND OTHER CARESSES

Consuela, an escaped novice, is taken home by a man whose voice she admires to the point of falling in love with the owner. He is greatly impressed by her innocence and beauty. After he has got her something to eat and drink, he looks into her eyes. "What do you see in −1.23 my eyes? Devils? Angels?" As she says this she projects her face closer as though to give him a better look. He kisses her. "What did you see?" she asks. "Devils," he replies. "Oh no, look again!" This time he changes it to angels, and again kisses her. "Can't you find anything else?" she queried, pushing her face still closer.

a. RELATIVE NUDENESS, HINTS IN CONVERSATION, ETC., SEEM CALCULATED TO AROUSE HIS SEX IMPULSES, BUT APPARENTLY COQUETTISHLY RATHER THAN SERIOUSLY

−1.51 Lola, a singer in a dance hall, has been escorted home by a young man she has met there. They arrive at her apartment house, and in the lower hall he bids her goodnight. She says, "Wait a second, I want to show you a new step I learned; won't you come in?" He replies that he must go. She proceeds to demonstrate the step at once. She lifts her dress considerably above the knee, tosses her head in accompaniment to the tune she is humming, winks and smiles at him very suggestively.

c. GIRL, FOR A THRILL, LEADS A MAN INTO THINKING SHE LOVES HIM BY BEING SOLICITOUS OF HIS WELFARE

−1.67 Arline likes thrills—and new men. She met Bill at a dance one night and from then on she was constantly asking him about his business, advising him to take care of himself and not work too hard, and in other similar ways making him think that she was intensely interested in him—loved him in fact. But Arline was playing the game—nothing more.

f. GIRL PRETENDS TO AVOID APPROACHES AFTER INVITING THEM

−1.70 At a garden party on a large estate two of the guests happen to be Sally and Roger who have only recently met. Sally leans against a tree and when she catches Roger's eye, she winks ever so slightly and tosses her head in invitation for him to come and talk with her. She waits until he is near and then suddenly turns and runs away, leaving the nonplussed man watching her. Her actions are again repeated—and the game is on.

a.   HER CONDUCT AND MANNER SEEM CLEARLY
INTENDED TO INVITE SEX RESPONSES

−1.83

Kelley tries to stay away from Polly but he can't resist the temptation. He goes to her room determined to tell her that he can't see her again, and that he is going away. She is lying back on a sofa strumming a guitar and singing. She jumps up when he enters, throws back her negligee, revealing her only clothing to be a brassiere and step-ins. She goes and gets him a drink. One strap over her shoulder slips down. She neither replaces it nor closes her negligee, but stands before Kelley until he has finished his drink, and then takes his hand and draws him over to the sofa.

AGGRESSIVENESS OF A GIRL IN LOVE–MAKING

MOTIVE: Spontaneous Expression or Thrill.
TECHNIQUES: Direct Approaches.

    a. Directly invites a man to companionship by word or deed.
    b. Shows special solicitude for a particular man.
    c. "Pursues" a man.
    d. Resorts to physical manipulation.
    e. Takes the initiative in avowing love.
    f. Directly invites avowal.
    g. Indirectly avows love, as in a song or in an expression of solicitude.
    h. Argues for companionship or for marriage.

a.   A GIRL LETS HER ROOMMATE, AN INTIMATE FRIEND,
ARRANGE A DATE FOR HER, FOR A DANCE

+ .34

Mary and Sue are roommates at a small college for girls. Mary is of the serious, studious type; her companion quite the opposite. Sue enters the room in time to see Mary hurriedly dry her eyes and pretend to be deeply interested in a book lying open before her. Sue: "You're not getting a bit of fun out of this college, young lady. Dan's friend wants a date for the hop tomorrow night, and you are it, get me?" After considerable protesting on the part of Mary, she finally gives Sue the permission to call Harry and arrange the details.

a, c.   A GIRL ASKS A MAN TO WRITE TO HER

+ .21
Ken Gardner is going to another town where the company for which he works has sent him. Today, when he chances to meet Louise Huddleson on his way home for dinner, he tells her that he is leaving and bids her good-by. As they are about to separate Louise asks him to write to her as she would be interested in knowing how he likes his new work.

a.   JOKINGLY INVITES A MAN TO CALL UPON HER AT HER HOME

+ .03
Phyllis and Paul have known each other for only a short time. They chance to meet at the beach one afternoon and engage in a very commonplace conversation. They joke and tease one another in a good-natured manner. "Kid," says Paul enthusiastically, "I wish I could see you oftener." "Well," replies Phyllis, half-teasingly but half hopefully, "you know where I live, don't you?"

a.   GIRL INVITES MAN TO COME TO HER HOME

−0.12
Joyce and Tom have been out to a dance. When they return home, Joyce turns to her escort and says: "Won't you come in for a little while; it isn't very late yet?"

c.   GIRL ACTS UPON THE SUGGESTION OF A MAN THAT SHE MEET HIM AT AN APPOINTED TIME AND PLACE

−0.26
"I have to work late tonight, but if you could call for me about nine we could still go out and have us a time." Alice was willing and so at the appointed time she went to the Fulton building, where she met Fred as he got off the elevator.

a.   A GIRL ASKS A MAN TO DANCE WITH HER

A group of young people have drifted together at the dance pavilion in the park. They laugh and talk about

−0.28 the times they had together in school. Suddenly the music starts and Jane grabs Bob by the hand saying, "Come on, old boy, let's dance."

b. MARRIED WOMAN CONFESSES HER LOVE FOR OLD SWEETHEART

Through a misunderstanding Janet and Gaylord, though loving one another, separated, and married others. Years later they meet in New York and go for a ride
−0.49 through the park in Janet's carriage. The conversation centers about themselves. Finally Janet, dreamily reminiscing says: "You are the only man I have ever loved, Gaylord."

a. A GIRL JOKINGLY PROPOSES HERSELF AS PARTNER FOR A DANCE

Edna flirts with Monte at the lunch counter where she is employed. She is very attentive to him, and smiles sweetly at him on the slightest pretext. She succeeds in
−0.63 drawing him into conversation, during which she mentions the Engineer's Ball to be held the following Saturday night. In answer to his negative reply and excuse that he hasn't a girl, she laughingly says, "I'm not going with anyone special."

f. BY GESTURES AND QUESTIONS ATTEMPTS TO FORCE A DECLARATION OF LOVE FROM HIM

Lola and Juan are partners in a song and dance act. He escorts her to her home. As they converse on the
−0.71 doorstep she gives him a light caress and says, "I do what you wish, but you do not say that you love me."

a, c. MILDLY FLIRTS WITH MAN TO GET HIM AS PARTNER IN DANCE OR TÊTE-À-TÊTE

Pauline is "crazy" to have Mr. Flanders as partner for a dance or a talk this evening and she does not hesitate to show it by signs that he ought to be able to understand. As they pass in the dance she bestows upon him
−0.99 her most inviting smile. When this is not enough she

takes a seat by a vacant chair and, as he comes along alone, begins to talk with him. When he pauses for conversation she grasps his hand and draws him into the vacant chair beside her.

d. PRESSES HIS ARM AND NUDGES HIM FAMILIARLY DURING A CONVERSATION

−1.04 Mabel has only recently met Mr. Blake. As they are walking through the park, Mabel grabs Mr. Blake's arm when she wishes to call his attention to anything, and continually nudges him with her elbow to accentuate certain outstanding points in the conversation.

c. A GIRL FOLLOWS A MAN TO TRY TO PREVENT HIS LEAVING HER

−1.07 Alexander and Jeanette are talking together at a party in a Vienna café when Alexander chances to see his former sweetheart. He immediately loses interest in Jeanette and follows his former girl from the room hoping to have a word with her. But Jeanette pursues him, takes him by the hand and tries to persuade him to remain in the café in company with her.

a. GRASPS HIS HAND AND PULLS HIM AWAY FROM A CROWD TO TALK OR DANCE WITH HER

−1.25 Phyllis has just been introduced to Henry at a house party. She is the type of girl who seems to take great delight in seeing how many men she can actually "make." After dinner the party go into the club room to dance. During intermission, Henry is talking to a group of girls and Phyllis walks over to him, smiles, and puts herself into the conversation. When the dance starts and he makes no move to invite her to dance, she seizes his hand and laughingly pulls him onto the floor.

a, c. A GIRL REPEATEDLY ASKS A MAN TO WRITE TO HER

Edith would certainly like attention from Dan Perry, but he seems more or less indifferent. At present he is working in another state. Edith has asked him to write

−1.28   to her, but when she received no letter she took the
initiative and wrote to him. After that she frequently
wrote several letters to each one received from him, and
if he was rather tardy in writing she would insistently
urge him to write to her more often.

a, c. Relative Nudeness, Hints in Conversation,
etc., Seem Calculated to Arouse His Sex
Impulses, but Apparently Coquettishly
Rather than Seriously

Lola, a singer in a dance hall, has been escorted home
by a young man she has met there. They arrive at her
apartment house, and in the lower hall he bids her good-
night. She says, "Wait a second, I want to show you
−1.51   a new step I learned; won't you come in?" He replies
that he must go. She proceeds to demonstrate the step
at once. She lifts her dress considerably above the knee,
tosses her head in accompaniment to the tune she is
humming, winks and smiles at him very suggestively.

f. A Girl Insinuates Herself into a Man's Private
Quarters in Order to Invite His Caresses

Bingo accidentally stumbles over Andy while she is
walking about the deck of a ship. He helps her rise.
She smiles at him and by her insinuations invites further
acquaintance. Later she comes to his cabin window
−1.63   which is open, sticks her head in and starts talking with
him as he shaves, minus his shirt. A little later she sees
him leave the cabin. She goes in; falls asleep on the couch
while she is awaiting his return. When he comes back,
she is awakened by the noise he makes, talks with him,
and asks him if he is going to kiss her good-night.

c. Relative Nudeness, Hints in Conversation, etc.,
Accompanied by Certain Gestures, Suggests No
Great Reluctance to Be Approached with
Sex Advances

Molly, an habitué of a public dance hall, has so successfully "vamped" Harry that he asks permission to

−1.79 take her home. They arrive at her apartment, enter, and take seats on the davenport. Molly's dress is somewhat abbreviated in all dimensions, so that when she sits down, not a great deal is left for the imagination. She assumes a half-reclining position and pulls Harry down beside her. She strokes his hair, unties his tie, and opens his shirt collar after having told him to remove his coat and vest, "Because it is awfully warm in here."

AGGRESSIVENESS OF A GIRL IN LOVE–MAKING

MOTIVE: Real Love.
TECHNIQUES: Direct Approaches. I.
    a. Directly invites man to companionship by word or deed.
    b. Shows special solicitude for a particular man.
    c. "Pursues" a man.
    d. Resorts to physical manipulation.

a. A GIRL WAITS IN APPARENTLY COMPLETE INDIFFERENCE FOR ALL ADVANCES TO BE MADE BY THE MAN

+0.32 Anne is firmly convinced that the man should always be the aggressor in any field, particularly that of love-making. When she is in the company of any man, the conversation remains strictly conventional, nor does she smile at him without cause. She is not dumb nor ignorant, but merely feels that she should not protrude herself in any "unlady-like" manner.

a, b. SERIOUSLY INVITES A MAN TO CALL UPON HER AT HER HOME

−0.06 They were both naïve country folk. Jennie had not received much attention from boys and wished to have a beau "like the other girls." As Charles helped her on with her coat, she said: "Come to see me sometime, won't you?"

a. Girl Invites Man to Come to Her Home

−0.12   Joyce and Tom have been out to a dance. When they return home, Joyce turns to her escort and says: "Won't you come in for a little while; it isn't very late yet?"

c, d. A Woman, Secretly Adoring a Man, Gives a Hint of Her Love by Stroking His Shoulder

−0.13   Kate, a none-too-handsome middle-aged lady, has long served as secretary to the elderly bachelor, Mr. Fellows. She is secretly in love with him but has hitherto expressed her love only by her solicitous care for his welfare, and by her faithfulness to duty. But tonight as she remarks that he needs a new suit, that his old one is getting shiny on the back, she strokes his shoulder very lightly and caressingly for an instant, then as quickly draws her hand away as if frightened by her act of familiarity.

a, c. Girl Asks a Young Man to Ride with Her in Her Auto

−0.18   Sally spies John Richards, for whom she entertains somewhat more than a passing fancy, in the yard as she drives by in her auto. She stops, and after a few minutes' conversation, invites him to take a ride with her.

d. Presses His Arm as They Walk Along, Ostensibly to Accentuate Certain Climaxes in the Conversation

−0.19   Phil and Joan are strolling through the park one Sunday afternoon. Joan is quite in love with Phil, but neither of them has ever taken the initiative in confessing their affections. Her hand rests lightly on his arm, and as she tells him of a show she saw the night before, she presses his arm sharply as she reaches the somewhat romantic climaxes of the story.

a, d. Girl Goes to Considerable Effort to Get a Man Interested in Her

After Dorothy met Archie there was only one man in the world as far as she was concerned. But although he

−0.31 was very pleasant and congenial company, Archie was not disposed to be more than a very good friend. But she wanted more attention and to this end would frequently invite Archie to her home for dinner, or take him with her to a party as her guest.

a, c.   GIRL FOLLOWS A MAN IN HOPES OF KEEPING HIM

−0.49 Ann has long loved Jim much more deeply than he realized. Only a few days before he is scheduled to move his headquarters to another city they have a little quarrel, and he leaves, lightly saying good-by. Ann, realizing that she may pass out of his life, follows him to his office in order to press for renewal of their former relation.

c.   GIRL COQUETTISHLY SMILES AT, AND CUDDLES AGAINST, MAN WHILE DANCING

−1.05 At the first strains of the waltz, Earl Patterson makes his way across the dance floor to his sister's group where he claims the dance with her college classmate, Marjorie, who is spending the holidays with the Pattersons. As they start to dance she places her left hand on his arm in the accustomed way but she smiles and holds his gaze all the while they exchange a few words. As the lights are turned low and the music softens, Marjorie slips her left hand around Earl's neck, clings closer to him, lays her head against his so that their cheeks touch, and with a sigh closes her eyes.

c.   A GIRL FOLLOWS A MAN TO TRY TO PREVENT HIS LEAVING HER

−1.07 Alexander and Jeanette are talking together in a party in a Vienna café when Alexander chances to see his former sweetheart. He immediately loses interest in Jeanette and follows his former girl from the room hoping to have a word with her. But Jeanette pursues him, takes him by the hand and tries to persuade him to remain in the café in company with her.

a, d. A Girl Seriously Proposes Herself for a Dance and a Tête-à-Tête

Tillie, a plain but somewhat attractive girl comes to the realization that if she is ever to be married it must be soon. She has met a Mr. Harrington and has fallen in love with him, although she has no reason to believe −1.08 that he shares her feelings. Seeing him in the stag line of the ball given in the hotel, she goes over to him and says, "Good evening, Mr. Harrington, would you care to dance this one?" After the dance she informs him that "there are some swell stars up on the roof—uh—a— will we go up and see them?"

d. Girl Resorts to Petting in Order to Arouse Love Impulses in the Man of Her Desire

Jeanne is greatly in love with Harry but he is not inclined to become serious. Hoping to arouse some manifestations of love from him, Jeanne resorts to petting. When −1.11 they are alone she playfully ruffles his hair, sits on his knee, and occasionally puts her arms around him while she gives him a kiss.

a, c. A Girl Repeatedly Invites a Man to Call upon Her at Her Home

Rita, a chorus girl of good repute, meets at a party given by one of her friends, Steve, for whom she entertains secret hopes. She invites him to call upon her at her apartment, but he declines the invitation on the plea of a previous engagement. She changes the date to a −1.13 night later. He keeps the appointment, and enjoys a perfectly conventional evening, but as he is leaving, Rita asks him to come around the following Tuesday for a bridge party she is giving. On another occasion she asks him to call despite the fact that he gives her no encouragement, extends to her no invitations, and attempts to find plausible excuses for not accepting hers.

a, c. SERIOUSLY APPEALS TO A MAN TO CALL UPON
HER AT HER HOME

−1.17

Zinna meets Martin and engages him in conversation about moving pictures. She tells him that she is an actress out of a job, and consequently has a hard time to make ends meet. She tells him that her divorced husband was terribly cruel to her, and paid her no alimony. During the course of the conversation she dabs her eyes frequently with her handkerchief. She mutters something about being extremely lonely and invites him to call at her apartment next evening.

d. GIRL EXCITES A MAN'S PASSION IN ORDER TO WIN
HIS LOVE

−1.54

Betty, a student of psychology, is "wise" to the connection between love and sex activity. Desperately anxious to win George, she purposely, though subtly, manages to stimulate his erogenous zones so as to excite sex passions.

d. GIRL LURES A MAN TO SEXUAL INTERCOURSE IN
ORDER TO WIN HIM

−1.65

Mabel was very far from "loose" in her sex life. In fact she had, up to this time, been perfectly "straight." But she had so set her heart on Jim that no price seemed too great to pay to get him. When other techniques had failed to work she went to the extreme limit—captured him through luring him into sexual intercourse.

AGGRESSIVENESS OF A GIRL IN
LOVE-MAKING

MOTIVE: Real Love.
TECHNIQUES: Direct Approaches. II.
    e. Takes the initiative in avowing love.
    f. Directly invites avowal.
    g. Indirectly avows love, as in a song or in an expression of solicitude.
    h. Argues for companionship or for marriage.

g. Girl Lets It Be Known Delicately to Man That She Feels Kindly toward Him

+0.24
Dick and Katherine are old friends, and while they have been together a great deal, their love for each other has never been mentioned. Dick is an aviator. One day as he is about to leave on a particularly long and dangerous flight Katherine tells him: "If anything happens to you I don't know what I would do."

g. Girl Offers Herself to Man in Danger

+0.10
Don is leaving home and will be gone for some time on a rather dangerous trip. Rose begs to be taken along, saying: "I must be near you; take me·with you." When he shows her that that would be impossible she adds: "Well, if anything happens to you and you need me, send word; I'll be waiting and ready to come."

e, f, h. A Girl Lets It Be Known to Her Intimate Friends That She Would not Be Averse to a Date with a Particular Man, but Gives No Hint of Such a Thing to Him

+0.03
Lydia has always been a backward girl. When teased about the boys, she has habitually pretended that she has no interest in them. But tonight, when she and Sally are alone, Lydia blushingly confesses that she would give anything to have Bill Treymore for a beau, but she doesn't know how to get him. "Leave that to me," says Sally, and to Lydia's anxious query, "Do you think you really could?" Sally replies, giving her a little push, "You'll see."

f. Girl Asks for Redeclaration of Love

+0.01
Juan and Rosita are lovers, and although Juan's work keeps him away a great deal, he comes to Rosita when he can. As they meet in the garden one day and are engaged in lover's banter, Rosita becomes serious and asks: "Juan, do you really love me?"

g. ADDRESSES A SENTIMENTAL SONG TO THE MAN SHE
LOVES TELLING HIM IN THIS WAY OF HER LOVE

+0.01

Sunny had known Bill very well while she was engaged
as an entertainer in the soldiers' barracks in France.
In fact she had grown quite fond of him, but never displayed her feelings. When they meet after a long absence,
she sings to him a song that they had both sung and
enjoyed years before. This time she accompanies the
words with glances and looks that betray her real feelings.

e.   SERIOUSLY AVOWS HER LOVE FOR HIM AFTER
KNOWING HIM ONLY A SHORT TIME

−0.28

Pierre has been sentenced to life imprisonment at a
penal colony in the South Sea islands. Because of his
good conduct he is assigned to the position of servant in
the warden's house. One of his duties is to accompany
the warden's wife on her shopping expeditions into the
town. She is a beautiful and talented woman, and Pierre
takes pleasure in helping her in many ways about the
house. She apparently becomes greatly attracted to him,
suggests that he make his escape, helps him with his
plans, and shows him that she is deeply interested in his
welfare. On the eve of his departure, he asks her why she is
so much concerned with him, a convict. She replies, after
countering the question for a time, "God help me, but I
love you, and it is better for us both that you leave."

f.   GIRL ASKS POINT BLANK FOR A DECLARATION OF
LOVE

−0.33

John and Susanna have kept steady company for some
time. John has shown affection by his conduct and indirectly by his talk but has made no direct avowal. This
evening as they sit in the swing Susanne, becoming serious,
asks point blank, "Tell me John, do you really love me?"

e, h.   A GIRL FOLLOWS A MAN IN THE HOPES OF
MARRYING HIM

Anne has loved Jim for a long time, but conditions
were such that she could not express any other feelings

−0.37   than those of friendship. Suddenly all obstacles between them were removed. Anne learning that Jim was sailing that night for Europe, engaged passage on the same steamer, met Jim and explained the whole situation.

e. A GIRL TELLS A PARTICULAR MAN THAT HE IS THE
KIND OF FELLOW SHE WOULD LIKE TO MARRY

Catherine and John have been going together for some time, but he, while counting on her for steady company, has never mentioned love or marriage. John is an athlete and is very good at most sports. One day while a group is swimming, and John has been showing exceptional skill, a fellow swimmer needs help and John is the one to reach
−0.47   him and bring him to shore. Catherine, as soon as they are alone, compliments John on his skill and bravery and, hoping to encourage him in his affections toward her, says: "I'm proud of you, John. When I see you so strong, brave, and capable it makes me realize that you are the kind of man I would want to marry."

e.   GIRL LOOKS ARDENTLY AT A MAN

Joetta is introduced to Paul at a party and is immedi-
−0.49   ately impressed. She allows herself to gaze at him ardently, almost spellbound, for about a minute's time.

f. ASKS A MAN POINT BLANK IF HE CARES FOR HER

Jenny and Robert had been palling about quite a bit and they had grown fond of each other. One day a little quarrel caused a separation lasting about a week. Jenny
−0.51   grew rather tired of her inactivity, and chancing to meet Robert on the street one day, stopped him and said impetuously: "Say, are you my boy friend or not? I want to know!"

e. GIRL AVOWS LOVE FOR A MAN WITHOUT WAITING
FOR HIM TO TAKE THE INITIATIVE

Florence and Dick have known each other for a long time and have frequently been thrown together in busi-

ness, and in various social events. Florence loves Dick
and at several times has made slight approaches that
−0.63   might indicate that she would not be averse to some
attention from him. Although he realizes that he loves
her, Dick feels that he must devote more of his time to
business than to love-making. One day when they are
together, seeking to hasten their romance, she comes
close to him, smiles, and says: "I love you, Dick."

g. A Girl Would Attract Her Lover by Singing Love Songs

Lea happens to be sailing on the same ship as her
chosen lover. Peeping out of the port hole she sees him
−0.67   promenading the deck with another girl. She thrusts her
head out of the tiny window and sings the love song he
knows so well.

f, h.   Seriously Urges Marriage upon a Man

When Ruth, after the searchers had found her, tells
Steve she supposes it is the "White Way again for little
Ruthie," he answers: "Do you want me to kidnap you
again?" She replies, "Yes." He is amazed and exclaims,
−0.73   "What!" She counters: "If you can't hear me, come a
little closer." She then asks him if he loves her, and upon
his swearing that he does, she answers: "Oh, Stevie,
don't you see how impossible all of this is? Let's be
married and cut it all. I don't care if you don't have a
cent, we'll get along somehow. Shall we do it—huh?"

h. Girl Argues with a Man That He Should Marry Her

Jeannetta Williams has so long shifted for herself in
the business world that she has lost all respect for the
traditions that her sex should play only a passive rôle in
−0.77   life. When she has set her heart on Bob Jones and he,
while continuing to go with her and show affection, fails
to propose marriage, she herself proffers it and backs up
her proposal with arguments just as she would back up
any business proposition.

h. HER APPROACHES AND LANGUAGE PLAINLY SUGGEST
SERIOUS SOLICITATIONS FOR REPEATED KISSING
AND CARESSES

−0.85
Louise, seriously wishing to marry Alfred, asks him to forget her high social position and to act as though she were of his class. She moves closer to him, lays her head on his shoulder, takes his face between her hands and, looking longingly into his eyes, whispers, "Kiss me, Alfred."

g. A GIRL PULLS A MAN AWAY FROM A CROWD IN
ORDER TO DANCE AND TALK WITH HIM

−0.97
Polly and Kelley are employed as entertainers. Polly develops a "case" on Kelley. When Kelley proves slow about taking the initiative, Polly seizes his hand and pulls him to a table. They ask her to sing. She consents and addresses a sentimental song to Kelley. The orchestra then strikes up for the next dance. Polly puts her arms about Kelley's waist and asks him to dance with her.

e, h. A GIRL TELLS A MAN THAT SHE LOVES HIM AND
THEN PROPOSES MARRIAGE

−1.44
When Audrey first met Dick she decided that he was the man for her. When he failed to take any interest in her she took matters into her own hands. She frequently would call for him in her car and invite him to parties. Finally one day when she had called for him and had taken him to lunch, she told him that she loved him and proposed that they be married.

AGGRESSIVENESS OF A GIRL IN LOVE–MAKING

MOTIVE: Material Advantage.
a. Get a job or promotion.
b. Marriage or companionship for material advantage.
c. Money or presents.
d. Business for employer.

d. GIRL COQUETTES A LITTLE TO ATTRACT CUSTOMERS

−0.09

Marjorie is a very successful waitress in the cabaret in which she works. She supplements alert service by casting pleasant glances and winning smiles upon the men at her tables.

d. A GIRL, IN A SPIRIT OF FUN AND ENTERTAINMENT, SINGS A SENTIMENTAL SONG TO A MAN

−0.17

Criquette is the "headliner" on the program and is greeted with applause as she comes on the floor of the café for her number. As she sings and dances she ap-approaches some particular man and coquettishly addresses to him the sentimental words of her song.

b. GIRL ASKS TO BE ALLOWED TO ACCOMPANY MAN ON A JOURNEY

−0.31

Collette suddenly discovers that she must go to New York. Knowing that her friend, Dick Winters, is leaving in a few hours by aëroplane, she rushes to the airport and begs to be allowed to accompany him.

a. GIRL APPEALS TO A MAN TO GIVE HER BROTHER A JOB

−0.69

Ruth Atkinson has long known Theodore Knight, the manager of the leading theater in the town. Her brother is an excellent violin player and desires to play in the concert orchestra that is daily a part of the entertainment offered by the theater. Ruth arranges to see Theodore and appeals to him to give her brother the position. As she talks with him she acts coyly and holds the lapels of his coat as she smiles up at him saying: "You would do it for little Ruthie, wouldn't you?"

d. A GIRL MAKES PRONOUNCED LOVE APPROACHES TO CUSTOMERS OF A CABARET IN ORDER TO STIMULATE BUSINESS

Luke enters a cabaret. Fifi, a "hostess" in the cabaret, shambles up to his table, begins talking with him, asks

−0.97   him if she may sit beside him. He buys her a drink and
orders another for himself. Soon she is safely seated
on his lap with her arms about his neck calling for more
drinks for both.

a. Girl Flirts with Her Boss in Order to Gain Promotion

−1.22   Louise Johnson is private secretary to the manager
of the department store. She greatly needs a raise in
salary and feels that flirting with the boss would help
her cause. She begins by being especially nice to him
and is careful to see that flowers are placed on his desk
each morning. She smiles and jests with him, and as he
seems to give her a little more attention, she takes occasion to come close to him and once in a while let her hand
rest on his arm. Then one day, after some coquetry, she
proposes that she be given an increase in wages so that,
"Your little secretary may look her best when at work."

c. Flirts with a Man in Order to Gain a Favor

−1.40   It must be confessed that Miss Wench was pretty even
at her worst and she looked exceptionally beautiful in
the fur coat the proprietor of the little store was showing
her. But the price was higher than she wished to pay.
She resorted to the tactics she knew best in order to get
the price down—coquetry. With head tilted slightly to
the side, cheek resting lightly against the soft fur, and
an engaging smile playing over her pretty features, she
said coaxingly: "You'll let me have it cheaper so I can
always look cute when you see me, won't you?"

c. A Woman Extravagantly Flirts in the Hope of Getting Presents from a Wealthy Man

−1.75   Mabel, chorus girl far past the "flaming youth" age,
meets wealthy Mr. Blake. As he is somewhat portly,
she takes keen delight in tickling him, punching him, and
pounding him around as a means of showing her delight
in being with him. She takes him to a party at a hotel
where she lolls all over him and flirts with him unreserv-

edly. After the party, she suggests, and insists, that they go window shopping as she wants to show him the "darlingest" roadster, and the "cutest" fur coat. She pleads somewhat like this: "You'll buy poor little Mabel a fur coat won't you, deary? And I get so tired walking to and from the theater, a car would be such a help."

c.   Girl on Balcony Winks at Man in Street, Inviting Illicit Love

On the second floor balcony of a much traversed city street, a girl is fingering a rose as she studies the faces
−1.76   of men passing by. Finally she catches the eye of one of them. She smiles, kisses the rose, throws it to him, and nods her head toward the room behind her.

b.   Seriously Proposes Marriage to a Man She Does Not Love as a Means of Furthering Her Ambitions

In order not to lose sight of Bill, the man she loves, Sunny stows away on the same ship on which Bill and his fiancée are making a trip to the United States. She
−1.84   is caught before the journey is over, and realizing that she will be deported as soon as the vessel docks, she appeals to Jim, a friend of Bill's, to marry her on board ship, and take her with him as his wife.

c.   A Girl Resorts to Pronounced Love-Making Measures for the Purpose of Enticing a Man to Sex Responses for Money

Dan enters the saloon and orders a drink at the bar. While he is drinking it, a girl comes over to him and
−1.87   invites him to join her at the table. She sits on his lap, ruffles his hair, leans over, whispers in his ear, and at his shaking of his head, holds up two fingers, winks, and leads him out of the room by the hand.

KISSING AND CARESSING

In Private.

    a. By serious lovers or betrothed persons.
    b. By casual lovers.

a. Engaged Couple Exchange a Quick Greeting Kiss in Private

+0.50

Al has just returned from a successful basketball trip. He immediately calls upon his fiancée, Ellen, at her home. As she greets him he takes her two hands in his, then draws her to him, quickly kisses her and as quickly releases her again.

a. A Man Kisses His Fiancée Very Reverently in Private

+0.48

The scene was a beautiful one, no denying that; but for Roger it was enhanced by the fact that the girl whom he was going to marry was standing before him enjoying it too. He watched the soft breeze making little ripples in her hair; it was all too beautiful, too wonderful. Without seeming to be conscious of the act, he lowered his head and brushed Fay's hair with his lips.

a. Lovers Kiss Long and Ardently after Becoming Engaged

+0.46

Joan and Ralph are in love with each other. One night, while walking through the garden with Joan, he can keep the secret of his love for her no longer to himself, and asks her to become his wife. She answers him by slipping into his arms. They kiss long and ardently.

a. Betrothed Persons Exchange a Quick Kiss in Private When Parting

+0.43

Mark and Sara are engaged. After a dinner dance he escorts her to her home. As he leaves they exchange a quick good-night kiss.

a. Lovers Hold Hands in Private

+0.32

Wilma and Jack had wandered into a secluded dell and were seated upon a large rock overlooking the meandering stream with its dark pools where speckled trout swam. Wilma had slipped her hand into Jack's and he continued to hold it as they talked.

a.   BETROTHED PERSONS PET IN PRIVATE

John and Mary indulged in some petting after they became engaged, of course they did; but it was always
+0.31   done in private and limited largely to holding hands and other tender but mild caresses.

a.   BETROTHED PERSONS EXCHANGE A QUICK KISS IN PRIVATE WHEN PARTING

Mark and Sara are in love with each other. After a dinner dance he sees her home to her hotel room. She
+0.30   invites him to stay a little while. After a very brief conversation he gives her a quick good-night kiss and leaves.

a.   MAN KISSES THE HAIR OF THE GIRL HE LOVES

Oliver and Rose have returned from the theater and are sitting listening to the radio. Oliver goes to the
+0.30   radio to select a new program and on returning to his seat pauses back of Rose's chair, stoops, and reverently kisses her hair.

a.   BETROTHED PERSONS KISS LONG AND AMOROUSLY IN PRIVATE

In anticipation of their approaching marriage, George and Evelyn are fastening curtains in the home they are soon to occupy. When Evelyn takes George's place on
+0.21   the ladder to give the final finishing touches, her foot catches in the drapery and she falls toward him. George catches her. Clinging tightly to him she kisses George long and amorously.

a.   BETROTHED PERSONS EXCHANGE QUICK, UNOBTRUSIVE KISSES IN PRIVATE WHEN NOT PARTING

Julia is sitting under a tree a short distance away from her fiance whom she is watching as he sketches the distant mountains. They are alone. Suddenly Baron lays
+0.17   down his brush, shakes his head, and mutters that he cannot get the proper effect. Julia bounds up to him,

looks at the sketch, then gives him a number of short kisses as she says: "Don't be silly, dear. It will be a masterpiece."

b. Casual Lover Kisses Girl's Forehead in Private

A large engineering firm recognized the abilities of Carol Luberg, rising young engineer, and assigned him to a field job that would absent him from his regular office desk for a year. Every one made it a point to wish him +0.10   well. When Ruth, his secretary whom he secretly loved but to whom he dared not propose marriage until he made good, entered his private office and extended her hand to say good-by, he held her hand a moment, and kissed her forehead.

b. Casual Lovers Exchange a Quick Kiss in Private at Parting

Lola and Juan are both members of the evening sales force at the department store. Much of their work is in −0.13   close proximity to each other and they have found each other congenial and pleasant company. Tonight he walks home with her after work and lingers a few minutes at her door. They exchange a quick kiss at parting.

b. A Feint at Kissing Repulsed at the Last Minute

Under the spell of the music, the dance, and especially the romance of the moonlight as they walk in the garden, the courtship of Mary Kennedy and Kenneth Brown develops apace. Mary is thrilled at her adventure, but −0.18   when Kenneth, taking advantage of a little playful pretense at quarreling that has brought their faces close together, makes an approach to kiss her, she first seems to accept the advance but at the last moment turns away her face and repulses the proffered kiss.

a. Engaged Couple Engage in Highly Sensuous Kissing in Private

Dick and Puff have been engaged for about two months, and although they see each other quite frequently, that

−0.34 fact doesn't deter them from throwing a real honest-to-goodness "necking" party whenever they chance to be alone at her home.

a. LOVERS EXCHANGE DRINKING CUPS IN MILD SYMBOLISM FOR KISSING

−0.40 Sam may have been lacking in words with which to express his love for Miriam but intuition provided him another way. After both had sipped a little from their glasses of water, Sam reached over, took Miriam's glass, turned it to the place her lips had touched and drank from it. Miriam slyly accepted Sam's glass in exchange for hers.

a. BETROTHED PERSONS KISS LONG AND AMOROUSLY ON A COUCH IN PRIVATE

−0.46 Grischa and Babka have shared the rough life of a soldiers' camp in the World War through a hard winter. They are passionately in love and have become engaged. Grischa must leave. In their parting moments Babka lies down on the couch with him and they kiss long and ardently.

b. CASUAL LOVERS EXCHANGE A QUICK PLAYFUL KISS

−0.46 Meredith is visiting with a girl friend and a date has been arranged for her with Art Johnson. They prove to get along admirably and at the picnic engage in much playful banter. That evening as they are alone for a few minutes Art suddenly takes her in his arms and, lifting her from the floor, gives her a quick, impulsive kiss.

b. CASUAL LOVERS EXCHANGE A NUMBER OF KISSES

−0.59 It is a beautiful moonlight night. Roy has taken Edith, a week-end guest of his sister, for a boat ride on the lake. Upon returning to the landing they sit upon a near-by rock where Edith reclines upon his shoulder as he holds her close to him. A little later they exchange a kiss, and again kiss ardently as they are about to go back to the house.

b.   Slight Acquaintances Kiss Long and
            Passionately in Private

-1.09
Sara is to have Alfred Melchner, the handsome guest, as her dinner partner. Tired of the dancing that follows, they stroll into the garden and seat themselves in the farther arbor which they are certain no one will enter. He keeps moving closer, puts his head on her shoulder, kisses the back of her hand, the palm of her hand, calls her "Sara," and finally kisses her long and passionately.

a.   Lovers Loll over Each Other and Engage in
            Much Kissing

-1.25
Jane and Bud are in love and spend much time "playing around" together. This evening they are together in Jane's apartment. She is dressed in lounging pajamas. He leans on her semi-prostrate body and they engage in sensuous kissing, lolling over each other on the davenport.

b.   Slight Acquaintances Loll over Each Other in
            a Private Room

-1.39
Angelina and John are together in courtship for the first time. As they sit on the couch Angelina hugs John and pulls him toward her. There follows a long spell of ardent kissing and hugging while they loll over each other.

b.   Slight Acquaintances Engage in Highly Sensu-
            ous Kissing Anticipatory of Sexual Intercourse

-1.71
After the fiesta, where they have met, the Colonel and Peggy have a dinner in her apartment. The dinner over, he puts his arms around her and kisses her, which she accompanies with an "um-um." The final kiss between them is a prolonged one. She throws her arms wildly about him, wiggles ecstatically, and again "um-um," as he remarks of their future pleasures and relationship.

b.   A Married Woman Kisses "Another Man"

Mrs. Fellows feels neglected by her husband, who spends not only all his days but almost all his evenings

−1.85   at his office. This evening she leaves the dance floor to sit out the dance with an admirer in the garden within sight of the office where her husband is still working over his correspondence. As she looks up toward her husband's window she wonders, coquettishly, what he would say if he knew what his wife was doing at that moment. Her partner, understanding the hint, takes her in his arms for a prolonged kiss. This is repeated several times while they joke with each other about the blissful ignorance of the husband.

b.   A MAN KISSES A GIRL AGAINST HER WILL

−2.07   Bored with his own company aboard ship, Frank remembers the attractive maid that tidied his room that morning. In answer to his ring she enters his private cabin questioningly. He immediately takes her into his arms, smiles into her face, says, "I want you to be nice to me," and kisses her in spite of her resistance.

b.   A MARRIED MAN KISSES "ANOTHER WOMAN"

−2.26   Eileen is the rather coquettish secretary of the elderly Mr. Fellows, a married business man. As time goes on the conversations between Fellows and his secretary turn more upon personal rather than business matters. This evening, as they talk in this personal way, their faces are drawn closer and closer together until Mr. Fellows blurts out: "Eileen, you're wonderful!" She replies, coquettishly moving still closer to him, "Think so?" The next instant he has grasped and ardently kissed her.

KISSING AND CARESSING

BY SERIOUS LOVERS OR BETROTHED PERSONS, IN PUBLIC.
     a. Kissing.
     b. Caressing.

b.   BETROTHED PERSONS THROW KISSES IN PUBLIC

While other wives and sweethearts are saying good-by to their parting soldiers, Dave leans over the window of

+0.20   the car trying to say everything he has forgotten to tell his betrothed, Marian. The train begins to move. They both smile bravely, wave, and throw kisses until they lose sight of each other.

a. BETROTHED PERSONS EXCHANGE QUICK, UNOBTRUSIVE KISS IN PUBLIC WHEN PARTING

    Margaret and Bob had long been lovers and, during the past week of glorious house-party vacationing, they have become engaged. A message summons Bob back

+0.14   to the city at once. Although the others of the party gather on the porch to see him off, Margaret hurries down the porch steps to where he is seating himself in his roadster. They exchange a short; unobtrusive kiss.

b. BETROTHED PERSONS EMBRACE IN PUBLIC

    Miriam goes to the railroad station to meet her fiance, Gilbert, who has been away on a business trip for sev-

+0.14   eral weeks. As he steps off the Pullman, they embrace quickly but, withal, warmly, and hurry off to the waiting taxi.

b. FIANCE HOLDS AND PATS FIANCÉE'S HAND IN PUBLIC

    After dinner the whole party lounged about the stern of the yacht waiting for the moon to come dripping up

−0.03   out of the ocean. While the others exchanged anecdotes, Helen leaned against her fiance, who was sitting beside her with his arm lying on the rail behind her, and slipped her hand into his. He patted and held it.

a. BETROTHED PERSONS KISS LONG AND ARDENTLY IN PUBLIC

    Pauline and Andrea are engaged but have been kept apart for five years by an accident at sea. News finally reaches the little town that Andrea is aboard the ship

−0.04   that is to dock that day. Pauline hurries to the wharf. The ship is finally anchored—she sees him, the gangplank clangs into place—she is in his arms. She takes his face between her hands and kisses him long and passionately.

a. A GIRL KISSES HER FIANCÉ IN PUBLIC AS A MEANS OF ENCOURAGEMENT

The day of the big game has arrived. Bill, who has been on the bench practically the whole season, is to be given his big chance, for the 'varsity man at halfback had been seriously hurt in scrimmage a few days before.
—0.06 Bill is nervous, and he is not ashamed to tell his fiancée, Arline, his condition as they walk together towards the playing field. She stops him, turns him toward her and says: "Please, Bill, do your best—you know I'll be watching you all the time." With that, she kisses him full on the lips, and runs toward the stadium.

a. BETROTHED PERSONS KISS LONG AND ARDENTLY IN PUBLIC ON PARTING

Tamazine and Andrea have been engaged for only a short time, but the wedding date and all the plans have been fixed. Three days before the great day, Andrea is
—0.11 called away on a trip which will necessitate his being gone for several months. Just before he steps onto the gangplank of the ship, he turns to his fiancée—forgets the crowd, the world, everything—as he kisses her long and passionately.

b. LOVERS HOLD HANDS IN PUBLIC

John and Mary had come to care more for each other than for the company of others. And so they withdrew from the big reception room of the fraternity house into
—0.15 a somewhat less public side room. There they sat—on the davenport—talking. As they talked, John now and then placed his hand over Mary's and pressed it—which act, because they were lovers, Mary did not resist.

a. COUPLE, ON BECOMING ENGAGED, KISS IN PUBLIC

Tatiana and Prince Charles are guests of honor at a dinner party. Suddenly Prince Charles arises, calls for
—0.17 silence, and announces that Tatiana has just promised to be his wife. He takes her by the hand, and as she stands to acknowledge the plaudits of her friends, he takes her into his arms and kisses her.

a. A FEINT AT KISSING

−0.31 Grace and Paul have withdrawn from the ballroom and are together on the porch. Paul takes her hand and, as their faces are drawn close together, they are about to exchange a kiss when the sudden appearance of some other dancers interrupts them.

a. LOVERS EXCHANGE A LONG PARTING KISS IN PUBLIC

−0.36 Anna and Mat love each other, but Anna, realizing the circumstances that make their marriage impossible, proceeds to tell Mat that this must be the end. They are walking a little ahead of the others towards the ninth hole where they are to tee off. He forces himself to accept the truth for her sake, turns to her and says, "May I say good-by?" They exchange a prolonged kiss. It demonstrates the depth of their love, and the struggle in giving each other up.

a. LOVER KISSES GIRL'S HAIR IN PUBLIC

−0.54 Sarah and Bob have been going together for a little over a year. They were very much in love with each other, and on this particular occasion, a party at a friend's house, Bob could not resist the temptation to kiss Sarah, at least on the hair, when she chanced to be standing near him.

a. MAN STEALS A KISS FROM HIS FIANCÉE IN PUBLIC

−0.59 Roger has grown tired waiting for the great man to pass before the assembled multitudes, and he studies his fiancée's face as a bit of change in scenery. Rather unconscious of the people about him, he leans over and kisses Marie lightly on the cheek.

b. FIANCE KEEPS ARM LYING LOOSELY ABOUT HIS FIANCÉE'S SHOULDERS PUBLICLY

−0.63 Mary and Charles have announced their engagement and are being entertained by some friends at a theater party. After helping Mary remove her wraps, Charles takes the chair next to hers and, throughout much of the performance, keeps his arm lying loosely about the shoulders of his fiancée.

a. BETROTHED PERSONS EXCHANGE QUICK, UNOBTRUSIVE KISSES IN PUBLIC WHEN NOT PARTING

−0.63   Gordon has entered the room unannounced. When Dulcy, his fiancée, sees him she launches herself at him with an "Oh, Gordy" followed by several big hugs and some emphatic, but quite brief, kisses.

b. BETROTHED PERSONS WALK AND STAND IN PUBLIC WITH ARMS ABOUT EACH OTHER

−0.93   Smith meets his fiancée, Ruth, outside the coffee shop where they are accustomed to lunch together. When he has shared the news of his promotion and increased salary, they make a grimace at their old lunching place, turn on their heels, and walk down the street with arms about each other to the "Old Homestead Tea Room."

a.   SERIOUS LOVERS KISS ARDENTLY IN PUBLIC

−1.01   Of course they were in love, or they surely wouldn't have gone together this long. Everybody knew it, at home; and when John and Betty happened to be with a group of only slight acquaintances on a yachting trip, they did not allow this fact to hinder them from expressing their love. They met on the deck one morning, and kissed long and ardently even though several others were up and about.

a. ENGAGED COUPLE KISS AS THEY WALK ALONG IN PUBLIC

−1.07   It was one of those rare days in spring, and Joan and Kenneth were taking advantage of it by walking along the country road arm in arm. From time to time, and utterly disregarding the passing vehicles, Kenneth would lean over and kiss Joan on the cheek, or again, they would stop and do the thing right.

a. A MARRIED WOMAN, IN LOVE WITH ANOTHER MAN, ACCEPTS A KISS FROM HIM

−1.17 Unfortunately, Tonio was married to a man whom she did not love. When Marshall, a guest at the home, came into her life, she just could not help falling in love with him. In spite of the effort of both of them to suppress it, their love reached a climax at which she yielded herself to the embrace of Marshall while he ardently kissed her.

KISSING AND CARESSING

BY CASUAL LOVERS OR SLIGHT ACQUAINTANCES, IN PUBLIC.
   a. Kissing.
   b. Caressing.

a. A SLIGHT ACQUAINTANCE ACKNOWLEDGES AN INTRODUCTION TO A WOMAN BY KISSING HER HAND

−0.00 Grace Barnes is being fêted in the home of her uncle and aunt who live in Virginia. Colonel Morgan is announced and is properly introduced to Grace by her aunt Lucy. He acknowledges the introduction by bowing and kissing her hand.

a. SLIGHT ACQUAINTANCES KISS AS A GAME PENALTY

−0.24 A game is played where the boy that catches the girl may exact a kiss from her. Duke catches Fifi and she gives him a kiss. He asks for another but she says, "I should say not," and runs teasingly away.

a. A FEINT AT KISSING

−0.31 Grace and Paul have withdrawn from the ballroom and are together on the porch. Paul takes her hand and, as their faces are drawn close together, they are about to exchange a kiss when the sudden appearance of some other dancers interrupts them.

b. CASUAL LOVER THROWS GIRL KISSES IN PUBLIC

Sam has had a glorious time at this port with a little Irish waitress named Nellie, whom he met at a restaurant.

−0.38   His boat is due to leave in a very few minutes, so Nellie
        hurries with him to the wharf.   He scrambles up the
        gangplank, but before taking his place on deck, he waves
        her a good-by and throws kisses.

        a. Casual Lover Kisses Girl's Forehead in Public

        During a vacation holiday at a mountain resort Charles
        met Sara.   Having many interests in common, they
        shared many pleasures together in a "brother-sister"
        way.   The last evening they were together they dined
−0.46   and danced at a large party.   As they stood talking near
        the close of the evening, Charles thinking only of the
        fact that they would soon be parting and forgetting that
        curious eyes might be watching, stopped and quickly
        kissed the forehead of his partner.

        b. Casual Lover Has Arm Lying about Girl in
                            Public

        A friend of Jack's has telephoned that his Dad gave
        him the car for the afternoon.   "Get the girl friend, Jack,
−0.52   and I'll be right over."   In a few more minutes Jack is
        helping Joan into the rumble seat, has taken the seat
        beside her, and has placed his arm about her shoulders.

        a.   Lovers Exchange a Quick Kiss in Public

        It was the day of the big game and many of the boys
        were calling at the sorority house for their girls.   Several
        couples were on the porch when Anne came out on the
−0.54   porch to meet Bob who was standing on the steps.   He
        suddenly lifted her from her feet, gave her a quick kiss
        and deposited her on the sidewalk amid the good-natured
        laughter of the crowd.

        a.   Old Friends Exchange a Quick Kiss upon
                      Meeting in a Restaurant

        When they were young together in the town in which
        they lived, this little group of boys and girls had had
        plenty of good times together.   But their life work had
−0.68   caused them to drift apart so that it was probably about

twenty years until Gus and his wife chanced to meet two
of their former friends in a New York restaurant. Gus
immediately rushed to his old friends and greeted each
of the girls with a kiss on the cheek.

b. CASUAL LOVER HOLDS AND PATS GIRL'S HAND IN
PUBLIC

Every Saturday night Clarence takes Molly to the
movies. When the feature picture is flashed on the screen
−0.71 he takes her hand in his and holds it throughout the entire show. At moments of intense drama or sentiment
he squeezes or pats it.

b. CASUAL LOVERS WALK WITH ARMS ABOUT EACH
OTHER IN PUBLIC

The stimulating autumn air and the brilliant glory of
the trees turning brown or golden in the wake of early
frost, evidently had their lure for "the rising genera-
−0.82 tion." For the mountain roads were dotted here and
there with little groups of hikers. Some lads maintained
a dignified aloofness from their ladies, a few were content
merely to lead each other by the hand, but many strolled
along with arms about each others' waists.

a. A MERE ACQUAINTANCE KISSES ANOTHER AS A
SYMBOL OF GRATITUDE

Sally is very grateful to Blair, the go-between, for
−1.02 having asked his friend to dance with her. To thank
Blair she runs to him, kisses him lightly on the lips, then
as suddenly disappears into the crowd.

a. SLIGHT ACQUAINTANCES KISS LONG AND
PASSIONATELY IN PUBLIC

Seeing Duke enter the cabaret at Harve, the dancing
girls run up to him, caress him, etc. When Duke sends
off the man who has been offending one of these dancers,
−1.15 Fifi, she winks at him, asks him how she can thank him,
then proceeds to accept his invitation to nestle on his
lap. They exchange long, passionate kisses as he crush-
ingly embraces her.

a. SLIGHT ACQUAINTANCES ENGAGE IN UNABASHED
CARESSING IN PUBLIC

−1.26 The Delta Mu Omicron's were celebrating House Party. After the dance on Saturday night, couples could be seen lounging about in chairs, davenports, etc., kissing and caressing entirely unmindful of the presence of others engaged in the same pastime.

a.   A WOMAN BESTOWS KISSES FOR MONETARY REASONS

−1.37 Marie operates a shop in France where meat is sold. A soldier comes in just before leaving for the front. When he wants to kiss her, she says, "One dollar, one sausage, one kiss." The soldier then gives her a dollar and she gives him the sausage followed by an energetic kiss.

a.   SLIGHT ACQUAINTANCES KISS IN PUBLIC

−1.39 Perhaps a sedan automobile seems to the occupants to give more shelter than it actually does. At any rate either Grace and Charles thought so or else they cared little about the gaze of passers-by. In spite of the fact that they had by no means reached the stage of betrothal, one looking in that direction at the right moment could have seen them "spoon" and kiss.

b.   CASUAL LOVERS LOLL OVER EACH OTHER IN PUBLIC

−1.83 Having nothing to do, the volunteer fire company takes out the ladder wagon for a joy ride. They pick up a load of girl acquaintances—a lassie for each laddie. When, an hour later, the wagon returns to its unloading place each girl is lolling over her boy—head on his shoulders, sitting on his lap, or even reclining on his semi-prostrate body.

KISSING AND CARESSING

MARRIED PEOPLE.
  a. In private.
  b. In public.

a.   MARRIED PEOPLE HOLD HANDS IN PRIVATE

+0.76
Although Mr. and Mrs. Swartz have been married a good many years they have not stopped the caressing that characterized their courtship days. Often when they are alone in the living room, the husband will sit by his wife holding her hand as they talk.

a.   HUSBAND AND WIFE EXCHANGE A BRIEF KISS IN PRIVATE

+0.73
At times husbands are more sentimental than at others. This evening as Mrs. Waverly sat upon the davenport idly listening to the radio program her husband came up behind her and gently kissed her on the cheek.

a.   HUSBAND AND WIFE EXCHANGE LONG AMOROUS KISS IN PRIVATE

+0.73
Judie and Martin have been married a number of years. One day he comes home with a huge box of flowers for her; he has remembered her birthday. She throws her arms around him and they kiss long and ardently.

a.   HUSBAND AND WIFE KISS ARDENTLY IN PRIVATE AFTER BEING SEPARATED FOR SOME TIME

+0.64
Bill Williams had been sent to South America by the mining concern for which he worked and had been separated from his wife for nearly a year. Upon his return they first meet in the living room of their home. He has surprised his wife by returning a day earlier than he had planned. They kiss long and ardently.

b.   HUSBAND THROWS WIFE A KISS IN PUBLIC

+0.61
A great crowd has gathered to see the brave aviator who is about to start on his lone continental flight. The aviator examines the motor, crawls into the cockpit, then scans the crowd. Suddenly his face lights up for he has caught sight of his wife waving him a farewell. With a sigh and a smile he throws her a kiss and is on his way.

b. HUSBAND PRESSES WIFE'S HAND IN PUBLIC UPON PARTING

+0.58   Each day Mr. Lodge visits his wife at the hospital, where she is recovering from the serious injuries she received in an automobile accident. All too soon the nurse appears to announce that his visit must be concluded. He rises from the bedside, presses his wife's hand warmly, and with a cheery remark, takes his leave.

b. HUSBAND TAKES WIFE IN HIS ARMS AND KISSES HER TENDERLY IN PUBLIC

+0.58   The elderly statesman leaves the bedside of his sick wife to attend a celebration where he will be given honors toward which he and his wife have yearned for years. Almost at the climax of the celebration the wife silently enters the great room. The surprised husband takes her into his arms and kisses her tenderly.

b. HUSBAND AND WIFE EXCHANGE BRIEF PARTING KISS IN PUBLIC

+0.51   With the approach of the hot summer months, Mrs. Wilkins leaves the city for their summer home in the White Mountains, where her husband will join her later for his month's vacation. Mr. Wilkins accompanies his wife to the railway station, and as she is about to leave, he kisses her lightly on the lips.

b. HUSBAND HOLDS AND PATS WIFE'S HAND IN PUBLIC

+0.50   With the assurance that the caller is a nurse who has brought news of their son who was reported wounded at the front, Mr. and Mrs. Boyd welcome her and invite her confidence. As they are sitting on the divan listening to the nurse's story, Mrs. Boyd slips her hand into Mr. Boyd's. He pats it gently and holds it.

b. MARRIED COUPLE EXCHANGE PARTING KISS IN PUBLIC

Previous to the opening of the baseball season the squad is about to leave for the "sunny South" for their

+0.32 annual spring training. The young pitcher's wife has accompanied him to the local railway station where he will embark to join his comrades. Just as the train pulls in, he embraces and kisses her several times and then hurries to join his mates.

b. HUSBAND KISSES WIFE'S HAIR REVERENTLY IN PUBLIC

+0.30 The Greens were not so young as they once had been but you could not have made them believe so. When a group of friends was joking them about their age, George looked down at his wife's hair, just beginning to turn gray, and a recollection of their long companionship overwhelming him, he lightly pressed his lips upon her crown.

b. HUSBAND AND WIFE KISS ARDENTLY ON MEETING IN PUBLIC

+0.14 It was back in those earlier days when the West was still somewhat rough. Earl Stanford had left his young wife, and together with three other men had gone the long journey from the mining settlement to the nearest railroad town to sell their bullion. Upon their return, almost the entire village of about fifty inhabitants came together in the one main street to greet their brave young men. As Earl spied his wife he ran to her and they exchanged a number of ardent kisses.

b. HUSBAND GIVES WIFE A QUICK GREETING KISS IN PUBLIC

+0.06 Mrs. Reese has come to the city a few days in advance of her husband. He meets her first when she is seated in a restaurant. They exchange a very quick greeting kiss.

b. HUSBAND AND WIFE EXCHANGE A LONG, AMOROUS KISS IN PUBLIC

"If you young people think that mistletoe was put there for just your use, we'll show you." With that

−0.27   Bruce deliberately offered his arm to his wife, led her
under the mistletoe, and to the amusement of the whole
party, kissed her long and amorously.

b. HUSBAND AND WIFE EXCHANGE A NUMBER OF LONG, ARDENT KISSES PUBLICLY

From the side of the stage Marie has watched her
husband's every movement as he held his audience spellbound. Having finished, he acknowledges the thunder-
−0.33   ous applause and hurries from the stage. But before his
many back-stage friends can crush their way to his side,
Marie has slipped into his arms. They embrace and kiss
long and ardently several times in succession.

b.   HUSBAND AND WIFE EXCHANGE A KISS FOR PUBLICITY PURPOSES

Blair, an internationally known athlete, has just married Sally at an elaborate church wedding. As they are
−0.52   coming out of the church a photographer shouts, "Kiss
your bride." Obediently the bride and groom pose with
a prolonged kiss.

b. MARRIED COUPLE LOLL OVER EACH OTHER IN PUBLIC

Luke and Grace, who have just been married, are
among a group of relatives that is talking and lounging
−1.47   about in the living room. Indifferent to the presence
of the others, she climbs on his lap, ruffles his hair, caresses
his cheek, kisses his forehead, entwines her arms about
his neck, and nestles against him.

DEMOCRATIC ATTITUDES AND PRACTICES

THEME: Race relations, General.

WHITE MAN SACRIFICES POLITICAL AMBITIONS, SUCCESS, AND FRIENDS TO ADVOCATE FULL RIGHTS AND CITIZENSHIP FOR THE INDIANS

Yancy Cravat was a nominee for governor of old Okla-
homa when the question of Indian rights came to the
fore. In the face of adverse public opinion, Yancy at

once took up the cause of the Indians, championed their rights, and by means of forceful political addresses and +1.09 terse newspaper editorials advocated full citizenship privileges for the male Indians. He knew all the while that he was sacrificing his chance to become governor, that his political life was as good as dead, and that he was making many enemies, but none of these considerations swerved him from his devotion to the cause of the cheated Indians.

An Indian Played Up in a Favorable Light

In this story chief Cachan was portrayed as tall, erect, and dignified in appearance. In character he possessed some of the vanity of a primitive race yet was on the +0.49 whole sportsmanlike and of sound practical sense. Although he was revengeful toward his enemies he was ready to be just, or even generous, to those who dealt fairly with him.

Rate: the propriety of playing up an Indian in a favorable light.

Chinese, Mexicans, and Other Similar Races Played in Attractive Rôles

Occasionally Chinese, Mexicans, and persons of other similar races are played up in books and in motion pic- +0.36 tures in rôles that show these people in a favorable light. The Chinaman or Mexican is shown as intelligent and manly and as exhibiting a human nature as attractive as that of American characters.

Jews Played Up in an Attractive Rôle

In a certain movie a Jewish family was played up in an attractive manner. The members of the family loved one another, the children respected their parents, and the +0.32 parents sacrificed and solved their domestic problems as best they knew how, just as the better families of any other race might do.

Thing to rate, playing up a Jewish family in an attractive rôle.

THESE GIRLS MINGLE WITH NO RACE ANTIPATHIES

It was strange how free from race consciousness these girls were. The majority of them were Americans but over here was a Jewess of pronounced Hebrew type, over there an Italian girl, and beyond her a Negro lass. But +0.29 they all chatted in unconstrained friendliness while awaiting the start of the machines. From the frankness with which they teased one another about their prospective "dates" you would not have judged that their prospective gallants ranged all the way from blond to black.

HIS INTELLECT ADMITS RACIAL EQUALITY BUT HIS FEELINGS AND HIS CONDUCT LAG BEHIND

Although Bolonius accepts as an intellectual proposition the idea that there should be no discrimination against Negroes, Indians, and colored races, he does not in fact feel quite as much at home with them as with −0.47 members of his own race. When circumstances compel him to ride in the same seat with one of them, instead of entering into a genial conversation as he would with one of his own kind, he remains "glum" or confines himself at most to brief and rather cold comments.

FORBIDS MARRIAGE ON ACCOUNT OF SMALL STRAIN OF COLOR

Sally Morgan is the daughter of a wealthy ranch owner in the West. There is an Indian reservation near by and one of the boys who has only a little Indian blood in his −0.51 veins frequently visits the ranch. Sally falls in love with this young man. But her father strenuously opposes the match on the ground of the color strain, and Sally is finally obliged to give up her lover.

AN INDIAN GIRL DOES NOT FIT IN THE SOCIAL LIFE

It was not that the girls disliked Hilda. And certainly it was not that she made herself in any way offensive. Indeed, realizing that because she was half-breed Indian she would need to watch her step carefully if she were

to make a place for herself in the laundry, she put her-
−0.79   self to pains to avoid any offense. But somehow when
she would join in the conversation, the social atmosphere
would be immediately chilled; her own little hopes seemed
out of place among those of the white girls. Hilda, soon
coming to detect this, became content to listen and to
say only to herself the thoughts that came to her mind.
Thing to rate, that the girl's race made a difference.

Jews Played Up in an Unattractive Rôle

Very frequently in moving pictures a Jewish character
is played up in an unattractive way. He is very often
−0.92   made to appear grasping and miserly. He is presented
in the person of a character with heavy face, shaggy
whiskers, and offensive gestures. Not infrequently he is
assigned a criminal rôle.

She Holds a Latent Prejudice against Jews

Sally is showing Mabel a coat that she had purchased
a short time before, and is complaining that the cuffs
−1.02   are about worn through. "Well, Sally, I warned you not
to get it from old Levi—what could you expect from a
Jew?"

Chinese, Mexicans, and Other Similar Races Played in Unattractive Rôles

Very often Chinese, Mexicans, and persons of other
similar races are played up in unattractive rôles. They
−1.02   are made to appear cruel and crude in manners and
appearance and dirty in personal habits, and are often
played in criminal rôles.

Exploits All Races Other than His Own

Both in theory and in practice Mr. Kettering was a
thorough convert to the doctrine of the superiority of the
Nordic race. In his political ideas he held to the desirability of debarring from every public office all but "hundred
per cent Americans." He was for shutting out from the
labor unions all "inferior races" and for restricting the

−1.17   area of their economic activities to menial labor while the descendents of North-European stocks took the directive positions. And in his own private business in the Orient he had no scruples whatever about the most thoroughgoing exploitation of the native colored peoples; from his point of view nature had made them for the benefit of his superior race.

INDIANS TREATED AS INFERIOR TO WHITE MEN

A political mass meeting was to be held in a large open amphitheater. The crowd of whites and Indians far exceeded the number the grandstand could hold. The Indians were immediately barred from a grandstand seat and arrangements made for them to sit on crude,
−1.25   improvised bleachers, since it was believed that the Indians couldn't appreciate good seats anyhow; that they would not understand the speakers' messages no matter how much of them they heard; and that the Indians certainly had to be made to understand that, since white men are of a superior race, the latter have first claims.

THEY DON'T LIKE A DUTCHMAN

Van Horn is a Pennsylvania German who inherited a large southern plantation. The people of the South
−1.36   resent his presence a little as shown by such remarks as: "That old Dutchman," and "He better mind his own business."

THIS MAN DESPISES JEWS

Horace James, an otherwise kindly and generous publisher, harbors a peculiarly strong dislike for the sons of Israel. He will not tolerate them about him, and none
−1.52   dare appeal to him for employment. He takes frequent occasion to print articles and editorials discrediting, and sometimes slandering, them. He refuses to subscribe to any of their charities in any manner whatsoever.

TALKS DISPARAGINGLY ABOUT OTHER RACES

"Ah, what do I care, he's only a Wop!" "Indians? Greasers? Humph! one's as crooked as the other. Not

-1.60   a truthful thought in their heads. Just as soon steal from a baby as not. Mexicans, rot!" Typical of Mr. Godfrey's attitude toward all foreigners are the above phrases. He doesn't like them, but he confines his prejudice to talking ill about them.

DEMOCRATIC ATTITUDES AND PRACTICES

THEME: Race relations, Negroes.[1]

DEFENDS COLORED MAN'S RIGHTS AT EXPENSE OF HIS OWN SAFETY

It was whispered in advance that the crowd would not let the Negro speak. When he arose to begin his address it became clear what the plan was. A tomato, and then another, whizzed by the stand and hands-in-coat-pockets indicated that many more were to come. But Professor Berry, who had long held high ideals of political equality for blacks and whites alike, mounted +0.84   the platform and stepped before the scheduled speaker. In a well-controlled but commanding voice he called out. "Just wait a minute." And then, at the risk of both his social position and his job in the border college, he rebuked the crowd for its lack of Americanism and demanded that the Negro have the privilege of free speech which had been guaranteed to him as a fundamental democratic right.

Thing to rate, Professor Berry's act.

A NEGRO IS PRESENTED AS SOMETHING OF A HERO

Rastus had been played up in a certain movie as a somewhat stupid Negro. He wished to be an expert electric repairman, though he had none of the mechan-

---

[1] Since our scale-makers were prevailingly from the north and the west, the evaluations on this scale doubtless express a sectional point of view. Where mores differ so much as they do on this question it would probably be necessary, in order to give an adequate description of the mores of our society, to have separate scales describing the approvals of the several groups. To throw all of the evaluations together into a single composite would tend to give all zero values and really describe the mores of no group at all. This is true not only of this race element but of every mos in respect to which there is a negative correlation between groups.

ical ability to make him so. One day the telegraph wire
was torn in a terrific storm, just at an hour when the
governor needed to send a telegram to save an innocent
+0.75   man's life. Rastus finds the break but is unable to bring
the ends of the wire together. The loyal Negro therefore
grasps the two wires in his hands, makes electric connection by means of his watch chain, and stands through
the storm until exhausted holding the wires so that the
connection may not be broken—long enough to permit
the sending of the life-saving message.

Rate the propriety of playing up a Negro as a hero.

A WHITE BOY IS OPENLY A FRIEND OF A NEGRO

When Sam, the faithful and innocent Negro servant,
is discharged in disgrace, Joe, one of the white aristocrats
and friend of the employers' family, meets him in the
+0.58   stable and bids him an affectionate farewell. "If you
ever need a friend," says Joe, "call on me." When later
Joe finds Sam serving in a restaurant the white boy shows
unbridled joy at seeing him again and the two engage in
a hearty exchange of pleasantries.

A NEGRO SERVANT PLAYED UP IN AN ATTRACTIVE RÔLE

Throughout a certain motion picture Sam, a Negro
servant, is played up in a modest but attractive rôle.
He is kind to his horse, even chummy with him. When
Jack, his employer's son, proves false to Sam, this Negro
boy does not counter but instead loyally takes on himself
the blame for Jack's misdeed. Discharged by his em-
+0.52   ployer for this supposed misdeed, Sam maintains a fine
optimism, sings a song about "What's the use of worry-
ing?" and, along with regrets at leaving the family he
has so long served and loved, modestly but confidently
asserts that he will find some way of taking care of himself. His conduct is so presented as to arouse the warm
admiration of spectators.

Thing to rate, the propriety of showing a Negro in
such a favorable light.

COLOR NO BARRIER TO FRIENDSHIP

+0.28

Marie was preparing in college for work as a foreign missionary. To the college there came a Negro girl—a rather unusual thing for that institution. She was likely to be snubbed, and certain to be friendless. But Marie resolved to begin her missionary work at home, she took the Negress as suite-mate and fraternized with her about the campus in as free and friendly a manner as if she had not been colored.

HE FRATERNIZES WITH NEGROES AS HE WOULD WITH OTHER FOLKS

+0.14

Van Horn can, somehow, never get acclimated to the social atmosphere of the South, at least in respect to treatment of Negro workmen. He persists in slapping them on the back in a friendly way, "messing" with them, and swapping stories. In consequence there grows up between him and his "niggers" a fellow-feeling and a mutual admiration that is not paternalistic or patronizing but genuinely fraternal.

HE FEELS "SQUIRMISH" TO BE WALKING WITH A NEGRO

−0.54

If you search your own heart perhaps you will not find it unnatural that Jinks should feel a little "squirmish" to be walking down a business street with a Negro workman. He was entirely decent to the colored man, it is true, but he did hope that none of his aristocratic friends would see him, and was heartily glad when they arrived at the corner where their ways parted.

HE IS DISTINCTLY UNCOMFORTABLE SITTING BY A NEGRO

−0.86

When the train reached Stanton Station there remained no unoccupied full seats in the coach. The Reverend George Washington Johnson, colored pastor of the Stanton African Methodist Church, was therefore obliged to "double up." He took his seat by Thomas Winton. Winton straightened up, evidently feeling uneasy to be seated by a Negro, and surveyed the accommodations of the coach. After a while he got up, left his seat, and moved to another part of the car where he could share a seat with one of his own race.

A Negro Not to Be Called Mister

−0.89

Carl Jacobs was from the North and was consequently somewhat naïve about race relations. Wishing to find the home of a certain Negro, he inquired of some white men where Mr. Amson lived. After conferring among themselves these men replied that no such person lived in that neighborhood. Finally it occurred to one of them to say: "Oh, that's Jake Robb's nigger. Young fellow, we don't call niggers mister around here."

Colored Athlete Refused Admittance to New York Hotel

−1.08

Lee is a member of the college cross-country team. He is a good runner but is handicapped due to his race; he is colored. The boys on the team like Lee and treat him as they would any other member. On a trip to New York he is taken to the hotel with the rest of the team but the manager refuses to give him a room because of his color—much to his personal embarrassment and to the dislike of the team. He is forced to secure quarters in another part of the city.

This Negress Was Unwelcome in the High School

−1.08

Very few Negroes had yet been seen within the classrooms of the high school of Okaloosa, Minn. But Minerva was especially brilliant and especially ambitious, so that she overcame the barriers that had hitherto kept her race out of high school of this aristocratic little city. But she soon discovered that not all the barriers were on the outside. She was out of everything—except what the law guaranteed her. Every group she approached with proffers of companionship greeted her with only a stony stare. Her scholarship all had to admit, but in comradeship she was as lonely as if she had lived on a desert island.

He Hates an Ambitious "Nigger"

It was no wonder that all of Saul's enemies, and some of his friends, called him "nigger hater." For the rise of the Negro race toward social and economic equality with the whites was his chief phobia. He was ready to admit, to be sure, that "niggers" have their place and are all right as long as they keep in their place; but it was evident that the place to which he would assign them was complete servitude to the whites with no glimmer of ambition to rise to a place of dignity and prestige of their own. And thus it was very natural that his home should be the rendezvous for mobs bent on frightening Negroes from casting votes and on driving "dangerous" ones out of the country.

−1.23

DEMOCRATIC ATTITUDES AND PRACTICES

Theme: Treatment of Employees and Subordinates.

Employer Places Confidence in His Employees

It was the policy of Russ Stoad to show confidence in his employees. Even when at heart he was not entirely convinced of the ability of particular ones to meet certain emergencies, he would still maintain an outward attitude of confidence. This he did not do for the sake of extra profits but out of respect for the dignity and the personality of his employees.

+1.06

He Treats His Subordinates as He Would Be Treated

It was not that Jacobson was "soft" as a boss. He knew, and so did his men, that the company would check up on what the gang was accomplishing and would demand from it as much as from any other gang. But Jacobson had laid on his heart that he would do by others as he would be done by, and he carried this principle into his foremanship. When the job was especially heavy he did not feel too dignified himself to take a hand along with his men. If reprimand or correction was to be given,

+1.05

it was done with keen recognition of the sensibilities of
the man. He was often known to take his place in the
ditch for an hour at a time to care for the work of a
subordinate rather than to have the fellow "docked" for
absence.

EMPLOYER GIVES PRESENTS TO EMPLOYEES

Old Man Zupper paid and treated his office force exceptionally well. He knew also that they were doing their
very best to show their appreciation. Vacation time came,
+1.05 and as each man in his turn was about to leave, Zupper
would call him into his office, hand him ten or twenty
dollars extra "for the wife and kiddies" or make him a
present of a traveling bag, or some other timely gift.

EMPLOYER HEARTILY CONGRATULATES HIS EMPLOYEES AFTER THEY HAVE COMPLETED A PARTICULARLY BRILLIANT BIT OF WORK

"Horseshoes," cub reporter for the *Evening World*,
had just sent in a scoop of great importance to the City
Editor. There was nothing particularly difficult about
getting the story, and "Horseshoes" considered it noth-
+0.95 ing more than part of his day's work. When he sauntered
into the office sometime later, the City Editor jumped
up, grabbed his hand, slapped him on the back, and con-
gratulated him on his brilliant piece of work.

EMPLOYER TREATS EMPLOYEES KINDLY AND FAMILIARLY

Thinking he had made a mistake in his work, Brady
went to Mr. Krist's office for advice. When his employer
saw Brady he smiled, and greeted: "Hello, Jack, old boy!
+0.91 Are you still plugging away at that blue-print?" Then
as he pushed a box of cigars toward Jack, he added:
"Take a puff at one of these and relax a moment, son,
while I look at it."

EMPLOYER TREATS SERVANT WITH RESPECT

Mr. Lawrence never thinks of Clark, his butler, as a
mere servant but rather as a friend and gentleman. As

+0.87   such, he asks his advice on many questions, weighs and
follows out his suggestions, and always treats Clark with
respect.

Treats Prisoners Firmly but Considerately

+0.81   Warden Healy realizes his responsibility, and enforces
to the letter all the rules he has laid down in order to
maintain discipline in his Penitentiary. However, if the
men have any complaint he listens to them, and either
corrects the situation or explains to the inmates just
why such an alteration cannot be effected.

An Army Officer Goes Out of His Way to Be Kind to a Common Soldier

+0.80   Colonel Sarig took a particular liking to young private
Dick Rust, so he was more than kind to him. Though
he selected Dick as his orderly, he would at no time permit Dick to unlace his superior's boots. Though Dick
was a mere private the Colonel never considered him as
such, but granted him privileges and leaves. One night
Colonel Sarig insisted that Dick go with him to a special
party. When Dick hesitated to accept, the Colonel said,
"Come on, Dick. We're brothers under the skin."

Man of Royal Standing Does Not Want Servants to Act Humbly before Him

+0.79   Prince William has just added a new member to the
servants of his royal household. The new servant immediately bows himself to the floor before his master; but the
Prince speaks, saying: "My servants need not bow before
me."

He Is Open to Approaches and to Advice

+0.65   Mr. Salisbury, president of a large men's clothing establishment is very much concerned about the attitude
of his employees toward the store policy. He calls a
meeting of all his employees once a month, at which
grievances, suggestions, or opinions as to methods are
discussed. He urges his help to bring their ideas to him

but uses discrimination as to what advice to accept. He is friendly at all times and only reasonably strict in enforcing the various rules of the establishment. He permits some of the older men to call him by his first name in private—and is habitually addressed about the store as "chief."

TREAT SERVANTS WELL, BUT PERMIT NO FAMILIARITY

Mr. and Mrs. Williston show their servants every consideration that they possibly can. Each has his afternoon and evening off. The servants may entertain their friends in their quarters whenever they please. They +0.58 are permitted to use one of the cars when it is not required by the members of the family. They know, however, how far they dare go, being servants. If they presume beyond this sphere, the Willistons very firmly but kindly tell them about it, with a warning that it must not happen again.

THE BOSS IS EXACTING WITH HIS MEN BUT EQUALLY EXACTING WITH HIMSELF

Swede Johnson is fire-foreman, third shift, on the S. S. Empiric. His men must be kept on their toes for four hot, dirty, labor-filled hours shoveling coal beneath the hissing, screaming boilers. Swede, handling the shovel +0.31 and bar as hard and as steadily as his men, stops only long enough to bark or threaten someone who happens to be "loafing" on the job. The boss is thus very exacting with his men but no less exacting with himself.

EMPLOYER TREATS HELP KINDLY BUT NOT FAMILIARLY

At precisely 8:55 A. M. the side door of the First National bank opens admitting a short dapper little man, Mr. Garrett, the cashier. Each morning for the past twenty years at identically the same moment and in the same manner Mr. Garrett's cheery "good morning" would be acknowledged and answered by his force of assistants. Woe betide anyone who would report for work after the "chief" had arrived. Mr. Garrett was

+0.29   not a severe man, but he treated his employees with a slight air of superiority, although never attempting to bulldoze them. He helped them both in business and in personal matters and, although he joked and teased with them, he never permitted familiarity. Nor did he ask their advice, though a complaint or a suggestion would be given fair consideration. He never took his employees into his confidence, nor would he permit himself to be made a confidant.

The Boss Is Somewhat More Distant and Harsh than the Average

The new boss the men found in charge Monday morning was somewhat "distant" and severe. He did not curse his men for loafing or for inefficiency but he did talk to them in an authoritative tone of voice and in a −0.32   way that invited no familiarity. The general comment of the men after sizing him up was that, while not cruel nor unjust, he was somewhat more distant and harsh than the average boss.

This Prison Guard Is Somewhat Harsher than the Average

Murphy rather enjoys exercising the authority his position as guard in the prison gives him. In consequence, he orders the prisoners around in an autocratic manner −0.95   and is ready to impose penalties upon them for little refractions of the rules. He is not extremely cruel nor particularly unjust but gives the benefit of the doubt to harshness rather than to kindness.

His Foremanship Makes Him "Different" from Ordinary Workers

Foreman Klein was not brutal, as railroad bosses go. But he did feel that, now that he was boss, it would be beneath his dignity to take a hand at work. You could see him, therefore, standing off a few paces calling "Heave! Heave!" when the men were lifting a heavy rail, or lying −0.96   on the bank with a straw in his mouth when the routine of work was moving smoothly. He did claim, of course, as his natural right, the first drink when the water bucket was brought up, which right his men accorded him with no apparent resentment. It was merely his philosophy that when one becomes a boss he is no longer "a common pick-swinger."

THIS BOSS IS BOSS—WITH AN IRON HAND AND A FACILE "JAW"

It is sometimes said that a man who has risen from the ranks makes a harsher boss than one who comes from the top. At any rate that theory would fit the case of Tony, our road-construction boss. He continually swears at his men and drives them by stinging remarks. He will take no "back talk" from anyone, and he includes

−1.03 in back talk any suggestion that a job be done at all differently from the way he suggests. Perhaps his men sense that he is not so hard at heart as his rough ways imply and that explains their meekness, but at any rate he acts out in practice the theory that if you are to get along with this class of workmen you've got to tell them in plain language what's what and who's who.

TALKS CURTLY TO SERVANTS

Rascob used rather curt and direct ways in talking to the servants in his home. When he would say: "Is

−1.13 there any mail" or "Get me my hat," it would be in a dictatorial tone that showed clearly he looked upon them as *servants*.

DOES NOT CONSIDER THE HARDSHIP TO WHICH DISCHARGED EMPLOYEES WILL BE SUBJECT

Montkern held that the money he possessed was his own and that he had the right, therefore, to hire and discharge employees exactly as he saw fit. When any

−1.44 workman displeased him, or when it was at all to Montkern's financial advantage to make a change, he would immediately discharge the workman without any regard as to what hardship the man would be subject to before finding another job.

DISREGARD OF THE RIGHTS OF SUPPRESSED PEOPLE

−1.60 An American corporation had set up in the Mexican plantation a model plant for the care of the stock. The corporation piped pure mountain water directly through the village, all the inhabitants of which were laborers for the company. But no outlet was provided from their water system in the village, and its inhabitants were obliged to subsist on the muddy water that the neighboring ponds provided.

SERVANT DISCHARGED BECAUSE OF HIS AGE

−1.67 Old Zeb had been with the former owners of the hotel for many years. When the management was changed, the new bosses found Zeb too old and weak to serve in the capacity of porter. Instead of finding something easier for him to do, they forcibly discharged him despite the fact that he was poor, and despite his willingness to do whatever work was assigned to him.

EMPLOYER DRIVES HIS EMPLOYEES FOR MAXIMUM PROFITS

−1.71 For Smith business was business. He drove his laborers at as high speed as possible. Throughout the grove where the men were gathering cocoanuts you could hear the constant clamor from the foremen to hurry. Whoever faltered a moment on the job was "bawled out," or even kicked, to compel him to get back to work.

TALKS SHARPLY TO A WAITER

−1.71 Whether or not the coffee was too cold, I cannot say; but, at any rate, Jim Ralston took occasion to talk sharply to the waiter about it. "What do you think I am, an alligator? I didn't ask for iced coffee, did I?" he blurted out in an impatient tone of voice. "And I'm in a hurry; don't keep me waiting here all day."

CONTRACT PRISON LABOR TREATED WITH GREAT
SEVERITY

The prison-labor contract assigned John Ratshaw to
digging coal, in spite of the fact that he was not at all
hardened for manual labor. Notwithstanding his bleeding hands and aching back he finally got the last car
loaded to fulfill his quota for the day. But a scheming in-
spector removed from the car John's tag and placed on it
−1.90   another tag. In consequence Ratshaw was reported short.
He tried to explain to his boss that he had done all his
work and showed his bleeding hands in a plea for justice.
But the boss merely cursed him as a good-for-nothing jail
bird, pitied himself for having to manage such "damned
trash," and ordered him to the whipping post for discipline.

DEMOCRATIC ATTITUDES AND PRACTICES

THEME: Social Status: I. Attitude of Those of "Higher"
Social Standing toward Those of "Lower" Standing.

MAN OF WEALTH AND "BLUE BLOOD" PREFERS TO
"STAND ON HIS OWN"

Jack McKelvey was the son of a rather wealthy,
aristocratic family. But Jack had ideas of his own and
+1.19   instead of living a life of ease, he chose to strike out
from civilization, get a job as a common laborer, keep
his identity a secret from his fellow workmen, and actually "make good on his own."

HE WOULD LOSE MONEY RATHER THAN EXPLOIT
SUBMERGED CLASSES

Bill Johnston had long struggled against great odds in
making his way as a lawyer. He desperately needed a
"break." Such a break seemed to be in sight when the
great Amalgamated Steel Company sent him an invitation to call at the central office. The company has, the
vice president pointed out, a number of suits all of which
involve the same principle—the integrity of a contract
in which the company had deliberately deceived its em-
+1.04   ployees. Would he take these cases? "But that," replied

Johnston, "involves dishonest treatment of these men."
"Oh," shot back the vice president, "what are they?
Only a lot of hunkies and dagoes." Then Johnston
straightened up in his chair. "These men," he said with
whitened face, "are faithful workers for your company;
they did their part; they have their families to maintain.
When I set my hand against such folks my name will
no longer be Bill Johnston."

He Prefers to Be Just "One of the Group"

+1.02 That he was a successful business and professional
man meant little to him. When on a trip with old friends
or in making new acquaintances, he preferred to be
known merely as Henry Baldwin.

A "Blue Blood" Treats Considerately Persons of Lower Social Stratum

Mr. Findlay was just as considerate of the sensibilities
of the commonest folks as he was of those of the socially
élite class to which he personally belonged. If one made
a social blunder, or intruded upon Findlay's presence
+0.99 when he had no right to do so, or differed from this
prominent man in an argument, the fellow was never
made the butt of ridicule but was taken with the same
seriousness, and treated with the same courtesy, as if he
were one of the "blue bloods."

Man of Royal Standing Does Not Want Servants to Act Humbly Before Him

Prince William has just added a new member to the
servants of his royal household. The new servant immedi-
+0.79 ately bows himself to the floor before his master; but the
Prince speaks, saying: "My servants need not bow before
me".

One of High Estate Faces Social Disapproval to Show His Great Respect for a Common Show Girl

Peter Van Horn has fallen in love with an actress.
The Van Horn family is very wealthy and the mother

especially is very sensitive about social prestige. At the betrothal party it becomes known that the girl has been a "common show girl." But the elder Van Horn, +0.79 who has come to see that she has a heart of gold in spite of her low social status, takes her arm and, proudly with great dignity, marches with her to her carriage past the shocked guests. As these two proceed, Mr. Rombeau, the most aristocratic of the "blue-stockings," steps up, takes her other arm, and walks with them.

Does Not Cut Old Friends because They Are Ordinary Laborers

Although Jiggs has become rich he still likes common folks best. He has a glad hand for Crogan and the rest wherever he meets them, regardless of the fact that they are plumbers, draymen, or other common laborers. In +0.76 fact he likes better to sit at their card parties and to attend their balls than he does to associate with members of the "Four Hundred" who live an artificial social life. But he has no objections to association with the socially élite—if they are good sports.

He Likes to Mingle with Common Folks

He was not a politician seeking votes. Nevertheless, Johnston liked sometimes to sit on a box at the country +0.65 store and swap stories with the rural folks in spite of the fact that he would have been welcome at all of these times at the country club where men of his own social level were assembled.

Prefers the Naïve, Honest Man to High Society

The Peterses had gone to Paris to make a grand display—at least that was the ambition of Mrs. Peters. But the Mr. was not of that type; he was a common, blunt man of the West. His bluntness desperately mortified the aspiring mother because she was sure it would drive out of their social life Marquis Rhambeau whom she had induced to attend her ball. But the Marquis was

+0.56 different. He slipped away from the rest of the guests to eat pie with Mr. Peters in the kitchen and to swap stories. Morning found these two in bed together, the blue-blood Marquis and the crude but honest-hearted country store-keeper—jovial chums. As the Marquis left he slapped Peters on the back and promised to come again—to eat some more pie and to swap some more stories.

Treats Considerately (with Slight Preference for Himself) People of His Own Social Class

Mr. Pomeroy would be counted a good neighbor, and even a passable church member. He is decently consider-ate of the rights and sensibilities of the people in his own neighborhood and, indeed, of his social and occupational
+0.16 level wherever he meets them. In a business deal he looks, naturally, first to his own interests, but not in a way that involves cheating his fellowmen or even putting them to unfair disadvantage. He is, in fact, just about like most of the rest of us—enough good and enough bad in him to strike a fairly even balance.

Newly Rich Pattern after Those with Social Prestige in Order to Become One of Them

The Barlows became fabulously wealthy over night and immediately aspired to become recognized by high society. They bought a home in the fashionable part of
−0.48 town, hired the best servants and an efficient social secretary. In order to establish contacts with society folk, they sent their children to the schools attended by the children of the "society" people, and attended the church of these people.

He Somewhat Feels His Superiority

When Mr. Osgood goes on a journey he is inclined to be slightly aware of his worldly success. When he makes
−0.88 new acquaintances or mixes with a group at the home of a friend, he prefers to be known and introduced as the president of the firm of Osgood and Osgood.

Wealthy People Attempt Newspaper Publicity and Show to Gain Social Recognition

-0.93

The Sawyers were determined that they would be recognized by the "400," if money could do the trick. They tried to outdo all the wealthy, not only in homes and cars, but in contributions to charity, and in spectacular social affairs that would give them newspaper publicity. When their daughter became of age, they arranged a brilliant "coming out" party, inviting all the people of recognized wealth and social prestige, even though they knew them only slightly.

A Prince Supposed to Be of Different Stock from a Common Man

-1.17

Prince Sergi has seduced the naïve mountain girl, Nadja, who, according to the custom of her tribe, is put to death for her "shame." Yegor, her brother, vows vengeance on the heartless prince responsible for his sister's disgrace. But the prince is the brother of the princess, Vera, who is deeply in love with the picturesque Yegor. At length Yegor gets his chance and chokes Sergi to death. When Vera finds her brother slain she cries out, dropping to her knees beside her brother: "Oh, Sergi! Sergi? Killed by this dog." Yegor pleads that it was his *sister* for whom he did it, that Sergi had ruined his sister's life. But Vera merely screams again:

"Who are you to kill a prince of Russia for *your* sister?"

Thing to rate, Vera's comparison between the prince and Yegor.

Mother Arranges Marriage of Daughter in Order to Gain Social Prestige

-1.37

When Mrs. Brooks inherits a fortune from what was thought to be a worthless estate, she immediately tries to break into New York's leading society. Finding herself unable to be the social luminary that she had hoped, she tells her daughter that they are going to England. Here again she is snubbed by society, but is able to arrange a meeting between her daughter and a handsome young Englishman whose only asset is a title of nobility. Sir Thomas is glad to accept the encouragement offered by Mrs. Brooks, and although Ellen finds his company very boring, she agrees to marry him so that she and her mother may have the social prestige that they crave.

She Feels Uncomfortable When Placed with Those of Lower Social Position

The name of Morris stood quite high in the business and social world and Mrs. Morris was fully conscious of her elevated standing as a member of that family. As she and her daughter were seated in the Union Terminal
−1.45   Building awaiting the departure of their train, a family belonging distinctly to the laboring class took seats next to them. Mrs. Morris became much disturbed and edged farther away from them and finally, with a look of contempt, took a seat in another part of the station.

Speaks Condescendingly of a Person Whose Occupation She Considers on a Lower Scale than Her Own

Polly owns and operates a high class beauty shop, catering to the upper stratum of society. Polly, herself, has by sheer good fortune risen from the ranks, finan-
−1.49   cially. When her niece's beau, who is a respectable and hard-working postal employee, is referred to, Polly says in a rather bored tone of voice: "Oh, but he's only a mail clerk."

She Expects Deference from Others because of Her Social Position

When Mrs. Curtis enters a store or a hotel she expects attention at once. Accustomed as she is to wealth and its prestige, she takes it for granted that all "common
−1.52   folks" with whom she comes in contact will be meek and subservient toward her and she is considerably annoyed when she encounters one who does not show such deference.

Feel Ill at Ease, and Take Little Pains to Be Agreeable, When Thrown with Others Who Are Considered to Be of Lower Social Status

−1.52 The Babsons were not very well pleased when the Thompsons stopped at their table for an after-lunch visit. For, although Babson and Thompson had been schoolmates, Thompson had somehow failed to keep the pace and had come to be recognized as just about down-and-out, while Babson had had good luck and was in a fair way to social success. It was evident from the furtive glances that the Babsons cast over the restaurant that they were ill at ease to be seen talking with these common folks and were hoping that none of their friends would observe them; while the brevity of their answers and their lack of initiative in keeping up the conversation suggested, even to social amateurs, that they wished their troublesome old friends would move on.

Disregard of the Rights of Suppressed People

−1.60 An American corporation had set up in the Mexican plantation a model plant for the care of the stock. The corporation piped pure mountain water directly through the village, all the inhabitants of which were laborers for the company. But they provided no outlet from their water system in the village, and its inhabitants were obliged to subsist on the muddy water that the neighboring ponds provided.

Common People Regarded as Worthless

−1.94 It was in the days immediately preceding the French Revolution. Some peasants were assembled along the route of the royal carriage. Presently along came the King in a carriage drawn by eight horses. The driver made no effort to check his steeds as they dashed into the scampering crowd. Some, unable to clear the way fast enough, were run down and a child was killed. When the carriage stopped, forced to do so by the crowd, out of the window projected the head of the King. "Are the horses hurt?" he inquired in an irritated voice. "Lash these curs out of the road. If any of them dare to get in our way again I'll have the whole set beheaded."

CONSIDERS SELF TOO GOOD TO WORK

The stock market disaster ruined the wealthy Brein family and caused the sudden death of Mr. Brein. Neither of the Brein children had ever done work of any kind, but the daughter, Bonnie, faced the situation squarely and sought work at once. When she challenged her
−2.20 brother's indifference to their poverty and suggested that he go to a friend of their father who would surely give him a teller's job in his bank, Jack stormed: "What! Stand in a case six hours a day and count coins? No! Not that job or any other; I've never worked, and being a Brein, never intend to."

DEMOCRATIC ATTITUDES AND PRACTICES

THEME: Social Status: II. Attitude of Those of "Lower" Social Standing toward Those of "Higher" Standing.

CLINGS TO POOR BUT HONEST AND KINDHEARTED FOSTER PARENTS

These men who had reared Sally were, it is true, very crude in appearance and manners. Their straggly beards, heavy faces, and bad grammar revealed too plainly Hebrew stock of the alley type. But they were kindhearted and ready to share the best they had with their foundling child. But when it was discovered that Sally's real mother belonged to a wealthy and aristocratic family
+0.88 and that this family was willing to accept the child and give her the luxuries of her rightful home, the alley protectors, who had reared and loved her, were ready, though in sorrow, to give her up. But when the rulers of the new home laid down the law that these crude alley folks might not visit in the home, and used disparaging terms in talking about them, Sally told her new

parents in very plain language what she thought of their fine ways—and cast her lot again with the alley folks.

Rate—Sally's choice.

He Is Not Stampeded by the Presence of Prominent People

+0.75　The fact that the wealthy and the socially prominent Van Pelts were at the little party caused no flutter in the heart of Sam Jones and no manifestations of excitement in his conduct. He shook hands with them with the same naturalness, spoke to them with the same directness, and let them pass out of his attention with the same ease as he did with anybody else at the party.

Insists That a Nobleman Work as a Basis for Recognition

+0.20　The daughter of a wealthy American gun manufacturer falls in love with an aristocratic Frenchman while in Venice. The father objects to the match because he considers the man "no good," but says that if the lover makes good in his manufacturing plant he'll give his consent to the marriage.

Thing to rate, expecting a nobleman to earn his living by work.

That She Is a Countess Does Not Excite This Man

+0.04　The Countess Tatiana is at the inn where the famous singing bandit, Yegon, comes. Tatiana, exercising the prerogative of her class, sends word to him that she wishes to see him and that he should come to her room. "You go up and tell your countess," Yegon replies to the messenger who brings the request, "that if she wants to see us she must come down here."

Thing to rate, Yegon's answer to the countess.

A Selfish Rich Man Humiliated

Mr. Paul is a millionaire speculator on Wall Street, but thoroughly selfish and brutal to his wife. Far away from civilization he falls into the hands of Lopez and his

men for whom only true manhood counts, not wealth
nor power. Lopez recognizing the selfishness of the man
and undaunted by his wealth and social standing in the
big eastern city, cuffs him around like a common cur, and
puts him in a most humiliating light.

+0.02

Thing to rate—failure to treat the man with dignity
to which his wealth would seem to entitle him.

They Have Great Respect for Those of Wealth and Nobility

The people of the province of Fenway held Lord
Algernon in great respect. At times when he was to
arrive from the city to spend a few days at his palatial
home, they would assemble with the community band to
escort him from the railway station to his estate. They
were constantly solicitous of the welfare of their lord
and reverent in their treatment of him.

−0.05

Husband Unwilling to Mingle with Fasionable Society

When the Renbeaus newly acquired wealth opened the
way to social recognition, Mr. Renbeau was found un-
interested in such recognition. He could see little pleasure or value in mingling with fashionable society. Hence,
whenever his wife planned a dinner or theater party, he
often pretended to be called out of town on business, to
be detained at the office, or to be suffering from a severe
headache.

−0.31

Rebukes a King in Spite of His Royalty

Young king Andrea of Robisonia is more of a gallant
than a king. When the members of his cabinet seek him
to report to him an acutely dangerous situation in the
country, they find him engrossed in the contemplation
of a picture of a beautiful American girl in his newspaper.
Certain that his personal charms and his royal standing
will get him any girl he wants, he starts at once for
America and begins an aggressive and cocksure courtship.

−0.40

But the lady is not so overwhelmed by his royal highness; right out in public she snubs him when he seeks a dance. To his amazed inquiry, "Why?" she flings back over her shoulder: "If I want to smell garlic I don't need to go to Robisonia for it."

Thing to rate, such a way to treat a king.

FEVERISHLY COURTS THE OPPORTUNITY TO BE WITH THE WEALTHY OR WITH THOSE OF HIGH SOCIAL POSITION

−1.29 Mrs. Jiggs is extremely anxious to get into "high society." Whenever a Duke or a rich man comes into town she manages in some way to get him to call at her home or to be seen with her husband. When with such company she is very self-conscious about her manners, extremely fearful lest she or her husband reveal some evidence of their lowly origin. No matter how much Mr. Jiggs may be bored with these "social lights," she insists that he entertain them or go with her to visit them, and is greatly disgusted with his preference for ordinary folks.

RELATION OF PARENTS TO CHILDREN

THEME: Companionship with Children.
     a. Delight in the presence of children.
     b. Expression of love for children.
     c. Participation in entertainment.

c. PARENTS ASSOCIATE WITH CHILDREN A GREAT DEAL IN ORDER TO GIVE THEM COMPANIONSHIP, AND TO TRAIN AND EDUCATE THEM PROPERLY

+1.07 Jack and Agnes are the parents of two children who, they believe, should be afforded all the training that they can give them. They do not go out and have big times at the party or dance while the children are left at home in the custody of a maid. Instead, the entire family frequently goes together on a picnic, or takes a trip to the museum or park. The summer before the children were to enter high school, their parents took them on a

trip to most of the interesting places in the United States.
Mr. Lane frequently goes hunting with his boy, while
Mrs. Lane is always willing to help Ellen entertain her
friends with a party.

c. Parents Associate with Children at Shows or Entertainments

Elsa desires to attend an entertainment this evening,
+1.05   but needs the company of her father. He gladly assents
to go and accompanies her to the café where he is very
congenial to her, and strives to think only of her pleasure.

c. Father Entertains Children by Singing

John is not the kind of a father to be bored by the
play of children. He is a companion to all the young
+1.01   folks in the small community in which they live. His
wife frequently gives parties to their own and the neighborhood youngsters, while John is often seen with all
the children, singing to them and telling them stories.

a. Married Couple Hopes for, and Plans for, Children

From the time the Smiths married they looked forward with happy anticipations to the time when they
+0.90   might have children of their own and planned their house
and their finances to make room for the babies for which
they hoped.

b. Parent Expresses Love for His Children

Expression of love for his children did not need to be
forced or artificial for Roger Babson. He could sit down
with his son and express to him his affection by both word
+0.78   and deed. When his grown daughter appeared for break-
fast, or when she left for a journey, he would talk to her
in endearing terms and kiss her just as he had done when
she was a child.

a. Parents Greet Son Warmly

When Hugh returns from college for the holidays, he is
met at the door by his father who greets him in a jovial

+0.44   and boisterous manner. They shake hands warmly, dance about the room together, and slap each other frequently on the back.

a.   PARENTS LOVINGLY FONDLE THEIR INFANT

Little Pete had had a good nap and was in fine spirits. Every time the proud father would pinch the baby's toes up would go the tiny feet and a gurgle of laughter would rock the little form. At last the mother, unable to restrain +0.39   longer the impulse to hug him, caught the child up in her arms, pressed him ecstatically to her bosom as she rocked him to and fro, saying as she did it: "Ain't he just the darlingest little angel?" And the broad grin on the father's face showed that on that question, at least, these two were one.

b.   PARENTS EXPRESS CONCERN AND ANXIETY FOR THEIR CHILD

When Mary Allen married Bert Coslow, she went to live with him in a sparsely inhabited outpost in the far north. Living conditions there were not so comfortable as in the home that she had known with her mother and father in Virginia, and her parents were concerned for +0.28   their daughter's happiness and safety. Letters from the far north were few, and on the receipt of each one we find the family anxiously gathered together as the epistle was read. The parents would remark that they were glad Mary was still happy, but were concerned over the hardships she must encounter.

a, b, c.   PARENTS AND CHILDREN LIVE TOGETHER IN ORDINARY FASHION

It was not that the Morrises were deliberately negligent of their family. They were just like most of the rest of us; they did not succeed as the days went by in always +0.20   living up to those high ideals of example and discipline urged by magazine writers. But even if life in the Morris family was somewhat prosaic, there was not absent a reasonable degree of patience and courtesy, and even of affection, among the members.

a. FATHER EDUCATES BOY AND THEN ALLOWS HIM TO SHIFT FOR HIMSELF

−0.48 Mr. Harper believes that manhood is developed by facing the realities of life. He himself is a lawyer of the hard-boiled, matter-of-fact type. He generously provides his son with money so that he is enabled to graduate from law school. "Now, young man," his father tells him, "you are well educated and it is up to you. Get away from here, locate in another state, don't count on any more help from me, and I don't want to hear from you until after you have made good and have a thriving law business."

b. MOTHER IS RETICENT ABOUT SHOWING AFFECTION FOR CHILD

−0.56 Min has her daughter, a girl about eighteen, assist her in the duties of running the hotel of which she is the proprietress. Her natural gruffness is not softened in her relationship with her daughter; she orders her around in a harsh voice and domineering manner. The reason she displays so little affection for her daughter is not because she does not love the child but merely because it is just not Min's nature to display her tender emotions in any way whatsoever.

a. MARRIED COUPLE DELIBERATELY AVOID CHILDREN

−0.87 The Joneses were normal in every respect and economically able to rear children. But they did not wish to be tied down by such responsibilities. They therefore decided between themselves not to have any children.

a. MOTHER ABANDONS ILLEGITIMATE CHILD

−1.21 Ruth Larkin successfully conceals from society the birth of her illegitimate child. When it is a few months old she carries it to the door of an Orphans' Home, where she leaves it with the expectation that it will be found and taken care of.

a. Child Reared in Home without Companionship of Parents

−1.32   Jane and Bobbie Wellington are abundantly supplied with beautiful clothes, toys, and entertainment. They are under the watchful care of a nurse and tutor, but seldom see their parents who are busily engaged with business and society. In fact, until after they were two years of age they scarcely knew who their mother and father really were.

b. Parents Over-Express Love for Children

−1.42   Mr. and Mrs. Carson love their children so dearly that they are always gushing, "Darling, come here," or "Now mother's sweetheart must not do that," and similar endearing terms from morning until evening. They hug and fondle their children at every opportunity, reward and praise them for the smallest acts of courtesy, see no reason for disciplining or correcting their children in the slightest degree.

a. Child Indifferently Left with Relatives

−1.43   After the death of Anne's mother, Mr. Christie sends his daughter to the home of relatives so that he will not need to take her to sea with him. He takes no further consideration of her welfare other than writing an occasional letter to her.

a. Parents Refuse to Help Their Children Solve Their Problems

−1.58   Freddy is perplexed. It is one of those situations where a problem has presented itself to his young mind and he feels that his father is the one who can put him right about it. But Mr. Conlon is reading and in answer to his boy's query replies: "Oh, run away. I can't be bothered with your childish problems."

a. Parents Provide No Care for Children

Both Mr. and Mrs. Miller care more about parties and dancing than they do about their first-born child.

−1.61

The baby is frequently given a bottle of milk, put to bed, and left alone for an afternoon and evening while the parents are out for golf, dinner, and a party. When the child is a little older it is allowed to drift about the streets in a filthy, poorly clothed, and nearly starved condition. A few friends protest against this neglect, but the parents maintain their indifference toward the child until the intervention by the Humane Society brings punishment to the parents and another home is secured for the boy.

a.   PARENTS CAST CHILD OUT FROM HOME

−1.91

When Donnie is fourteen years old, his parents turn him from their home. They tell him that he is lazy and a loafer, when in reality the boy has been spending a great deal of time in drawing and painting pictures in the garret of their house. Donnie is cut off entirely from his family and drifts about until taken in by some kind people in an adjoining village.

RELATION OF PARENTS TO CHILDREN

THEME: Discipline.

a. Discipline through discussion, reason, or rewards.
b. Impulsive *versus* purposive discipline.
c. Coöperation of parents in discipline.

a.   MOTHER COMMENDS HER CHILD FOR DOING HIS WORK WELL

+0.97

Dick Snyder has been given the task of weeding his mother's flower bed. His mother is talking to a neighbor when Dick comes to tell her that he has finished. The three of them walk together to inspect the finished piece of work. When Mrs. Snyder sees how well the job has been done she thanks young Dick and tells him that he has done well.

a.   MOTHER REASONS WITH DAUGHTER TO KEEP HER FROM WRONG CONDUCT

Helen has announced that she is going on a motor tour with three girl friends of hers and will be gone

+0.93 about two months. Mrs. Wills wants her daughter to have a good time and to "see the world"; but she does not think that young girls should be traveling alone far from home. However, instead of arbitrarily forbidding the trip, she talks with Helen about the matter, stating her reasons for disapproving it and patiently meeting any points that Helen may have to offer.

a. FATHER COUNSELS WITH SON TO DISSUADE HIM FROM A COURSE BELIEVED TO BE WRONG

+0.63 When Winnis, part Indian, has been rejected as suitor to a white girl but still believes there is a chance for him, his father, Black Eagle, has a long and sympathetic talk with him about the matter. Showing no impatience with the boy's impulses, and matching ideas with him frankly and fully, the father points out to him in detail why it would be better for the lad to return with him at once to their own people.

a. PARENT COMPLIMENTS HIS CHILD

+0.52 Mr. Huston is working in his office when his daughter enters. The father notices her fine appearance and greets her with the words, "Getting stylish, aren't you?" and then compliments her on her neatness.

c. ONE PARENT, THOUGH NOT APPROVING OF THE OTHER PARENT'S KIND OF DISCIPLINE, WILL NOT INTERFERE AT THE TIME

+0.41 The baseball game was so interesting that William Green simply couldn't leave until it ended. But dinner hours will come despite baseball games; hence when William hurriedly took his place at the table his mother and daddy were eating their dessert. "Just a minute, young man," said Mr. Green, "It's time you are given a reason to remember our dinner hour. You shall have no dinner and shall go to your room for the rest of the day." Mrs. Green pitied her hungry son and would not have punished William thus, but she gave no sign of this to either father or son.

Rate Mrs. Green's conduct.

b. Son, after Frequent Failures, Refused Further Money with Which to Go into Business

+0.32 Young Jim Lane has tried several different kinds of business and each time failed. Each time he has come to his father for more money with which to back a new adventure and his father, having faith in his boy's ability, has given it to him. Finally, when Jim approaches him for more money in connection with his latest scheme, the father refuses him help entirely and tells him to take the regular business measures, get money from the bank, and take the responsibility for his success on his own shoulders.

b. Daughter Refused Car for Character-Building Reasons

+0.27 The Fullertons are very wealthy and the children are allowed liberal amounts of money for their own use. Ruth, one morning, asks her father for a car of her own; but her mother objects, saying that it will lead to greater neglect of her studies, and that it is not good training for a girl to get used to such a high standard of living as is suggested by the personal ownership of a car merely for pleasure.

b. Mother Punishes Child to Teach Her a Lesson

+0.05 Mrs. Kearns has told her little three-year-old daughter that she must not cross the street in front of their house, as there is some danger that she may be hit by a car. Little Helen frequently plays about the house, but has never crossed the street. One day while she is playing, some older children ask her to come across and play with them. At first she hesitates, but then after some coaxing, crosses the street to play. When her mother learns what has happened, she realizes that Helen was not greatly at fault, as she had been influenced by older children; but since crossing the street is very dangerous she feels that a lesson must be taught the child, and so punishes Helen by keeping her in the house for three days instead of allowing her to be out-of-doors where she loves to be.

b.   Annoyed Mother Scolds Children

−0.23
The Meyers children have been playing on the front lawn. In the midst of their enthusiasm they have destroyed some flowers which grow there. When Mrs. Meyers discovers the damage she is much annoyed and scolds the children severely, telling them that there will be no more play and that they must go into the house and read until dinner time.

a.   Father Commands Children Somewhat
Dictatorially

−0.44
The childen were waiting around the living room after the time for them to go to bed had passed. Mr. Henry looked up from his paper and said, in the commanding voice slightly annoyed parents have been tempted to use from time immemorial: "Now you children get to bed! John, Mary, get to bed! Go on!"

b.   Father Educates Boy and Then Allows Him to
Shift for Himself

−0.48
Mr. Harper believes that manhood is developed by facing the realities of life. He himself is a lawyer of the hard-boiled, matter-of-fact type. He generously provides his son with money so that he is enabled to graduate from law school. "Now, young man," his father tells him, "you are well educated and it is up to you. Get away from here, locate in another state, don't count on any more help from me, and I don't want to hear from you until after you have made good and have a thriving law business."

a.   Father Promises His Boy a Gift if He Behaves
Well

−0.55
In an effort to teach Roy to be more kind to his little sister, Mr. Walton promised the boy an air rifle if he would not be mean or rough to Betty for a week.

a.   A Parent Threatens the Child with Punishment

"You may go with the girls to the show, Anne, but if you don't come home promptly after it is over I won't

−0.58 allow you to go again for a week." Thus spoke Mrs. Wil
son to her young daughter as she was about to accompany a group of her friends to the local theater.

a, b. ANNOYED PARENT PUNISHES CHILD TO KEEP HIM FROM REPEATING THE ACT

Mr. Appledorn dislikes dogs, and to have them about
annoys him greatly. His young son, on the contrary, is
fond of pets and offers companionship and a meal to
any homeless dog he happens to find. He often brings
stray dogs home with him, and after getting them some
bread from the kitchen, allows them to sleep in the
−0.63 garage. There the dog is discovered when Mr. Appledorn
goes for his car in the morning. After warning his son on
two occasions of the consequences, he again finds a dog
waiting to greet him when he opens the garage door on
Saturday morning. He immediately goes to the house,
gets the boy out of bed and tells him that he cannot go
with the Boy Scouts on their week-end trip, and that
there will not be any allowance for two weeks.

a. FATHER ENFORCES HIS DECISION WITHOUT GIVING REASONS

Mr. Robinson is a well-meaning but a silent father.
He has what he considers good reasons for not permitting
John to use the car to go to the fair. But he holds to the
theory that children—even eighteen-year-old boys—
−0.89 "should be seen and not heard." So when John ventures
to argue with his father about why he should not use the
car, the elder Robinson merely replies sternly: "Haven't
I told you that you can't use it? That ought to be enough
for you. I usually know what I am doing."

c. ONE PARENT, IN PRESENCE OF CHILD, ARGUES AGAINST PUNISHMENT BY OTHER

Bobby has disobeyed and is about to be punished by
his father when Mrs. Hazlett comes into the room. "I
−1.42 don't think you ought to punish him, daddy," pleads
Mrs. Hazlett. "Bobby is a good boy, and won't disobey

again, will you, son? Now please don't punish him this time."

c. ONE PARENT RELIES ON OTHER TO DO ALL DISCIPLINING

William Garver was playing with his little neighbor, Louise, in the sand box in sight of Mrs. Garver who was sitting on the porch with her mending. In the process of the play Louise picked up William's sand shovel. When William saw this he became infuriated. He rushed —1.44 at her, wrenched it from her, beat her with it—all this before Mrs. Garver could intervene. When she did intervene Mrs. Garver simply insisted that he come into his own yard, and threatened: "Wait till your father comes home. I'll tell him of this and he will attend to you!" Mrs. Garver made no attempt to punish William herself but told the father on his return home, who administered the delayed penalty.

c. ONE PARENT INTERFERES WITH OTHER PARENT'S IRRATIONAL DISCIPLINE

Mr. Welles is practicing on his fiddle in a corner of the dining room while his wife is clearing away the dishes. Charles, their seven-year-old son, guides his tricycle from the kitchen into the dining room to his father's side, —1.45 shouting all the while in play. The annoyed father scolds the little son and orders him to put the velocipede on the back porch. Mrs. Welles, in the presence of the son, rebukes the father for impatience with the boy and tells Charles he may go on playing as before.

b. MOTHER SCOLDS AND NAGS HER SON

"You unthoughtful boy! Just look at the dust on those shoes and soon you will have it tracked all over the house. Won't you ever learn to keep clean? Your hands are dirtier than ever, and how did you tear the button off that shirt? Now get cleaned up as I want you to take care of the baby. And for goodness' sake don't —1.62 be dumb about it and let the child get hurt. You are about the most awkward boy I know and not nearly the help to me that your older brothers were when they were your age. Well, don't stand there looking at me, HURRY." Thus spoke Mrs. Brown to her thirteen-year-old boy as he entered the house in response to her call.

e. ONE PARENT INTERFERES WITH DISCIPLINE BY THE OTHER

In a quarrel John had broken his little brother's toy wagon. After thinking the matter over John's father made up his mind to punish the lad by withholding his —1.69 allowance of spending money for the week and giving it instead to the brother. But John's mother interfered. She said John must not be robbed of his money and proceeded to hand it to him out of her own purse.

c. PARENTS DISAGREE BEFORE CHILD REGARDING KIND OF PUNISHMENT

Dorothy should be punished. Both parents were agreed on that; but they did not agree on what the punishment should be. So, while little Dorothy stood —1.80 in anxious fear of the discipline she was to receive, her father and mother continued to argue as to how she should be punished.

b. MOTHER WHILE IN A PASSION WHIPS HER SON

It may be that sixteen-year-old Charlie was daydreaming so that he gave too slight attention when his mother called him to let that chicken out of the coop. At any rate he opened the wrong box. When mother —2.00 saw, strutting across the yard, the hen she intended for tomorrow's dinner, she flew at once into a rage and, seizing a whip, laid a series of stinging blows across the lad's back. Those blows hurt his flesh,—but they hurt his feelings more.

FATHER WHIPS BOY BRUTALLY

Behind the door hangs an old razor strap. And if Jim does anything that displeases his father, that strap sees

−2.37 service. Dinner is ready and the family are all there but Jim. He arrives just as the meal is over, having been detained as a result of watching a school baseball game. Immediately the father grabs the boy, shakes him viciously, throws him to the floor several times, and then proceeds to whip him with the razor strap until Jim cringes helplessly on the floor.

RELATION OF PARENTS TO CHILDREN

THEME: Tolerance of the Point of View of Children.
    a. Appreciation of the child's love affairs.
    b. Bolstering the dignity and the morale of children.
    c. Sharing confidences.
    d. Willingness to forgive error.

c.   FATHER AND SON TREAT EACH OTHER WITH CONFIDENCE

+1.41 Hugh and his father are real pals. There is a fine spirit of fellowship between them so that Hugh feels free to talk to his father about his problems and the father in turn is confidential with Hugh.

a.   MOTHER SYMPATHETICALLY SHARES THE ROMANCE OF HER DAUGHTER

+1.09 Mrs. Golder was not the kind to treat with levity the love affairs of her daughter. On the contrary she took the keenest interest and delight in Marie's romance. In consequence, Marie felt free to approach her mother with all her joys and trials and to seek from her sympathetic advice on all the problems that typical romances involve.

c.   FATHER TAKES DAUGHTER INTO CONFIDENCE

+0.93 Mr. Jones has recently met some financial and social reverses that, although not particularly serious, have caused him considerable worry. His daughter, Milly, noticing that something has been preying upon her father's mind, asks him if she can do anything to help him. He puts his arms around her shoulders, tells her all his troubles, and asks her advice as to the manner in which the situations should be handled.

d.   FATHER FORGIVES DAUGHTER

+0.80   Anna has been living at the home of her relatives while her father has been away at sea. During this period of neglect, Anna becomes ensnared in evil ways and becomes a prostitute. When her father returns to her and learns of her immoral life, he realizes his neglect of his daughter, forgives her for her waywardness, takes her to live with him, and does all that he can to make her happy in her new life.

d.   A MOTHER "STICKS TO" HER ERRING DAUGHTER

+0.78   Ellen has been seduced by a faithless lover and has borne an illegitimate child. In a court trial it has been shown that the girl had had a prior record in connection with a "speak-easy" and had been in jail for disorderly conduct—a set of facts hitherto unknown by her mother. But the mother retains her faith in the fundamental goodness of her daughter, continues to treat her and the baby tenderly and lovingly, and patiently helps her adjust her relations with the father of the child.

a.   PARENTS, THOUGH NOT APPROVING OF THEIR DAUGHTER'S CHOICE OF HUSBAND, CONSENT TO THE MARRIAGE AT THEIR OWN SACRIFICE

+0.63   The parents of Florence Durant had high hopes that she would marry James Holmes some day; for besides being a promising young man, he would be able to provide the kind of cultured life to which she was accustomed. But Florence loved Ralph Stone of whom her parents did not entirely approve. Though Mr. and Mrs. Durant were much disappointed in their daughter's choice, they consented to Florence's marriage to Ralph notwithstanding the sacrifice of their own hopes.

a.   PARENTS ENCOURAGE SON IN LOVE-MAKING

Carl's parents own the large southern plantation where they live. As Carl leaves to see a girl one evening his

+0.48   father tells him that he is glad the boy is in love. When Carl returns with Dixiana, to whom he has become engaged, they give a large party in celebration of the occasion.

b.   Father Speaks Laudatorily to Others Concerning His Child

Mr. Barnes and his old crony, Jim Walters, are on their way to spend a day hunting. During their con-
+0.29   versation Walters asks his friend, Barnes, how his son is getting along in school. "Great," replies Mr. Barnes. "Jim, that boy of mine is sure a fine chap and as capable and ambitious as they make them."

d.   Parents Defend Children against the Law

Richard is one of a gang of adolescent boys who are continually doing pranks to damage property, steal small articles, and cause disturbances in general. He has been caught by the police on two occasions, and both he and his parents warned of the consequences. His next prank is to steal a bicycle, for which he is taken into custody
−0.08   by the police. The juvenile court wants to send him to a reform school, but his parents offer to meet any requirements that the state may make of them and beg that they be allowed to take the boy home. They will pay all damages and be responsible for any further wrong acts.

d.   Parents Forgive Son, but Can't Forget Completely

William had committed a misdemeanor that was somewhat worse than the average for a boy of eighteen. He
−0.70   promised his parents very sincerely that he would behave from now on, and they forgave him. The thing hung over them, though; they just couldn't treat him as warmly nor with as much confidence as they had formerly.

c.   Parents Admit Children Only Partially into Confidence

John and Mary Willis are old enough to understand and appreciate the good and bad things in life. But

when their father has met with serious financial reverses, their mother takes them aside and says: "Now children, there is no use in my explaining what has happened;
−0.84 you wouldn't understand it anyhow. But from now on, all of us must be careful with our money. Your allowances will have to be stopped for awhile, and neither of you can go to the seashore next week. I'm awfully sorry, but it can't be helped." To their anxious queries she replies: "Now, now, I have told you all that is necessary for you to know."

b. MOTHER DAMPENS THE SPIRITS OF HER DAUGHTER

The Williams family has lived in the poor neighborhood of the same community for three generations. Molly Williams is an ambitious member of the present family, who longs for the better things of life. She asks her mother one day if she might use some old wall paper, which the man at the community store had given her, in order to make their home more attractive. But her
−1.20 mother refuses her, saying that only rich people paper the walls of their home. Instead of being content to be a maid in the home of some more wealthy person, Molly asks her mother if she may use the money she makes in order to go to night school and learn to be a stenographer or a secretary. Mrs. Williams says that that might be all right for some people, but that the Williams family are common people and not bright enough to learn from books.

a. PARENTS TREAT LOVE AFFAIR OF DAUGHTER DISPARAGINGLY AND TEASINGLY

Mary is quite old enough to be thinking seriously about the boys, and in fact, has met Bill, with whom she has had a few dates, and whom she really loves. Her par-
−1.25 ents, however, chide her unmercifully about being too young to have a beau, saying that she doesn't know what love means. They laugh and tease her when she announces that she is going out with Bill, although they have, in fact, nothing against him personally.

b. Mother Speaks Disparagingly of Her Children

Mrs. Osman is talking over the back fence to Mrs. Murphy. The conversation turns to Mrs. Osman's two children, Ted and Don. To Mrs. Murphy's question, −1.41 "And how are the boys getting along in school?" the mother replies: "Well, not so well. Teddy doesn't seem to have any brains at all,—just can't get his lessons; while that imp, Don, is just too contrary and mischievous to get down to his studies."

d. Parents Outwardly Forgive Child, but Make No Effort to Forget

John is caught taking some money from the cash register by his father. Questioning brings forth the information that this time was not the first. Upon John's solemn promise never to repeat his actions, his parents −1.49 forgive him, and his father allows him to keep his job in the store. Both parents, however, repeatedly refer to this occasion when reprimanding him for other slight misdeeds, or cast it up to him, at times, without the least provocation.

b. Father Does Not Trust His Son

John Phillips is a youngster of twelve years. His cousin, Benny, who is one year younger than John, is visiting at the Phillips home for two weeks. Mr. Phillips −1.64 finds one day that he must have some nails from the store a few blocks away. He calls the boys to him, informs them of the errand, and then gives the money with which to buy the nails to Benny instead of to his own son. John felt hurt at this seeming distrust by the father.

a. Father Consults His Own Pleasure Rather than His Daughter's in Regard to Her Marriage

Sally loves Onetka, but her father absolutely forbids their marriage because Onetka is part Indian and the father thinks that he would not like him as a son-in- −1.64 law. But he does like the companionship of his friend,

Sheriff Wells, and therefore maneuvers so that the Sheriff and Sally should be together much of the time. He arranges a wedding between the two without consulting his daughter's feelings in the matter.

b. FATHER TALKS DISPARAGINGLY TO SON

−1.74   Whatever started Mr. Swanson to talking to John the way he did is hard to say. But at any rate he is now in the habit of calling his son "stupid" or "good-for-nothing" or even "idiot."

a. DAUGHTER FORCED TO MARRY FOR MONEY

−1.87   Mary and Sean are in love with each other, but Sean is a poor young man whose only asset is his ability to sing. Mary's mother, a social climber, is determined that her daughter shall marry wealth. She makes life so unpleasant for her daughter that the girl finally marries a rich man whom she really doesn't love. But the mother at least enjoys the prestige of a rich son-in-law.

d. PARENTS WILL NOT FORGIVE CHILDREN

−1.96   Henry is the only son of a very wealthy man who had planned that his son should go to college as "all respectable people's sons are doing." Then the boy was to study law. Henry never cared for school, and simply hated college, with the result that he "flunked-out." This was a great disappointment to his parents and a great blow to their pride, making them stone-hearted in whatever Henry was concerned. They disowned him and refused to forgive him.

RELATION OF PARENTS TO CHILDREN

THEME: Sacrifice by Parents for Children.

MOTHER GIVES HER LIFE TO SAVE HER CHILD

A great tenement house in New York city is on fire. The Meade children have been playing alone while the mother was out working. The mother, attracted by the

+1.23 fire, runs home in time to burst into the room where the baby is still sleeping. She snatches the child from its bed, and shielding it from the heat and flames she dashes with it to safety. But in so doing she inhales flames so that she dies a few minutes later.

Parents Sacrifice Time, Money, and Effort to Help Children Prepare for Their Life Work

+1.10 Mr. and Mrs. Hays want to give their boys all the help they can in preparing them for successful careers. They are able to live comfortably, but only by virtue of much economy and rather frequently denying themselves new clothes, a new car, and a possible vacation. Jim wants to go into business, so his father provides him with the initial capital. Bob desires to be a lawyer, so he is sent to college and the law school. Both parents have great faith in their boys and their ability to succeed.

Parents Give Money to Save Child from Vice

+0.99 The Smiths are moderately wealthy, but their mode of life has probably given the impression that they are much more wealthy. Their little girl is kidnapped and held for ransom of $50,000. This sum will completely wipe out their fortune, but they quickly get it together and give it to the bandits in order to save their child.

Mother Uses Her Small Savings to Buy Clothes for the Children

+0.89 When school starts in the fall and the children must go, the Stuarts are confronted with the problem of providing clothes for them. Times are hard and Mr. Stuart has lost much money. Mrs. Stuart has set her heart on a new dress to wear at her sister's wedding, and has slowly saved a little money with which to buy it. Nevertheless, now that the children need clothes, she takes this money and spends it on them so that they may be well dressed.

Parents Allow Children All the Privileges They Have to Offer

+0.87
The Boyds are a respected family in the community where Mr. Boyd is in the real estate business. They have three children, each of whom is well taken care of, and allowed to go to school until he has been thoroughly prepared for a life work. The parents have faith in their children, and try to show them their mistakes, and share in their joys and sorrows.

Parent Unwilling to Bring Up Children in a Bad Town

+0.85
Two towns were possible locations for the new home of the Millers. In discussing the desirability of locating in either, Mr. and Mrs. Miller were reminded that the one community was practically controlled by gambling politicians, and at the same time offered poor schools and no clean recreation centers for children. "I simply wouldn't think of Bernard growing up in such a town," concluded Mrs. Miller.

Father Uses the Last of His Savings to Give Son Opportunity to Make Good

+0.83
Juan's father has encouraged him to develop his voice so that he is now a fine singer. Juan has the usual difficulty of getting recognition so that he may appear before the public in leading theaters. In order to give his son the great opportunity, Juan's father secretly uses the last of his savings with which to hire a large theater for his son's initial performance.

Parents Give Children Gifts

+0.73
The family and friends gather about Clara West and her husband to say good-by as they are about to leave on a journey into a distant country. As they are about to leave, Mr. West comes to Clara and places a package in her hand, saying, "These are some books I prize highly which may give you comfort too." When mother

West kisses Clara good-by, she slips a necklace about her neck with the comment, "Just a keepsake from mother."

PARENTS DEPRIVE THEMSELVES TO BUY CHRISTMAS PRESENTS FOR CHILDREN

+0.66 "Mother dear, do you think Santa will bring me a violin?" It was a hard question for Mrs. Landsberg, but knowing how greatly the child desired the instrument she tried to answer bravely in spite of their extreme poverty. That day she took her last five dollars and bought the boy the gift he wanted.

PARENTS, THOUGH NOT APPROVING OF THEIR DAUGHTER'S CHOICE OF HUSBAND, CONSENT TO THE MARRIAGE AT THEIR OWN SACRIFICE

+0.63 The parents of Florence Durant had high hopes that she would marry James Holmes some day; for besides being a promising young man, he would be able to provide the kind of cultured life to which she was accustomed. But Florence loved Ralph Stone of whom her parents did not approve entirely. Though Mr. and Mrs. Durant were much disappointed in their daughter's choice, they consented to Florence's marriage to Ralph in spite of the sacrifice of their hopes.

PARENTS MAKE EMERGENCY LOANS TO CHILDREN

+0.45 If John got into a financial "jam" he could always count on his father to lend him sums of money or to sign the son's note as security, even though this cost the father some inconvenience. But to get this aid it was necessary for John to show that his need was due to a real emergency, not merely to carelessness or to habits of extravagance.

SON, AFTER FREQUENT FAILURES, REFUSED FURTHER MONEY WITH WHICH TO GO INTO BUSINESS

Young Jim Lane has tried several different kinds of business and each time has failed. Each time he has come to his father for more money with which to back a new adventure and his father, having faith in his boy's ability, has given it to him. Finally, when Jim approaches him for more money in connection with his latest scheme, his father refuses him help entirely and tells him to take the regular business measures, get money from the bank, and take the responsibility for his success on his own shoulders.

+0.32

Parents Are "Tight" about Giving Gifts to Children

It may or may not be true that Mr. and Mrs. French had a philosophy back of withholding gifts from their children. At any rate John and Mary got but few gifts and but small sums of spending money. Birthdays were customarily entirely forgotten, "pin money" allowances were meager, and Christmas gifts were much less expensive than most parents of equal financial circumstances are in the habit of giving to their children.

−1.05

Parents Parade and Show off Children in Order to Bring Glory to Themselves

When Paul Baumer returns from the front on a furlough, he quickly exchanges his uniform for more comfortable civilian dress. It is good to feel himself in ordinary street clothes again. But his father cannot understand why the son should be tired of army clothes; he himself gets a great deal of satisfaction and pride as he sees his son about town being admired by the village people. The father therefore insists that Paul wear his uniform regardless of the boy's dislike to do so.

−1.35

Father Values His Money More than He Does His Daughter

"You won't take my daughter, will you? I'll give you anything you ask." Thus spoke Mr. Hardy to the leader of a bandit gang who was threatening to kidnap his daughter. "All right," replied the bandit chief, "make it one hundred thousand dollars and we will go."

−1.51 At mention of that amount of money, Hardy staggered and said, "But that will almost clean me out." Hardy was willing to allow them to take his daughter and he would take a chance on securing her release from the bandits, rather than part with his money.

PARENTS COMPEL CHILD TO GO TO WORK

As soon as Raymond is sixteen and past the age of compulsory school attendance, his father does not permit him to realize his desire of becoming a mechanical engineer. He puts the boy to work in his lumber business.
−1.55 Raymond drives a truck to deliver lumber each day, receiving in return for his services merely his board, room, and clothes. Raymond's father thinks it is a boy's duty to work for his father to repay his parents for the sacrifice they have made in rearing him.

PARENTS PROVIDE NO CARE FOR CHILDREN

Both Mr. and Mrs. Miller care more about parties and dancing than they do about their first-born child. The baby is frequently given a bottle of milk, put to bed, and left alone for an afternoon and evening while the parents are out for golf, dinner, and a party. When the
−1.61 child is a little older it is allowed to drift about the streets in a filthy, poorly clothed, and nearly starved condition. A few friends protest against this neglect, but the parents maintain their indifference toward the child until the intervention by the Humane Society brings punishment to the parents and another home is secured for the boy.

SON MUST LOOK AFTER HIMSELF

Buddy's father is a heavy drinker and as a result is very poor and works very little. Buddy is a youngster of about fourteen years, whose only home is the one room he shares with his father in the basement of a store
−1.79 building. The father takes no care of his son beyond providing shelter for him. Buddy attends school irregularly, does what little work he can get to do, and is

largely dependent upon the neighbors for food and clothing.

Father Tricks Son for Own Selfish Gain

At his mother's death Jose had been abandoned by his bandit father, Pedro. Many years later, overhearing some of his father's men tell of his parentage, Jose resolves to find his father and tells the men that he is the son of their leader. When Pedro hears of his son's proposed visit, he fears dire results to himself. He has his men stage a fake hold-up while Jose is on his way to visit him and plant robbery evidence on his son. In the meantime Pedro has hinted his suspicions of Jose to men of the law who, in face of the evidence found, send him to jail.

−1.85

Child Must Go without Clothes So That Parents Can Have Them

Mr. and Mrs. Wise have high social aspirations. They frequently attend theater parties, bridge parties, dances, etc., and are always dressed in good but elaborate taste. But the children pay-up in part for the money the parents spend on themselves. They go, not only in dingy clothes, but even ragged and dirty and, in winter, with insufficient clothing to keep them warm.

−2.00

APPENDIX B

TABLES

Table XXXVII

Sigma-Values at the Three Quarter-Points for Approvals (Admirations Plus Half Neutrals) for the Several Groups on the Aggressiveness Scale

Groups	Real Love, Coquetry			Spontaneous, Coquetry			Spontaneous, Direct			Real Love, Direct			Total		
	Q₁	Q₂	Q₃	Q₁	Q₂	Q₃	Q₁	Q₂	Q₃	Q₁	Q₂	Q₃	Q₁	Q₂	Q₃
College sen., male	.16	− .07	− .55	.08	− .32	−1.05	.20	− .17	− .65	.25	− .09	.49	.19	− .14	.76
College sen., female	.28	− .10	− .59	− .08	− .31	−1.09	.09	− .18	− .51	.17	− .16	− .54	.17	− .17	.75
College sen., total	.23	− .09	− .52	.27	− .23	−1.05	.17	− .19	− .60	.21	− .15	− .45	.23	− .17	− .73
Young miners	− .23	− .56	− .93	− .67	−1.01	−1.53	− .15	− .59	−1.04	− .31	− .60	−1.79	− .26	− .70	−1.12
Adult miners	− .20	− .59	−1.03	− .56	−1.03	−1.41	− .15	− .54	−1.04	− .13	− .63	.93	− .21	− .65	−1.08
Graduate students	.00	− .31	− .69	− .10	− .61	−1.13	.01	− .29	− .65	.03	− .17	.71	.00	− .36	.90
Young Brethren	.05	− .14	− .38	− .05	− .63	−1.00	.16	− .19	− .43	.35	.19	− .37	.13	− .21	.48
Adult Brethren	.27	− .13	− .37	.03	− .33	− .69	.51	.14	− .18	.25	− .02	− .36	.26	− .03	.35
Business men	− .07	− .31	− .49	− .19	− .61	− .97	− .06	− .36	− .64	.02	− .34	− .79	− .05	− .39	.76
Factory workers	− .11	− .52	− .88	− .22	− .78	−1.52	− .12	− .41	−1.04	− .04	− .58	− .92	− .10	− .55	−1.08
Social leaders	− .02	− .43	− .87	.24	− .49	−1.25	.22	− .23	− .80	.14	− .35	−1.05	.00	− .37	−1.02
Hampton Negroes	− .03	− .20	− .36	− .12	− .54	− .92	.38	− .09	− .43	− .07	− .15	− .54	.04	− .24	.53
Lancaster preachers	.16	− .20	− .69	.45	− .07	− .88	.47	− .03	− .49	.20	− .26	− .54	.30	− .11	.64
Preachers, U. S.	.22	− .17	− .57	.14	− .18	− .80	.15	− .15	− .54	.18	− .82	− .58	.17	− .14	.62
Groups combined	.03	− .31	− .71	− .06	− .53	−1.16	.12	− .25	− .72	.16	− .28	− .70	.10	− .31	.81

Table XXXVIII

Sigma-Values at the Three Quarter-Points for Active Disapprovals for the Several Groups on the Aggressiveness Scale

Groups	Real Love, Coquetry			Spontaneous, Coquetry			Spontaneous, Direct			Real Love, Direct			Total		
	Q_1	Q_2	Q_3	Q_1	Q_2	Q_3	Q_1	Q_2	Q_3	Q_1	Q_2	Q_3	Q_1	Q_2	Q_3
College sen., male	−.01	−.28	.75	−.10	.74	−1.32	−.12	−.44	.93	−.06	−.33	.75	−.06	−.40	.97
College sen., female	.04	−.40	.79	−.14	.93	−1.41	−.11	−.37	.75	−.14	−.43	.76	−.08	−.53	.10
College sen., total	.02	−.36	.77	−.10	.62	−1.34	.14	−.36	.86	−.05	−.37	.74	−.01	−.40	.98
Young miners	−.39	−.70	−1.02	−.83	−1.33	−1.63	−.36	−.78	−1.27	−.27	−.79	−1.05	−.43	−.86	−1.23
Adult miners	−.43	−.77	−1.17	−.80	−1.24	−1.54	−.31	−.67	−1.11	−.26	−.79	−1.11	−.38	−.82	−1.30
Graduate students	−.21	−.56	.93	−.47	−1.01	−1.43	−.21	−.52	.89	−.18	−.63	.99	−.25	−.65	−1.15
Young Brethren	−.04	−.29	.51	−.13	.68	−1.08	−.03	−.30	.56	.06	−.23	.44	.00	−.36	.62
Adult Brethren	−.02	−.26	.52	−.02	.45	.86	.36	−.01	.41	.12	−.13	.53	.14	−.16	.53
Business men	−.20	−.40	.51	−.41	.86	−1.16	−.21	−.41	.84	−.17	−.54	.85	−.24	−.57	.92
Factory workers	−.28	−.61	−1.03	−.36	.99	−1.60	−.22	−.65	−1.28	−.18	−.69	−1.12	−.21	−.72	−1.26
Social leaders	−.35	−.77	−1.27	−.24	−1.16	−1.70	−.21	−.68	−1.30	−.31	−.94	−1.45	−.28	−.90	−1.42
Hampton Negroes	−.07	−.32	.69	−.31	.69	−1.03	.12	−.15	.62	.10	−.24	.58	−.06	−.33	.75
Lancaster preachers	−.15	−.58	.98	−.11	.71	−1.29	−.04	−.36	.77	−.13	−.41	.80	−.10	−.49	.96
Preachers, U. S.	−.19	−.55	.83	−.25	.85	−1.28	−.09	−.51	.83	−.12	−.48	.85	−.13	−.58	.97
Groups combined	−.16	−.45	.86	−.24	.81	−1.36	−.09	−.49	.92	−.04	−.46	.93	−.10	−.54	−1.08

TABLE XXXIX

SIGMA-VALUES AT THE THREE QUARTER-POINTS FOR ADMIRATIONS FOR THE SEVERAL GROUPS ON THE AGGRESSIVENESS SCALE

Groups	Real Love, Coquetry			Spontaneous, Coquetry			Spontaneous, Direct			Real Love, Direct			Total		
	Q_1	Q_2	Q_3	Q_1	Q_2	Q_3	Q_1	Q_2	Q_3	Q_1	Q_2	Q_3	Q_1	Q_2	Q_3
College sen., male	.32	.16	−.19	.43	−.10	−.49	.66	.13	−.27	.51	.12	−.22	.17	.10	−.26
College sen., female	.49	.18	−.21	.33	.22	−.55	.19	−.03	−.29	.42	.09	−.27	.40	.07	−.30
College sen., total	.31	.10	−.15	.42	−.04	−.41	.36	.06	−.23	.52	.11	−.22	.48	.08	−.24
Young miners	−.07	−.41	−.70	−.49	−1.09	−1.29	−.05	−.42	−.87	.01	−.38	−.81	−.12	−.47	−.91
Adult miners	−.02	−.29	−.79	−.32	−.83	−1.27	.02	.28	−.73	.03	−.45	−.83	−.06	−.47	−.90
Graduate students	.23	−.07	−.38	.09	.23	.64	.16	−.15	−.38	.24	−.11	−.42	.26	−.11	−.47
Young Brethren	.15	.02	−.28	.05	.27	.73	.20	−.02	−.39	.30	−.02	−.27	.25	−.04	−.38
Adult Brethren	.41	.07	−.14	.16	.17	.61	.62	.36	.04	.42	.20	−.12	.41	.17	−.12
Business men	.07	−.12	−.22	−.08	.56	.82	.07	−.16	−.41	.21	−.13	−.49	.09	−.19	−.51
Factory workers	.05	−.43	−.75	−.02	.71	−1.24	−.03	−.16	−.77	.07	−.30	−.85	.07	−.34	−.88
Social leaders	.34	−.04	−.39	.81	.07	.59	.58	.12	−.35	.84	.02	−.46	.63	.03	−.44
Hampton Negroes	.12	−.13	−.56	−.09	.43	−.86	.40	.05	−.36	.24	.00	−.32	.12	−.11	−.45
Lancaster preachers	.68	.08	−.17	.38	.50	.07	.41	.53	−.02	.43	.06	−.25	.52	.16	−.19
Preachers, U. S.	.50	.17	−.18	.20	−.02	−.21	.41	.10	−.18	.48	.14	−.16	.45	.12	−.17
Groups combined	.25	−.10	−.37	.20	.30	.78	.34	−.06	−.42	.34	−.04	−.45	.32	−.07	−.48

264

TABLE XL

SIGMA-VALUES AT THE THREE QUARTER-POINTS FOR APPROVALS (ADMIRATION PLUS HALF NEUTRALS) FOR THE SEVERAL GROUPS ON THE KISSING SCALE

Groups	Private			Public			Married			Total		
	Q_1	Q_2	Q_3	Q_1	Q_2	Q_3	Q_1	Q_2	Q_3	Q_1	Q_2	Q_3
College sen., male	.16	−.28	−.84	.13	−.19	−.65	.39	.02	−.20	.22	−.19	−.63
College sen., female	.15	−.22	−.56	.00	−.31	−.69	.27	−.08	−.36	.13	−.25	−.62
College sen., total	.11	−.24	−.71	.07	−.35	−.69	.34	−.05	−.30	.17	−.23	−.64
Young miners, male	.07	−.29	−.79	−.08	−.47	−.86	.50	.32	−.10	.09	−.30	−.65
Young miners, female	.12	−.32	−1.00	−.09	−.46	−.88	.38	.08	−.07	.07	−.37	−.81
Young miners, total	.12	−.27	−.85	−.02	−.42	−.93	.47	.25	−.08	.14	−.28	−.73
Adult miners, female	.28	.00	−.43	.15	−.24	−.59	.46	.44	−.16	.28	−.06	−.49
Adult miners, total	.21	−.09	−.48	.33	−.15	−.60	.44	.29	−.31	.33	−.06	−.55
Graduate students	.17	−.15	−.59	.21	−.04	−.42	.46	.10	−.21	.31	−.06	−.42
Young Brethren	.09	−.18	−.73	.05	−.33	−.77	.50	−.01	−.29	.18	−.24	−.68
Adult Brethren	.28	.15	−.24	.19	−.04	−.33	.43	.25	−.09	.33	.07	−.26
Business men	−.14	−.49	−.94	.19	−.24	−.65	.45	.23	−.23	.17	−.22	−.69
Factory workers	.23	−.17	−.52	.01	−.38	−.74	.24	−.16	−.67	.12	−.30	−.68
Social leaders	−.01	−.40	−1.10	−.04	−.47	−.99	−.12	−.22	−.74	−.04	−.44	−1.00
Hampton Negroes	.18	−.25	−.71	.18	−.21	−.44	.45	.23	.06	.22	−.19	−.41
Lancaster preachers	.20	−.10	−.43	.07	−.29	−.65	.26	−.17	−.50	.19	−.23	−.59
Preachers, U. S.	.21	−.12	−.47	.26	−.22	−.66	.30	−.11	−.31	.26	−.19	−.57
Groups combined	.17	−.17	−.65	.17	−.24	−.71	.41	.10	−.32	.25	−.18	−.65

TABLE XLI

SIGMA-VALUES AT THE THREE QUARTER-POINTS FOR ACTIVE DISAPPROVALS FOR THE SEVERAL GROUPS ON THE KISSING SCALE

Groups	Private			Public			Married			Total		
	Q_1	Q_2	Q_3	Q_1	Q_2	Q_3	Q_1	Q_2	Q_3	Q_1	Q_2	Q_3
College sen., male	−.36	−.72	−1.10	−.16	−.46	−.99	−.23	−.12	−.61	−.31	−.26	−.95
College sen., female	−.01	−.42	−.87	−.20	−.52	−.86	−.02	−.22	−.67	−.15	−.45	−.82
College sen., total	−.19	−.61	−1.02	−.13	−.46	−.95	1.06	−.19	−.72	−.12	−.47	−.91
Young miners, male	−.10	−.37	−.93	−.19	−.61	−1.03	.52	.28	.22	−.02	−.37	−.79
Young miners, female	−.70	−.47	−1.18	−.20	−.62	−.95	.28	−.01	−.23	−.08	−.50	−.81
Young miners, total	−.11	−.49	−.97	−.12	−.57	−1.04	.37	.13	−.28	−.03	−.51	−.86
Adult miners, female	.25	−.15	−.75	−.08	−.38	−.78	.44	.39	−.24	.15	−.25	−.71
Adult miners, total	.12	−.24	−.70	.20	−.25	−.68	.36	.15	−.35	.23	−.18	−.65
Graduate students	−.06	−.44	−.82	−.01	−.29	−.68	.23	−.08	−.45	.05	−.30	−.67
Young Brethren	−.08	−.50	−.90	−.05	−.44	−.88	.37	−.01	−.37	.04	−.38	−.79
Adult Brethren	.28	−.19	−.38	−.02	−.23	−.48	.33	.10	−.20	.20	−.15	−.40
Business men	−.28	−.73	−1.24	.05	−.35	−.71	.41	.13	−.43	.01	−.35	−.75
Factory workers	−.02	−.35	−.67	−.13	−.50	−.94	.01	−.35	−.82	−.09	−.44	−.86
Social leaders	−.15	−.60	−1.49	−.42	−.87	−1.22	−.18	−.30	−.94	−.34	−.68	−1.27
Hampton Negroes	.00	−.42	−1.04	.11	−.24	−.62	.34	−.35	−.17	.11	−.22	−.64
Lancaster preachers	.02	−.35	−.70	−.27	−.58	−1.05	−.11	−.28	−.97	−.19	−.50	−.93
Preachers, U. S.	−.07	−.37	−.69	−.14	−.58	−.86	−.04	−.18	−.50	−.12	−.50	−.75
Groups combined	−.09	−.42	−.88	.01	−.44	−.90	.25	−.12	−.48	.04	−.40	−.83

TABLE XLII

SIGMA-VALUES AT THE THREE QUARTER-POINTS FOR ADMIRATIONS FOR THE SEVERAL GROUPS ON THE KISSING SCALE

Groups	Private			Public			Married			Total		
	Q_1	Q_2	Q_3	Q_1	Q_2	Q_3	Q_1	Q_2	Q_3	Q_1	Q_2	Q_3
College sen., male	.39	.11	−.19	.33	−.00	−.27	.52	.28	−.04	.44	.10	−.21
College sen., female	.25	−.02	−.31	.27	−.09	−.44	.43	.11	−.12	.31	−.05	−.36
College sen., total	.32	.05	−.28	.30	.00	−.30	.52	.23	−.09	.38	.06	−.25
Young miners, male	.23	−.63	−.53	−.06	−.34	−.68	.61	.37	.03	.22	−.19	−.51
Young miners, female	.26	−.07	−.77	−.01	−.36	−.68	.48	.28	.00	.21	−.18	−.61
Young miners, total	.34	.00	−.53	.04	−.29	−.70	.51	.25	−.14	.28	−.13	−.58
Adult miners, female	.38	.07	−.15	.24	−.05	−.38	.42	.33	−.18	.37	.07	−.30
Adult miners, total	.28	−.04	−.35	.33	−.04	−.38	.42	.32	−.16	.33	.05	−.35
Graduate students	.30	.09	−.21	.37	.05	−.17	.58	.33	.02	.41	.17	−.16
Young Brethren	−.24	.00	−.36	.14	−.20	−.53	.58	.37	−.11	.28	.00	−.43
Adult Brethren	.37	.26	.05	.34	.07	−.17	.49	.39	.23	.40	.24	−.03
Business men	−.05	−.31	.54	.18	−.16	−.55	.52	.36	.90	.25	−.05	−.46
Factory workers	.22	−.03	−.41	.08	−.25	−.63	.45	.06	−.39	.25	−.15	−.54
Social leaders	.23	−.11	−.45	.10	−.12	−.53	.35	−.08	−.24	.24	−.12	−.48
Hampton Negroes	.37	−.01	−.39	.24	−.15	−.36	.47	.25	.33	.37	.00	+.30
Lancaster preachers	.39	.10	−.15	.33	.04	−.32	.44	−.03	−.29	.40	.06	−.27
Preachers, U. S.	.37	.19	−.06	.55	.11	−.36	.54	.19	−.14	.48	.15	−.23
Groups combined	.28	.04	−.36	.33	−.02	−.41	.54	.27	−.14	.37	.08	−.37

TABLE XLIII

SIGMA-VALUES AT THE THREE QUARTER-POINTS FOR APPROVALS (ADMIRATION PLUS HALF NEUTRALS) FOR THE SEVERAL GROUPS ON THE DEMOCRACY SCALE

Groups	Race—General			Race—Negro			Employees			Social Status			Totals		
	Q_1	Q_2	Q_3	Q_1	Q_2	Q_3	Q_1	Q_2	Q_3	Q_1	Q_2	Q_3	Q_1	Q_2	Q_3
College sen., male	.10	−.23	−.53	.24	−.17	−.68	.56	.06	−.58	.13	−.14	−.53	.27	−.12	−.57
College sen., female	.32	−.31	−.74	.29	−.29	−.64	.46	−.09	−.49	.30	−.13	−.63	.34	−.18	−.63
College sen., total	.14	−.25	−.62	.26	−.20	−.72	.49	.00	−.59	.21	−.11	−.54	.28	−.13	−.61
Young miners, male	.21	−.57	−1.04	.16	−.31	−.83	.59	−.09	−.96	.38	−.19	−.80	.33	−.32	−.93
Young miners, female	.32	−.63	−1.10	.54	−.53	−1.52	.43	−.27	−1.19	.66	−.54	−1.72	.53	−.52	−1.40
Young miners, total	.14	−.71	−.98	.40	−.45	−1.14	.46	−.03	−1.08	.43	−.25	−1.18	.38	−.37	−1.12
Adult miners	1.01	−.13	−1.20	.54	−.10	−1.27	.60	−.20	−.64	.37	−.28	−.83	.55	−.14	−1.10
Graduate students	.07	−.28	−.79	.34	−.17	−.64	.51	.15	−.39	.22	−.12	−.56	.26	−.12	−.63
Young Brethren	.10	−.45	−.72	.16	−.03	−.41	.60	.26	−.46	.36	−.10	−.63	.34	−.21	−.56
Adult Brethren	.17	−.47	−.87	.15	−.34	−.70	.68	.27	−.23	.47	−.01	−.38	.35	−.13	−.51
Business men	.56	−.24	−.75	.31	−.32	−.90	.27	−.14	−.80	.15	−.20	−.60	.31	−.24	−.75
Factory workers	.34	−.39	−.87	.43	−.10	−.63	.47	.06	−.72	.28	−.20	−.72	.38	−.18	−.73
Social leaders	.17	−.31	−.77	.30	−.38	−1.18	.47	−.10	−.69	.10	−.32	−.71	.26	−.28	−.85
Hampton Negroes	.11	−.38	−.79	.16	−.15	−.54	.53	−.08	−.25	.37	−.22	−.93	.33	−.21	−.69
Lancaster preachers	.19	−.21	−.74	.12	−.12	−.55	.25	−.22	−.68	.17	−.19	−.60	.18	−.19	−.64
Preachers, U. S.	.07	−.34	−.68	.24	.30	−.71	.61	.22	−.28	.46	−.07	−.55	.39	−.11	−.55
Groups combined	.16	−.27	−.76	.30	−.20	−.72	.50	.09	−.47	.15	−.18	−.73	.29	−.16	−.70

Table XLIV
Sigma-Values at the Three Quarter-Points for Active Disapprovals for the Several Groups on the Democracy Scale

Groups	Race—General			Race—Negro			Employees			Social Status			Totals		
	Q_1	Q_2	Q_3	Q_1	Q_2	Q_3	Q_1	Q_2	Q_3	Q_1	Q_2	Q_3	Q_1	Q_2	Q_3
College sen., male	.04	−.54	−.70	.04	−.64	−.84	.11	−.55	−.89	−.10	−.48	−.06	.02	−.54	−.87
College sen., female	−.12	−.65	−.88	−.06	−.51	−.83	.17	−.50	−.96	−.16	−.51	−.87	−.05	−.55	−.88
College sen., total	−.16	−.55	−.75	−.08	−.68	−.84	−.02	−.48	−.85	−.13	−.53	−.94	−.10	−.56	−.84
Young miners, male	.16	−.67	−.96	−.15	−.60	−.97	.21	−.35	−1.19	.03	−.52	−1.15	.04	−.55	−1.10
Young miners, female	−.07	−.92	−1.32	−.01	−.81	−1.68	.25	−.76	−1.31	.15	−.91	−1.96	.09	−.87	−1.59
Young miners, total	−.01	−.85	−1.10	.01	−.84	−1.50	.09	−.50	−1.24	.11	−.53	−1.38	.05	−.68	−1.27
Adult miners	.69	−.66	−1.33	.58	−.17	−1.12	.44	−.18	−.93	.28	−.44	−1.13	.50	−.38	−1.14
Graduate students	−.13	−.69	−1.11	−.16	−.60	−.81	−.04	−.51	−.74	−.04	−.48	−1.02	−.09	−.56	−.93
Young Brethren	−.15	−.60	−.74	.11	−.20	−.59	.32	−.06	−.53	.23	−.24	−.94	.15	−.23	−.72
Adult Brethren	−.17	−.72	−1.04	.08	−.41	−.84	.59	−.01	−.61	.17	−.37	−.58	.14	−.37	−.76
Business men	.21	−.59	−.95	.06	−.64	−1.00	.12	−.51	−1.03	.14	−.31	−.87	.12	−.52	−.96
Factory workers	.01	−.80	−1.06	.27	−.39	−.80	.21	−.36	−.93	−.09	−.57	−1.17	.07	−.56	−1.02
Social leaders	−.19	−.60	−.93	−.07	−.86	−1.25	−.11	−.53	−.91	−.20	−.61	−1.09	−.13	−.68	−1.03
Hampton Negroes	−.03	−.44	−.89	.03	−.31	−.76	−.43	−.51	−1.06	.16	−.71	−1.17	.16	−.49	−.97
Lancaster preachers	−.01	−.57	−.91	−.03	−.45	−.96	−.26	−.68	−.94	−.12	−.53	−1.07	−.11	−.55	−.99
Preachers, U. S.	−.22	−.58	−.76	−.07	−.62	−.86	.09	−.08	−.56	−.10	−.50	−.85	−.09	−.46	−.76
Groups combined	−.06	−.58	−.92	.06	−.57	−.90	.06	−.37	−.80	−.07	−.51	−1.03	.00	−.51	−.92

TABLE XLV

SIGMA-VALUES AT THE THREE QUARTER-POINTS FOR ADMIRATIONS FOR THE SEVERAL GROUPS ON THE DEMOCRACY SCALE

Groups	Race—General			Race—Negro			Employees			Social Status			Totals		
	Q_1	Q_2	Q_3	Q_1	Q_2	Q_3	Q_1	Q_2	Q_3	Q_1	Q_2	Q_3	Q_1	Q_2	Q_3
College sen., male	.37	.01	−.23	.38	.10	−.28	.60	.49	.07	.35	−.01	−.15	.42	.15	−.16
College sen., female	.30	−.05	−.39	.44	.07	−.17	.54	.32	.12	.52	−.25	−.15	.43	.16	−.16
College sen., total	.27	−.02	−.29	.40	.08	−.10	.67	.44	.05	.46	.11	−.50	.46	.15	−.15
Young miners, male	.35	−.40	−.82	.36	−.06	−.72	.62	.49	−.80	.41	−.05	−.26	.43	.03	−.71
Young miners, female	.55	−.20	−.86	.82	.05	−.93	.62	.17	−.90	1.04	−.12	−1.22	.80	−.05	−1.02
Young miners, total	.56	−.13	−.84	.62	−.01	−.69	.68	.34	−.79	.59	−.02	−.83	.61	−.02	−.79
Adult miners	.92	.37	−.91	1.33	.34	−.67	.77	.26	−.47	.59	−.05	−.65	.75	.25	−.60
Graduate students	.27	−.01	−.29	.55	.17	−.09	.74	.49	.17	.43	.05	−.15	.50	.18	−.08
Young Brethren	.20	−.26	−.66	.25	.04	−.23	.65	.42	−.05	.45	.04	−.24	.40	.09	−.25
Adult Brethren	.30	−.04	−.62	.35	.02	−.43	.73	.56	.26	.74	.38	−.10	.57	.24	−.29
Business men	.60	−.08	−.54	.39	.04	−.71	.47	−.07	−.43	.53	−.05	−.35	.51	.00	−.53
Factory workers	.40	−.27	−.69	.47	.11	−.33	.65	.37	−.46	.57	.16	.32	.53	.09	−.44
Social leaders	.31	−.09	.69	.49	.25	−.60	.69	.52	.10	.48	−.06	−.28	.52	.12	−.43
Hampton Negroes	.23	−.25	−.54	.24	−.02	−.31	.61	.00	−.56	.48	.02	−.62	.43	−.06	−.57
Lancaster preachers	.36	.11	−.55	.25	−.08	−.31	.38	.12	.34	.46	.10	−.27	.26	.06	−.38
Preachers, U. S.	.38	−.10	−.42	.43	.07	−.28	.84	.61	.25	.88	.21	−.16	.66	.22	−.15
Groups combined	.39	−.08	−.54	.46	.00	−.32	.67	.33	−.11	.53	.01	−.25	.52	.06	−.30

Table XLVI

Sigma-Values at the Three Quarter-Points for Approvals (Admiration Plus Half Neutrals) for the Several Groups on the Parents and Children Scale

Groups	Companionship			Discipline			Tolerance			Sacrifice			Totals		
	Q_1	Q_2	Q_3	Q_1	Q_2	Q_3	Q_1	Q_2	Q_3	Q_1	Q_2	Q_3	Q_1	Q_2	Q_3
College sen., male	.60	.06	− .32	.72	.10	− .49	.53	.08	− .37	.57	.12	− .68	.55	.09	− .47
College sen., female	.32	− .08	− .81	.26	− .25	− .58	.38	− .15	− .87	.44	− .18	− .68	.36	− .16	− .72
College sen., total	.41	− .05	− .64	.53	− .04	− .57	.50	− .05	− .65	− .52	− .02	− .65	.49	− .04	− .62
Young miners	− .17	− .48	− 1.01	− .08	− .59	− 1.28	.11	− .78	− 1.19	.30	− .49	− 1.26	.06	− .59	− 1.21
Adult miners	− .08	− .37	− .88	− .11	− .54	− .78	.12	− .64	− 1.15	.16	− .73	− 1.07	.03	− .57	− .94
Graduate students	.16	− .11	− .50	.13	− .24	− .52	.32	− .28	− .80	.60	− .08	− .72	.35	− .16	− .63
Young Brethren	.33	− .18	− .53	.11	− .22	− .75	.60	− .08	− .87	.54	− .08	− .82	.36	− .16	− .75
Adult Brethren	.11	− .12	− .54	.21	− .29	− .57	.63	.07	− .40	.69	− .41	− 1.12	.44	− .18	− .61
Business men	.14	− .16	− .45	.16	− .36	− .49	.42	− .03	− .64	.39	− .31	− .81	.30	− .21	− .58
Factory workers	.19	− .35	− .79	.13	− .38	− .70	.52	− .18	− .88	.58	.09	− .60	.38	− .21	− .75
Social leaders	.34	− .04	− .78	.26	− .14	− .41	.14	− .34	− .79	.33	− .13	− .76	.27	− .18	− .64
Hampton Negroes	− .04	− .32	− .68	.26	− .35	− .60	.42	− .15	− .69	.56	− .14	− .59	.31	− .26	− .64
Lancaster preachers	.21	− .17	− .61	.25	− .20	− .58	.23	− .42	− .90	.50	− .12	− .89	.32	− .23	− .71
Preachers, U. S.	.24	.11	− .41	.15	− .37	− .51	.22	− .41	− .69	.14	− .25	− .81	.18	− .16	− .58
Groups combined	.13	− .12	− .55	.15	− .29	− .68	.39	− .24	− .91	.48	− .38	− .91	.31	− .25	− .76

271

TABLE XLVII

SIGMA-VALUES AT THE THREE QUARTER-POINTS FOR ACTIVE DISAPPROVALS FOR THE SEVERAL GROUPS ON THE PARENTS AND CHILDREN SCALE

Groups	Companionship			Discipline			Tolerance			Sacrifice			Totals		
	Q_1	Q_2	Q_3	Q_1	Q_2	Q_3	Q_1	Q_2	Q_3	Q_1	Q_2	Q_3	Q_1	Q_2	Q_3
College sen., male	.12	−.27	−.62	.62	−.20	−.91	−.17	−.20	−.72	.28	−.34	−.98	.35	−.24	−.81
College sen., female	−.12	−.50	−1.08	−.09	−.46	−.88	−.09	−.64	−1.25	.33	−.42	−1.10	.01	−.51	−1.09
College sen., total	.05	−.38	−.82	.30	−.36	−.92	−.11	−.36	−1.00	.13	−.53	−.96	.15	−.39	−.33
Young miners	−.36	−.68	−1.22	.30	−.84	−1.40	−.41	−1.09	−1.33	−.34	−1.14	−1.47	−.35	−.92	−1.38
Adult miners	−.30	−.55	−1.10	.39	−.50	−1.06	−.23	−.75	−1.36	−.51	−1.21	−1.38	−.35	−.73	−1.22
Graduate students	−.22	−.37	−.75	.15	−.41	−.80	−.06	−.63	−1.00	−.11	−.49	−1.01	−.04	−.48	−.88
Young Brethren	.24	−.64	−.74	.14	−.55	−.95	.35	−.59	−.92	.20	−.45	−1.18	−.10	−.56	−.95
Adult Brethren		−.23	−.46	.28	−.47	−.65	.21	−.12	−.78	.35	−.63	−1.18	.10	−.35	−.81
Business men	−.14	−.37	−.59	.05	−.44	−.66	.07	−.42	−.80	.15	−.47	−.99	.01	−.42	−.72
Factory workers	−.19	−.66	−.97	.13	−.52	−.96	.07	−.58	−1.00	.23	−.15	−1.09	.00	−.49	−1.00
Social leaders	−.22	−.68	−.99	.05	−.35	−.72	−.24	−.61	−1.18	−.13	−.80	−1.25	−.09	−.59	−.99
Hampton Negroes	−.07	−.45	−.61	.04	−.43	−.94	.29	−.45	−.87	.32	−.33	−.80	.11	−.42	−.83
Lancaster preachers		−.38	−.88	.10	−.52	−.93	.38	−.74	−1.09		−.89	−1.19	−.18	−.56	−1.01
Preachers, U. S.	−.17	−.44	−.69	−.04	−.41	−.84	−.33	−.51	−.90	.22	−.24	−.80	−.07	−.40	−.82
Groups combined	−.16	−.40	−.87	.00	−.50	−.86	.05	−.69	−1.07	.06	−.75	−1.18	.01	−.58	−1.00

272

TABLE XLVIII

SIGMA-VALUES AT THE THREE QUARTER-POINTS FOR ADMIRATIONS FOR THE SEVERAL GROUPS ON THE PARENTS AND CHILDREN SCALE

Groups	Companionship			Discipline			Tolerance			Sacrifice			Totals		
	Q_1	Q_2	Q_3	Q_1	Q_2	Q_3	Q_1	Q_2	Q_3	Q_1	Q_2	Q_3	Q_1	Q_2	Q_3
College sen., male	.81	.46	.11	.99	.41	−.07	.46	.37	.00	.63	.53	−.24	.71	.43	−.06
College sen., female	.51	.22	−.35	.47	.12	−.34	.72	.33	−.15	.70	.54	−.10	.64	.31	−.25
College sen., total	.65	.23	−.11	.70	.21	−.24	.61	.32	−.07	.69	.40	−.09	.69	.29	−.13
Young miners	−.09	−.16	−.71	.17	−.42	−.96	.46	−.13	−1.00	.60	.36	−.93	.36	−.13	−.92
Adult miners	.08	−.18	−.61	.15	−.50	−.54	.48	−.02	−.92	.69	−.54	−1.08	.35	−.27	−.76
Graduate students	.39	.16	−.13	.29	−.04	−.25	.60	.39	−.26	.71	.33	−.33	.52	.22	−.24
Young Brethren	.56	.27	−.11	.29	−.10	−.40	.67	.22	−.54	.74	.43	−.17	.57	.14	−.33
Adult Brethren	.32	.15	−.24	.39	−.05	−.48	.70	.62	−.02	.64	.50	−.01	.50	.35	−.23
Business men	.38	.04	−.21	.24	−.16	−.45	.53	.28	−.05	.53	−.03	−.53	.53	.04	−.30
Factory workers	.39	.00	−.46	.30	−.26	−.54	.71	.37	−.36	.73	.49	.00	.54	.09	−.39
Social leaders	.44	.11	−.05	.38	.15	−.15	.45	.05	−.49	.46	.27	−.65	.44	.14	−.25
Hampton Negroes	.05	−.29	−.70	.35	−.15	−.42	.62	.09	−.54	.63	.34	−.01	.44	−.01	−.39
Lancaster preachers	.36	.13	−.42	.38	−.05	−.28	.49	.09	−.46	.59	.11	−.31	.47	.02	−.37
Preachers, U. S.	.36	.21	−.14	.18	−.17	−.42	.47	.12	−.44	.27	.39	−.04	.30	.06	−.26
Groups combined	.26	.02	−.23	.33	−.10	−.42	.65	.17	−.46	.83	.23	−.45	.51	.11	−.40

273

Table XLIX

SIGMA-VALUES AT THE THREE QUARTER-POINTS FOR REPORTED ACTUAL PRACTICES FOR CERTAIN SOCIAL GROUPS ON AGGRESSIVENESS

Groups	Real Love, Coquetry			Spontaneous, Coquetry			Spontaneous, Direct			Real Love, Direct			Total		
	Q1	Q2	Q3	Q1	Q2	Q3	Q1	Q2	Q3	Q1	Q2	Q3	Q1	Q2	Q3
College sen., total	-.13	-.59	-1.01	.53	.94	-1.48	-.19	.52	-1.10	.01	-.28	.76	-.15	-.59	-1.09
Young miners	-.50	-.92	-1.50	-1.19	-1.59	-2.21	-.49	-1.12	-1.51	-.32	-.92	-1.20	-.54	-1.17	-1.55
Adult miners							-.64	-1.29	-2.08	-.46	-.95	-1.48	-.53	-1.17	-1.89
Graduate students	-.21	-.57	-.91	-.45	-.92	-1.37	-.17	.40	-.98	-.08	-.42	.85	-.14	.55	-1.07
Young Brethren	.15	-.48	-1.09	.12	.94	-1.94	.07	.48	-1.16	.07	-.39	.92	.12	.58	-1.29
Adult Brethren	.06	-.17	-.65	.05	.49	-.99	.49	.05	-.66	.26	.01	.60	.16	.06	.67
Business men	-.20	-.61	-.96	.56	-1.07	-1.52	-.25	.75	-1.17	-.16	-.50	.95	-.26	.68	-1.14
Factory workers	-.17	-.84	-1.56	-.44	-1.19	-1.76	-.02	.79	-1.42	-.21	-.81	-1.29	-.18	.85	-1.50
Hampton Negroes	.18	-.26	-.67	.79	-1.12	-1.32	.02	.04	-.49	.03	-.11	.43	-.13	.31	.65

TABLE L

SIGMA-VALUES AT THE THREE QUARTER-POINTS FOR REPORTED ACTUAL PRACTICES FOR CERTAIN SOCIAL GROUPS ON KISSING

Groups	Private			Public			Married			Total		
	Q1	Q2	Q3	Q1	Q2	Q3	Q1	Q2	Q3	Q1	Q2	Q3
College sen., total	-.34	-.94	-1.88	.00	-.47	-1.21	.35	-.06	-.75	-.01	-.48	-1.33
Young miners	-.25	-.83	-1.70	-.31	-.74	-1.05	.37	.06	-.51	-.20	-.65	-1.18
Adult miners	-.31	-1.42	-1.98	.32	-.95	-1.69	.33	.04	-.63	-.20	-.94	-1.94
Graduate students	-.20	-.86	-1.64	.10	-.33	-1.05	.45	.14	-.40	-.08	-.38	-1.12
Young Brethren	-.15	-.84	-1.90	.05	-.32	-1.00	.53	.02	-.78	.09	-.39	-1.18
Adult Brethren	.21	.12	.38	.19	-.05	-.40	.62	.40	.17	.31	.17	-.20
Business men	-.20	-.63	-1.54	.06	-.51	-1.16	.37	.02	-.71	.07	-.45	-1.18
Factory workers	.18	-.25	-1.00	-.38	-.63	-1.03	.09	-.34	-.98	-.21	-.51	-1.01
Hampton Negroes	.25	-.05	-.88		.31			.54			-.17	

Table LI

Sigma-Values at the Three Quarter-Points for Reported Actual Practices for Certain Social Groups on Democracy

Groups	Race—General			Race—Negro			Employee			Social Status			Total		
	Q_1	Q_2	Q_3	Q_1	Q_2	Q_3	Q_1	Q_2	Q_3	Q_1	Q_2	Q_3	Q_1	Q_2	Q_3
College sen., total	-.62	-1.22	-1.77	-.78	-1.11	-1.56	.78	.51	-1.76	.16	-.69	-1.91	.00	-.85	-1.77
Adult miners	-.52	.68	.17	.74	.01	.75	.71	.45	-1.45	.39	-.91	-1.94	.33	.55	-1.49
Graduate students	-.36	.57	-1.74	.27	.58	-1.24	.43	.88	-1.89	.39	-.74	-1.93	.32	.75	-1.73
Young Brethren	.13	.74	-1.47	.43	.32	-1.24	.50	.07	-.45	.50	-.23	-.97	.38	.31	-.99
Adult Brethren	.10	-.61	-1.13	.29	-.54	-1.23	.21	.85	-1.24	.25	-.69	-1.54	.22	.63	-1.30
Business men	-.05	.50	-1.03	.11	-.14	-.90	.69	.42	-1.47	.51	-.64	-1.52	.36	.41	-1.32
Factory workers	-.13	.37	-1.48												
Hampton Negroes	-.84	-1.56		-.80	-1.16	-1.46	-.64	-1.31	-1.98				-.79	-1.37	-1.97

Table LII

Sigma-Values at the Three Quarter-Points for Reported Actual Practices for Certain Social Groups on Parents and Children

Groups	Companionship			Discipline			Tolerance			Sacrifice			Total		
	Q_1	Q_2	Q_3	Q_1	Q_2	Q_3	Q_1	Q_2	Q_3	Q_1	Q_2	Q_3	Q_1	Q_2	Q_3
College sen., total	.42	-.10	-.93	.17	-.58	-1.69	.29	-.61	-1.37	.49	-.43	-.95	.34	-.51	-1.32
Young miners	.06	-.90	-1.37	-.61	-1.54	-2.25	-.14	-.97	-1.55	.02	-1.16	-1.57	-.27	-.12	-1.60
Adult miners	.48	-.20	-1.03	-.32	-1.06	-1.88	.11	-1.08	-1.39	.38	-1.04	-1.73	.12	-.93	-1.52
Graduate students	.70	.20	-.90	-.09	.63	-1.45	.40	.77	-1.33	.42	-.74	-1.05	.38	-.43	-1.24
Young Brethren	.16	-.69	-1.35	.06	.89	-1.94	.32	.80	-1.70	.29	-.66	-1.69	.14	-.80	-1.70
Adult Brethren	.71	.02	.42	-.21	-.35	-1.14	.49	.03	.79	.61	-.44	-1.41	.50	-.20	-1.00
Business men	.59	-.02	-.81	-.15	-.79	-1.59	.21	-.77	-1.25	.11	-.40	-1.28	.15	-.54	-1.16
Factory workers	.08	-.84	-1.29	-.14	-.86	-1.51	.31	.54	-1.40	.74	.24	-1.11	.15	-.57	-1.36
Hampton Negroes	.82	.04	.57	.02	.98	-2.06	.69	.16	-1.19	.41	.34	-.80	.35	-.35	-1.25

TABLE LIII — INTERCORRELATIONS AMONG GROUPS IN VALUES DERIVED FROM THE ORIGINAL PROCEDURE IN MAKING THE SCALES

Groups	r	Means	
Kissing:			
Student and faculty	.888	(S) −.26	(F) −.60
Student and wage girl	.871	(S) −.26	(WG) −.06
Student and wage boy	.868	(S) −.26	(WB) −.69
Faculty and wage boy	.873	(F) −.60	(WB) −.69
Facult and wage girl	.873	(F) −.60	(WG) −.06
Wage girl and wage boy	.846	(WG) −.06	(WB) −.69
New York girl and student	.799	(NY) −.22	(S) −.26
New York girl and faculty	.801	(NY) −.22	(F) −.60
New York girl and wage girl	.802	(NY) −.22	(WG) −.06
New York girl and wage boy	.795	(NY) −.22	(WB) −.69
Democracy:			
Student and faculty	.914	(S) −.22	(F) −.44
Student and wage boy	.928	(S) −.22	(WB) −.66
Student and wage girl	.923	(S) −.22	(WG) .85
Faculty and wage boy	.905	(F) −.44	(WB) −.66
Faculty and wage girl	.902	(F) −.44	(WG) .85
Wage girl and wage boy	.890	(WG) −.85	(WB) −.66
New York girl and student	.820	(NY) −.32	(S) −.22
New York girl and faculty	.800	(NY) −.32	(F) −.44
New York girl and wage girl	.768	(NY) −.32	(WG) .85
New York girl and wage boy	.743	(NY) −.32	(WB) −.86
Parent-Child:			
Student and faculty	.961	(S) −.36	(F) −.43
Student and wage boy	.872	(S) −.36	(WB) −.49
Faculty and wage boy	.884	(F) −.43	(WB) −.49
Faculty and wage girl	.870	(F) −.43	(WG) −.10
Wage girl and wage boy	.802	(WG) −.10	(WB) −.49
Student and wage girl	.893	(S) −.36	(WG) −.10
New York girl and student	.896	(NY) −.41	(S) −.36
New York girl and faculty	.926	(NY) −.41	(F) −.43
New York girl and wage girl	.824	(NY) −.41	(WG) −.10
New York girl and wage boy	.834	(NY) −.41	(WB) −.49
Aggressiveness:			
Student and faculty	.857	(S) −.88	(F) −1.21
Student and wage boy	.790	(S) −.88	(WB) −.96
Student and wage girl	.859	(S) −.88	(WG) −.70
Faculty and wage boy	.792	(F) −1.21	(WB) −.96
Faculty and wage girl	.730	(F) −1.21	(WG) −.70
Wage girl and wage boy	.702	(WG) −.70	(WB) −.96
New York girl and student	.849	(NY) −.74	(S) −.88
New York girl and faculty	.810	(NY) −.74	(F) −1.21
New York girl and wage girl	.708	(NY) −.74	(WG) −.70
New York girl and wage boy	.660	(NY) −.74	(WB) −.96

APPENDIX C

SOME STATISTICAL FORMULÆ EMPLOYED IN OUR STUDY

A. Coefficient of Correlation (Pearson Product-Moment Formula)

Because some persons not technically trained in statistics may wish to do some correlation work of the sort we did in our study, we shall give the formula in a form that anyone with a little training in high school algebra can use. It is as follows:

$$r = \frac{n\Sigma XY - (\Sigma X) \cdot (\Sigma Y)}{\sqrt{n\Sigma X^2 - (\Sigma X)^2}\sqrt{n\Sigma Y^2 - (\Sigma Y)^2}}$$

The Σ is the Greek letter for S, the initial letter of "sum." It means you are to add together for the whole series the values that follow it. An X stands for a score in the one series and a Y for a corresponding score in the other series, in any form in which you happen to have these scores, provided only you keep consistently to the same kind of scores throughout the series. For example, the "aggressiveness" score on *Bad Girl* might be -1.35 and the box-office receipts from this same picture $5,362. The XY for that picture would be 5,362 multiplied by -1.35, which equals -7238.7. Each other picture in the correlation problem would also have a value for the product of the badness score and the commercial success score. The ΣXY would be the sum of all these products, the algebraic sign being treated in the customary way. The (ΣX) requires adding the badness values algebraically of all the pictures and the (ΣY) requires similarly adding all the box-office receipts. Then these two sums must be multiplied together and the product subtracted from the n times ΣXY, the n being the number of pictures in the correlation problem. An analogous procedure is followed in the denominator: the ΣX^2

requires that you square each badness value, then add these squares together; in the $(\Sigma X)^2$ you sum before you square. After taking the square root of each of the quantities under the radical, those square roots must be multiplied together and the product divided into the numerator to get r. Coefficients of correlation run from -1.00 to $+1.00$. Their practical significance in work like ours is discussed on pages 147–151.

B. Standard Deviation

You are very close to a standard deviation when working with the denominator of the correlation formula. You only need to divide the square root you have taken by n, the number of items in the series, to get sigma (which is the technical name for standard deviation). The formula, then, where X represents a score in any series, is:

$$\text{Standard Deviation} = \frac{1}{n}\sqrt{n\Sigma X^2 - (\Sigma X)^2}$$

The symbol used in statistics for standard deviation is the Greek letter corresponding to our small s, σ, the name of which is sigma.

C. The Spearman Prophecy Formula

Because so much of what we have said about reliabilities in our study turns upon the Spearman Prophecy Formula, we shall undertake to give to the fairly technical reader a notion of what is back of this formula in order that he may be able to judge how much confidence he can place in it. It will be recalled that this formula is used when we wish to predict how closely the findings we have from a few samples will correlate with findings from further trials in the future. We must have in hand at least two samples (or one that can be divided into two halves), then we can judge the expected agreement with future samples by means of the degree of consistency among the samples we have in hand.

We shall start our development with the basic correlation formula which, when the scores are put in terms of deviations from the means of the series in which they occur instead of in raw scores as in the formula given in our first section, is:

$$r_{xy} = \frac{\Sigma xy}{\sqrt{\Sigma x^2 \cdot \Sigma y^2}}$$

Now let the x be replaced by the sum of a series of scores (as the sum of ratings made by a number of judges), these elements being represented by $x_1, x_2, x_3, \cdots, x_a$; and let the y also be constituted by the sum of $y_1, y_2, y_3, \cdots, y_b$. Then

$$r_{(x_1+x_2+x_3+x_4+\cdots+x_a)\ (y_1+y_2+y_3+\cdots+y_b)}$$

$$= \frac{\Sigma(x_1+x_2+x_3+x_4+\cdots+x_a)\ (y_1+y_2+y_3+\cdots+y_b)}{\sqrt{\Sigma(x_1+x_2+x_3+x_4+\cdots+x_a)^2 \cdot \Sigma(y_1+y_2+y_3+y_4+\cdots+y_b)^2}}$$

Multiplying together our polynomials in the numerator and squaring those in the denominator as indicated, placing the summation sign with each member instead of before the expressions as wholes, and using a more abbreviated symbolism for the r between the sums,

$$r_{s_x s_y} = \frac{\Sigma x_1 y_1 + \Sigma x_1 y_2 + \Sigma x_1 y_3 + \cdots + \Sigma x_2 y_1 + \Sigma x_2 y_2 + \cdots + \Sigma x_a y_b}{\sqrt{[(\Sigma x_1^2 + \Sigma x_2^2 + \Sigma x_3^2 + \cdots + \Sigma x_a^2) + \Sigma x_1 x_2 + \cdots + \Sigma x_a x_n] \cdot [(\Sigma y_1^2 + \Sigma y_2^2 + \cdots) + \Sigma y_1 y_2 + \cdots}}$$

Let us now divide both numerator and denominator of the right-hand member of the equation by $n\sigma\sigma$, which also equals $n\sigma^2$, the sigma being the typical standard deviation of the series and the n the number of cases in any one of them. This involves the assumption that the samples we have in hand and also those about which we are attempting to predict in the future all have approximately the same variability and the same number of cases. We shall then have:

$$r_{s_x s_y} = \frac{\dfrac{\Sigma x_1 y_1}{n\sigma\sigma} + \dfrac{\Sigma x_1 y_2}{n\sigma\sigma} + \dfrac{\Sigma x_1 y_3}{n\sigma\sigma} + \cdots + \dfrac{\Sigma x_2 y_1}{n\sigma\sigma} + \dfrac{\Sigma x_2 y_2}{n\sigma\sigma} + \dfrac{\Sigma x_2 y_3}{n\sigma\sigma} + \cdots}{\sqrt{\left[\dfrac{\Sigma x_1^2}{n\sigma^2} + \dfrac{\Sigma x_2^2}{n\sigma^2} + \cdots + \dfrac{\Sigma x_1 x_2}{n\sigma\sigma} + \dfrac{\Sigma x_1 x_3}{n\sigma\sigma} + \cdots\right]\left[\dfrac{\Sigma y_1^2}{n\sigma^2} + \dfrac{\Sigma y_2^2}{n\sigma^2} + \cdots + \dfrac{\Sigma y_1 y_2}{n\sigma\sigma} + \dfrac{\Sigma y_1 y_3}{n\sigma\sigma}\right]}}$$

Having assumed that the standard deviations are approximately equal, so that any one sigma is reasonably representative of any other, all of the expressions of the type $\dfrac{\Sigma xy}{n\sigma\sigma}$ become equal to r_{xy}, and all those of the form $\dfrac{\Sigma x_1 x_2}{n\sigma\sigma}$ become r_{xx}. But since we are assuming the y series of samples to be similar to the x series we have in hand, r_{xy} will be the same sort of thing as r_{xx}. We may speak of all of these r's summed together and divided by their number as the *average intercorrelation* for which the symbol shall be r_{1I}. This symbol does not particularly fit the xy terminology in which we have developed the formula here, but it is the standard symbol and we shall employ it for the sake of uniformity. Evidently there are in the numerator ab of such r_{1I}'s, because each element of the x series, of which there are a in number, enters into combination with each element of the y series of which there are b. But in the denominator each enters into combination with one less than the whole series (itself being excluded by reason of having been used in the x^2 element); therefore the number will be $a(a-1)$ or (a^2-a), on the left and (b^2-b) on the right. The expressions of the type $\dfrac{\Sigma x^2}{n\sigma^2}$ each equals $\dfrac{\sigma^2}{\sigma^2} = 1$ (since $\dfrac{\Sigma x^2}{n} = \sigma^2$ where our units are in terms of deviations from the mean), and there are a of them on the left and b of them on the right. Keeping in mind all these equivalents, we may write,

$$r_{s_x s_y} = \frac{abr_{1I}}{\sqrt{a+(a^2-a)r_{1I}}\sqrt{b+(b^2-b)r_{1I}}}$$

This is the generalized Spearman Prophecy Formula for predicting the correlation between the sums of a sets of scores in hand and b sets of scores in a future series.

If a and b be equal, and both be represented by a, the formula simplifies to

$$r_{s_a s_a} = \frac{a^2 r_{1I}}{a+(a^2-a)r_{1I}} = \frac{a r_{1I}}{1+(a-1)r_{1I}}$$

If a is 2, which is the case where we split our sample into two halves so that the sum is twice each half and we wish to predict the extent of agreement with another sum equal to the same two halves,

$$r = \frac{2r_{1I}}{1+r_{1I}}$$

This is the well-known Spearman-Brown formula.

Let us go back to our generalized formula and see whether we could make b infinite, so that we would have the predicted correlation between the sum or the average of our set of judges and the sum or the average from an infinite number. If we substitute infinity for b we get infinity over infinity for our fraction, and that is of indeterminate value. Let us, therefore, divide both numerator and denominator by b. Then, remembering that the b must be squared when dividing under the radical,

$$r_{s_a \infty} = \frac{a r_{1I}}{\sqrt{a + (a^2 - a) r_{1I}} \sqrt{\frac{1}{b} + \left(1 - \frac{1}{b}\right) r_{1I}}}$$

The $\frac{1}{b}$ equals zero, since the denominator is infinity. Therefore

$$r_{s_a \infty} = \frac{a r_{1I}}{\sqrt{a + (a^2 - a) r_{1I}} \sqrt{r_{1I}}} = \frac{a r_{1I}}{\sqrt{a r_{1I} + (a^2 - a) r_{1I}^2}}$$

One may divide either or both of the series in a correlation problem by any factor without affecting the correlation. The correlation between the sums would therefore be the same as the correlation between the averages got by dividing these sums by their respective n's. Of course the one we have called infinity could not be entirely infinity and yet retain any mathematical meaning when divided by its corresponding n, which would be infinite. But it may be as large as we please. We may call the average of an extremely large number of scores (or judgments) the "true" score or the "true" judgment. The formula above will then give us the correlation between the averages of the ones we have in hand and the true averages.

D. Average Intercorrelation

The average intercorrelations needed for the formula in the preceding section may be computed directly. But, especially if the number of series is large (the number of judges), the task of computing them is very great. If the means and the standard deviations of the series are approximately equal, the average intercorrelation may be got by a much simpler process. We shall show the development of the formula, which we employed in computing the ·reliabilities of the ratings of motion pictures by our first committee.

Let s be the sum of scores x_1, x_2, x_3, x_4, $\cdots$, x_a on each picture, these being taken as deviations from the means. Then

$$\sigma_s^2 = \frac{\Sigma(x_1 + x_2 + x_3 + x_4 + \cdots + x_a)^2}{n}$$

Squaring the polynomial in the numerator and putting the n and the summation sign with each of the constituent terms,

$$\sigma_s^2 = \frac{\Sigma x_1^2}{n} + \frac{\Sigma x_2^2}{n} + \frac{\Sigma x_3^2}{n} + \frac{\Sigma x_4^2}{n} + \cdots + \frac{\Sigma x_1 x_2}{n} + \frac{\Sigma x_1 x_3}{n} + \frac{\Sigma x_1 x_4}{n}$$
$$+ \cdots + \frac{\Sigma x_2 x_1}{n} + \frac{\Sigma x_2 x_3}{n} + \cdots .$$

By multiplying both numerator and denominator of each of the expressions of the type $\frac{\Sigma x_1 x_2}{n}$ by $\sigma\sigma$, we shall have expressions of the type $\frac{\Sigma x_1 x_2}{n\sigma\sigma}\sigma^2$, which equals $r_{x_1 x_2}\sigma^2$. We shall treat the standard deviations $\left(\text{represented by the expressions of the type } \frac{\Sigma x^2}{n}\right)$ as equal, and the r's as an average. Just as was the case in our section above, there will be a of the sigmas and $(a^2 - a)$ of the r's.

Then
$$\sigma_s^2 = a\sigma_x^2 + (a^2 - a)r_{1I}\sigma_x^2$$

Transposing,
$$(a^2 - a)\sigma_x^2 r_{1I} = \sigma_s^2 - a\sigma_x^2,$$

and
$$r_{1I} = \frac{\sigma_s^2 - a\sigma_x^2}{\sigma_x^2(a^2 - a)} = \frac{\dfrac{\sigma_s^2}{\sigma_x^2} - a}{a^2 - a}$$

σ_s is the standard deviation of the set of sums across the columns and σ_x is the typical sigma of a single set of scores. It may be taken as the average of all the separate standard deviations of the individual series or, without much error, as the standard deviation of all the individual scores thrown into a single distribution. If there are three series (as three judges) and we have averages from them instead of sums, the σ_s^2 will equal nine times $\sigma_{\text{av.}}^2$. Our formula will then simplify to

$$r_{1I} = \frac{\dfrac{9\sigma_{\text{av.}}^2}{\sigma_x^2} - 3}{9 - 3} = \frac{3\sigma_{\text{av.}}^2}{2\sigma_x^2} - \frac{1}{2}$$

INDEX

Advertising motion pictures, Chap. X; adjectives employed, 130–134; pictures employed, 134–136

Aggressiveness in love-making, Chap. VI; scales for measuring, 15–16, 167–194; an illustrative rating, 52–54; practice regarding, 94–96

Art in relation to motion pictures, 137–142

Attractive *versus* unattractive characters, 67–68, 99, 111, 120

Correlation, effect of zero scores, 77; meaning of, 147–151; partial correlation, 150; formula for coefficient of correlation, 277–278; average inter-correlation, 281–283; *see also* Reliability

Democratic attitudes and practices, Chap. VIII; scales for measuring, 16, 212–238; practice regarding, 116

Folkways defined, 1

Group solidarity, 37–38, 45, 53, 56–58

Hypotheses about the effect of motion pictures, 65–68, 161; about relation of art to motion pictures, 137–142

Kissing in the movies, Chap. VII; scales for measuring, 17, 194–212; practice regarding, 106–107; propriety of displaying in public, 108; an illustrative rating, 55–56

Measuring mores of representative groups, Chap. IV; measuring relation of appeal of picture to morality, 142–151; relation to commercial success, 151–155

Mitchell, Alice M., on imitation of conduct in movies, 66–67

Moral profile charts proposed, 150–158

Morality and the mores, Chap. I; difficulty of studying scientifically, 7

Mores, defined by Sumner, 2; relation to morality, 1–5; impulsive rather than rational, 3, 12, 30, 45

Normal curve, nature of, 22–23; assumption of, 31–35; normal ogive curve, 39, 46–50

Number of raters needed, 73–75, 158–159

Parents' treatment of children, Chap. IX; scales for measuring, 17, 238–261; practice regarding, 126–127

Practice, in respect to certain mores, 60–62; in aggressiveness, 94–96; in kissing, 106–107; in democracy, 116; in treatment of children, 126–127

Reliability, of our scale values, 18–20; of measurement of mores, 61–63; of ratings on motion pictures, 75–82

Scales for measuring mores, principles for constructing, 9–10; technique of developing, Chap. II; method of using, 68–72

Scientific research needed, 153–155, Chap. XII

Spearman prophecy technique, 20, 73, 75–77; development of formula for, 278–281

Standard deviation as unit of measure, 24–25, 29–30; reducing different variabilities to a standard one, 34–38, 50–52; formula for, 278

Sumner, W. G., quoted on folkways and mores, 1, 2; on difficulty of studying morality scientifically, 7

Thurstone, L. L., on units of measure, 29

Tylor, E. B., quoted on conservatism of Dyaks of Borneo, 4

Westermarck, E., reference on tribal differences in mores, 3

Woody, Clifford, technique imitated, 46